Governing Societies.

Political perspectives on domestic and international rule

Issues in Society

Series editor: Tim May

Current and forthcoming titles:

Governing Societies:
Political perspectives on domestic and international rule

MITCHELL DEAN

Open University Press

Open University Press
McGraw-Hill Education
McGraw-Hill House
Shoppenhangers Road
Maidenhead
Berkshire
England
SL6 2QL

email: enquiries@openup.co.uk
world wide web: www.openup.co.uk

and Two Penn Plaza, New York, NY 10121–2289, USA

First published 2007

A catalogue record of this book is available from the British Library

ISBN-13: 978 0 335 20897 5 (pb) 978 0 335 20898 2 (hb)
ISBN-10: 0 335 20897 5 (pb) 0 335 20898 3 (hb)

Library of Congress Cataloguing-in-Publication Data
CIP data applied for

Typeset by YHT Ltd, London
Printed in Poland by OZ Graf. S.A.
www.polskabook.pl

The **McGraw·Hill** Companies

Contents

Series editor's foreword

The social sciences contribute to a greater understanding of the workings of societies and dynamics of social life. They are often, however, not given due credit for this role and much writing has been devoted to why this should be the case. At the same time we are living in an age in which the role of science in society is being re-evaluated. This has led to both a defence of science as the disinterested pursuit of knowledge and an attack on science as nothing more than an institutionalized assertion of faith with no greater claim to validity than mythology and folklore. These debates tend to generate more heat than light.

In the meantime the social sciences, in order to remain vibrant and relevant, will reflect the changing nature of these public debates. In so doing they provide mirrors upon which we gaze in order to understand not only what we have been and what we are now, but to inform ideas about what we might become. This is not simply about understanding the reasons people give for their actions in terms of the contexts in which they act, as well as analyzing the relations of cause and effect in the social, political and economic spheres, but about the hopes, wishes and aspirations that people, in their different cultural ways, hold.

In any society that claims to have democratic aspirations, these hopes and wishes are not for the social scientist to prescribe. For this to happen it would mean that the social sciences were able to predict human behaviour with certainty. This would require one theory and one method applicable to all times and places. The physical sciences do not live up to such stringent criteria, whilst the conditions in societies which provided for this outcome would be intolerable. Why? Because a necessary condition of human freedom is the ability to have acted otherwise and to imagine and practice different ways of organizing societies and living together.

It does not follow from the above that social scientists do not have a valued role to play, as is often assumed in ideological attacks upon their place and role within society. After all, in focusing upon what we have been and what we are now, what we might become is inevitably illuminated. Therefore, whilst it may not the province of the social scientist to predict our futures, they are, given not only their understandings, but equal positions as citizens, entitled to engage in public debates concerning future prospects.

This international series was devised with this general ethos in mind. It seeks to offer students of the social sciences, at all levels, a forum in which ideas are interrogated in terms of their importance for understanding key social issues. This is achieved through a connection between style, structure and content that is found to be both illuminating and challenging in terms of its evaluation of topical social issues, as well as representing an original contribution to the subject under discussion.

Given this underlying philosophy, the series contains books on topics which are driven by substantive interests. This is not simply a reactive endeavour in terms of reflecting dominant social and political pre-occupations, it is also pro-active in terms of an examination of issues which relate to and inform the dynamics of social life and the structures of society that are often not part of public discourse. What is distinctive about the series is an interrogation of the assumed characteristics of our current epoch in relation to its consequences for the organization of society and social life, as well as its appropriate mode of study.

Each contribution contains, for the purposes of general orientation, as opposed to rigid structure, three parts. First, an interrogation of the topic which is conducted in a manner that renders explicit core assumptions surrounding the issues and/or an examination of the consequences of historical trends for contemporary social practices. Second, a section which aims to 'bring alive' ideas and practices by considering the ways in which they directly inform the dynamics of social relations. A third section then moves on to make an original contribution to the topic. These encompass possible future forms and content, likely directions for the study of the phenomena in question, or an original analysis of the topic itself. Of course, it might be a combination of all three.

Mitchell Dean's book captures the ethos of this series through its interrogation of governing societies. At the outset, he is not content to allow his analysis to either drift into discussions of complexity and flows against the backdrop of allusion to globalization, nor to submit to a form of micro-analysis that leaves nation-states behind in its apparent concern for detail whilst missing the bigger picture and its profound effects upon the world. This means taking the political, with its accompanying threats of force, as well resistance and confrontation, seriously. It means refusing the banality that surrounds a great deal of discussion on globalization and instead taking law (including disregard of international law in the name of 'freedom'), diplomacy, violence and the proliferation of weapons, into account in order not only to challenge, but also re-build social and political thought for the twenty-first century. As Mitchell Dean puts it: "The project of governing societies, and its political character, cannot be blotted out by the 'withering sun of globalization' or fade to grey in the drab world of governance" (p. 14)

Accounts of government have often reverted to governance as reflective of a post-political world in which a liberal consensus apparently reigns supreme. As the end of history was being preached on the back of an extraordinary arrogance born not of the coming of age of reason, but of the end of the confrontation between two superpowers from which emerged only one, advanced liberal governing claimed to secure and defend individual liberty. At the same time it sought to intervene through the construction of particular forms of life around norms of autonomous and self-governing persons and those who represented exceptions to such norms. At a distance there are those whose commitment to alternative ways of governing and organizing has met with the erection of barbed wire fences and the use of force, whilst within the boundaries of the nation state there are those, such as the long-term unemployed, who are subject to the enforcement of obligation because they have not taken up the opportunities offered by its promises.

It is the process of naturalization of what are these political packages that has to be understood in the first instance (dilemmas). Much of what is political has been professionalized to the extent that politics is assumed to be administered and subject to issues associated with efficiency. It becomes process without purpose. A resulting de-politicization then reduces the scope for action in the political arena where struggle is its fundamental feature. Should it be apparent, it is often only 'after the fact', leaving a concern with politics to be confined to history as if that were an irrelevance to the present and future.

It is not only an account of the dilemmas that now face us that is required, but also a diagnosis in order to seek to understand the governing of societies without the traps that have been evident in deploying the value system of liberalism. Here the book unfolds into an analysis of the ways in which the concept of 'governmentality', from the work of Michel Foucault, has been selectively deployed to iron out differences between the programmes of policy and their real effects, and between their normative claims and their modes of operation. Here we find a 'reinscription thesis' in which otherwise heterogeneous powers are put together under a single rubric thereby ruling out an empirical examination of their interactions in any sphere of social and political practice. This conflates power relations with the idea, however useful, of government expressed as 'the conduct of conduct'. Instead, the powers of life and death bound to territory, population and sovereignty are brought into the frame of analysis. What is found is not simply a political rationality concerned with the exercise of restraint on powers such as sovereignty, but an extension of the powers within the state and the dispersion and delegation of sovereign powers onto all types of agents. What emerges is not simply a neo- or advanced liberalism but also an authoritarian liberalism.

As noted earlier, this happens both within the boundaries of the nation-state as well as outside them. Governing societies implies not simply a governing through freedom but the use of force to protect those forms of life described as freedom. Governing cannot be separated from violence and sovereignty. The latter operates to both include and exclude and relies as much upon violence as it does the law, but it is now also subject to dispersal. What then appears to be exceptional increasingly becomes more routinized in the desire to annihilate exceptions within the fabric of contemporary liberalism. Questions are then raised about the differences between democracy and absolutism as is apparent in the controversy surrounding the existence of Guantánamo Bay and other US facilities in the conduct of a war on terror (as discussed in chapter eight).

Overall, Mitchell Dean challenges those who have reproduced the claims of liberalism with their characterizations of contemporary forms of life in terms of mobilities and flows, as well as those who seek to flatten all before them in the name of a limited, analytic purity. This book successfully argues for nothing less than a paradigm shift in how we think about governing societies without retreating to an earlier statist position. Moreover, the purpose is highly practical: that is, to recover the political in the face of a universalism that seeks to flatten all before it and turn what is contentious into matters of efficiency in the name of limited ideas of how we ought to live together. It enjoins those who are satisfied with neither the conventional narratives of the social and political sciences nor their radical critiques to search for a new way of thinking abut how we govern and are governed in societies today. For that reason, this book deserves a wide readership.

Tim May

Acknowledgements

I must begin with my sincere thanks to Tim May for inviting me to be a part of this significant series and displaying extraordinary patience with me over the more than reasonable time it took to put this book together.

For a denizen of the Antipodes, this book has definite Nordic inspiration. Two kind invitations fostered many of the initial considerations of its themes. The first was to give a series of three public lectures called 'Governing Society Today' at the Universities of Helsinki and Jyväskylä in October 2001 and sponsored by the Finnish Academy. My sincere thanks to the organizers and principal interlocutors of these lectures, Ilpo Helén and Sakari Hänninen. Chapters 1 and 2 especially have their origins in these lecture series.

The second invitation was to a Visiting Professorship in the Department of Management, Philosophy and Politics at the Copenhagen Business School in the semester of 2002–3. This visit was organized by Niels Åkerstrøm Andersen to whom I must express my deep gratitude. During that time I had the privilege of participating in many seminars and conducting a PhD course. I would like to acknowledge the stimulating environment of the Business School and particularly that provided by the members of the Politics research group there.

Chapter 3 dates from that Copenhagen visit. It draws upon, but extensively reworks, Dean (2003a), 'Culture governance and individualisation', in H. Bang (ed.) *Governance as Social and Political Communication*, Manchester University Press. That paper was first published in Danish as 'Kulturstyring og individualisering' in C. Borch and L. Thorup Larsen (eds) *Perspektiv, magt og styring: Luhmann og Foucault til Diskussion*, Hans Reitzels Forlag, Cophenhagen. The argument of this chapter was developed during my stay in Copenhagen and extensively debated with Henrik Bang of the Institute of Political Science, University of Copenhagen.

Chapter 4 is a revised version of Dean (2002b), published as 'Powers of life and death beyond governmentality', in *Cultural Values: Journal of Cultural Research*, 6 (1/2): 119–38 (available at http://www.tandf.co.uk/ journals). The earliest versions of the paper were presented at the invitation of the Institute of Sociology, University of Copenhagen, and the 'Ethos of Welfare' conference at the University of Helsinki in August 2000. I thank Kaspar Villadsen and, again, Ilpo Helén, for those invitations.

Chapter 5 is also a revised version of an earlier paper, but one that has somewhat simplified and, I hope, clarified the earlier argument. That was published as Dean (2002a), 'Liberal government and authoritarianism' in *Economy and Society*, 31 (1): 37–61 (available at http://www.tandf. co.uk/ journals). This paper was first delivered at the Indonesian Studies Conference at the University of Tasmania in Launceston in December 2000 and at the Department of Sociology, Macquarie University, in May 2001. I thank Simon Philpott for organizing the first of these events and Robert van Krieken for his comments at the latter. I also thank Kevin Stenson for his written comments on this chapter. Paul Henman, Barry Hindess, Malcolm Voyce and Kaspar Villadsen provided valuable written comments on this chapter and were partners in different collaborations which I have been privileged to have. Barry Hindess offered helpful comments on the Introduction to this book.

The final three chapters are completely new material and somewhat uncharted territory for me. I am thus very grateful that Fleur Johns and Andrew Neal generously offered comments and critique of Chapters 6 and 7 at my request.

Finally, I would like to acknowledge the intellectual presence in this book of the late Paul Q. Hirst. Paul acted as an examiner of my doctoral thesis almost two decades ago and advised me on its publication (Dean 1991). While I would not claim great intellectual intimacy with Paul, we did meet a number of times over the years and he arranged a fellowship for me at Birkbeck College. I imagine that he gave me the same encouragement and assistance he gave countless numbers of research students and scholars. As I was finishing this book, it was Paul's posthumously published work that helped support many of the arguments found here (Hirst 2005).

Introduction: setting the scene

Many sociologists, political scientists and cultural theorists have made the mistake of thinking that the idea of 'governing societies' is outmoded for a whole variety of disparate reasons. In contrast, this book focuses on 'governing societies' as a distinctive political project that continues to define political life today. Some sociologists have argued that governing societies is no longer a coherent idea because the changed social conditions of the 'second age of modernity' (Beck 2000a, 2000b) have rendered the idea of society itself obsolete. Numerous political scientists, on the other hand, have replaced a focus on the state or on government with the somewhat nebulous catchall 'governance'.[1] In my view, much of both these disciplines has failed to understand governing society politically, that is, as something concerned with power, confrontation and appropriation, with struggle, resistance and combat, and with the use and the threat of force. Bedazzling themselves as much as their readers with the language of complexity, virtuality and mobility, and the metaphors of network, flows and spaces, they have failed to examine the task of governing societies politically, which means not simply to examine it economically but also legally, militarily and diplomatically. They remain mesmerized by changes in production and consumption and by technology and its cultural impacts.

At the other end of the scale, certain postmodernists and post-structuralists have in recent years told us that we must abandon 'global' analysis and be content to engage only in micro-political analyses. If this means – and it need not – that we must abandon analyses of national states, international alliances and organizations, and indeed questions of world order, then nothing could condemn us more to sterility and irrelevance in our current time. Yet they too, like their apparent opposites – the diag-nosticians of globalization, the sociologists of mobilities and flows, the theorists of global governance, and heralds of a cosmopolitan world order – have underestimated the continued force of the political.

That is, until recently. For today the most optimistic proponent of globalization has to confront the many local struggles against international agencies such as the World Trade Organization and the International Monetary Fund that have emerged since the protests in Seattle in 1999. The jet-setting theorist of mobilities might pause to consider the often horrific limits to the flows of people across borders and the effects of attempts to regulate those flows – effects captured by such words as refugee, asylum seeker, illegal immigrant, deportation, detention centre and statelessness. If not, he or she can consider the effects of their travel upon the Earth's biosphere. The most naïve theorist of governance must admit the continued exercise of sovereign state and non-state powers in the enforcement of order – not least in the proliferation of the (sometimes secret) camps in which the illegal immigrant or the 'enemy combatant' is to be found. The most optimistic cosmopolitan can find little solace in the continued existence of suicide bombers, often genocidal wars, the proliferation of nuclear, chemical and biological weapons among states and non-governmental 'networks' and the inadequacy, or indeed chaos, to which international law and order has often descended in the last decades – for example, in Rwanda in 1994, or with the invasion of Iraq in 2003. Even postmodernist theorists have to come to terms with a form of world order in which the United States acts in the position of the sole hegemon, adopts an uncertain relation to international law, and is capable of undertaking a permanent 'war against terror' in the name of humanity and freedom across the globe. Committed cultural pluralists have to accept that a radical Islamism has announced that the unipolar world and its understanding of the secular good life has a real and highly destructive enemy. As I suggest in this book and its engagement with various approaches to governing societies, there is an urgent need to understand, deploy and transform many classical concepts of sovereignty, states, exception, violence, war and peace, and world order, to prevent our understanding becoming a banal version of globalization narratives, whether those of the 'Washington Consensus' or its liberal cosmopolitan opponents.

While the aim of the book is modest, to explore the notion of governing societies from a particular perspective, it was written against the background of the history of the twenty-first century which has been marked by the significant analytic failure of social and political thought.

The 'long twenty-first century'

For many the political re-entered the contemporary scene with certain events of 11 September 2001, which have been reduced to four keystrokes, 9/11. The United States discovered it had an enemy or at least someone or something who unexpectedly had decided to regard *it* as the enemy. The shock, the symbolic violence and the sheer atrocity and terror of the events of that day in New York, Washington and rural Pennsylvania certainly inspired a sense of the political which involved violence and enmity rather than its anodyne treatment as 'governance'. They also suggest that the problem of 'world order' could not be quite so easily conjured away as the invocation of globalization might suggest. It was the kind of event that generated much commentary. It could be used to confirm or contest Samuel Huntington's 'clash of civilizations', the strengthening or decline of 'national sovereignty', the necessity or the limitation of international law, and so on. Against liberal cosmopolitanism, American conservatism would affirm the status of the United States as a world sovereign with true enemies (Harris 2004).

Yet, one might choose many other dates in close proximity to this one in the early days of the third millennium of the Christian West. Several come to mind. The first is 11 December 2000. That is the day the United States Supreme Court voted 5–4 along partisan lines that it would not be possible for Florida to set up a constitutionally adequate recount and that the recount must adhere to the official deadline for certifying Electoral College votes, which happened to be midnight that night. One of the dissenting Justices, Ruth Bader Ginsburg, scathingly remarked 'such an untested prophecy should not decide the Presidency of the United States' (in *Bush v. Gore*). For five weeks, US democracy had been thoroughly deconstructed to a global audience of satellite and cable news networks. American politics had become decidedly political and the outcome was based on a legal judgement that was thoroughly political in character. Such events might indicate an exercise of sovereignty in the world's paradigmatic liberal democracy that was neither liberal nor democratic and which consisted in a decision on what in other jurisdictions might have been regarded as a constitutional crisis or state of exception.

If we leave the United States, another date might be 20 July 2001. On that day, Carlo Guilliani, aged 23, was shot dead in Genoa by a conscript member of the Carabinieri, three years his junior, and then run over by a reversing police Land Rover. He was among the 'anti-globalization' protestors at the G8 summit, the group of the major industrialized nations, and a member of the 'White Overalls' group, whose uniform was meant to symbolize the condition of the 'invisible workers' without fixed contracts or security (Hardt and Negri 2004: 265). Whatever else might be said about this tragic incident, it was the day that those who would criticize and protest against globalization came to realize that what they were attacking would be defended if necessary by deadly force. Globalization could no longer be naïvely viewed as the pacific march of commerce; it was a perspective, a programme and a form of political action.

An event of another order unfolded only a couple of weeks before the fateful attacks on New York and Washington and at the other end of the Earth in the seas of the Indian Ocean between Indonesia and the islands that are part of Australian territory. On and after 26 August 2001, the

Norwegian freighter, the *Tampa*, was refused landing by the Australian government on one of these islands, Christmas Island, after it had saved 438 boat people, mainly from Afghanistan where they fled the Taliban regime, including 43 children (Marr and Wilkinson 2004). This day and subsequent events in Australia and parallel events elsewhere might stand as the day when we see national governments who espoused 'neo-liberal' policies of globalization as willing to use sovereign force to protect their borders and to use 'mandatory detention' for those who breach or seek to breach those borders without appropriate documentation. As shown by policies of indefinite mandatory detention, which includes the detention of babies and children, national citizenship means very much when you are without it – when you are 'stateless'. Even those who were not stateless but previously diagnosed as mentally ill could find themselves interned in a detention centre, as the German citizen and permanent Australian resident Cornelia Rau discovered, or deported to another country, as the Australian citizen Vivian Alvarez Solon found.[2]

There are events that are perhaps more terrible or even more fundamental than these – ones that have gained more or less media attention and others that have occurred under the media radar. We could mention the 'War on Terror' George W. Bush conducted in the aftermath of 11 September, the invasion of Iraq and the divisions amongst the United Nations, the revelations and pictures of torture at Abu Ghraib, the treatment of detainees at Guantànamo Bay, the revelations of secret CIA goals, the incidents involving the regular and careless killing of civilians in Iraq, emblematic of which was that of Haditha in November 2005. Indeed, the question of torture and the standards of interrogation practices permitted by the US government have been a running story of the second Bush administration. The Australian story above is linked to the revelations of the detention centres there and its policies of the 'Pacific Solution', which included the offshore housing of illegal immigrants in the impoverished island nation of Nauru. There are more tragic boat journeys than that of those who were picked up by the Tampa. Not long after, a boat labelled Suspected Illegal Entry Vessel X (SIEV-X) by the Australian authorities sunk in the same waters, leaving 351 drowned, amid a cloud of accusations about the actions and inactions of the Australian government.

The history of the twenty-first century has been marked by radical Islamism and terrorist attacks in Western cities and in holiday resorts. It has also been marked by urban riots and conflict with often an inter-ethnic character in cities as affluent and as different as Paris or Sydney. Indeed, the early twenty-first century is marked by an increasing cascade of events which force the political back into focus if we understand the political as the domain of antagonistic relations between groups, of the use and threat of physical force, of decisions that go beyond custom, precedent and even law and which often involve matters of life and death, and of the struggle for and exercise of sovereign control over populations and over territories of rule. At the symbolic or spatial edges or boundaries of the liberal-democratic world, its security is pursued with ruthlessness and violence. Deep in its heartland, however, we witness the drift to a law-and-order state and find the instruments of punishment being applied not simply to criminals and prisoners but to illegal immigrants and refugees, welfare recipients, unemployed youth, those exhibiting anti-social behaviour, negligent parents and those at risk of delinquency and criminality.

These years have also been marked by a very specific intellectual context in relation to both domestic and international affairs. In regard to domestic matters, virtually all mainstream social and political thought would assume the inexorable movement of globalization and argue that this requires the reform of existing national institutions in general and a strengthening of the obligations of individual to community and society on the other. This concern for the individual and his or her conduct has opened up a space for a range of projects that speak to the choice, prudence, planning capacities, virtue and even salvation of individuals and populations and how to attain it. There has been the emergence of a project for the reformation of character through the proper governance and cultivation of the individual. While many of these projects might be described as liberal or even neo-liberal, in that they seek to work through and shape the choices, capacities and aspiration of individuals, many others took a far more conservative cast and, in relation to certain economically or socially vulnerable groups, an authoritarian dimension. Practical political philosophy witnessed the recrudescence of non-liberal and even illiberal programmes and policies including 'tough love' and new paternalist approaches to social policy under the rubric of 'welfare reform', 'compassionate conservatism' that stresses the role of 'faith-based organizations', and even new forms of political theology including both Christian and Islamic fundamentalism. At first sight, these apparently illiberal techniques for enforcing obligation, and the use of sovereign and coercive means to govern certain populations, raise questions about the headline liberal-democratic values of freedom.

The postulate of globalization promised new economic freedom, geographic mobility and liberatory cosmopolitanism. But it also led to a kind of remoralization of the individual as a prudent, self-responsible actor, who rationally plans his or her own life and fulfils his or her obligations subject to more intrusive sovereign surveillance and scrutiny. In international matters, a similar double-take occurs. On one side, the imperative of what is called 'global governance' indicates a remoralization of the conduct of international actors, including states, in such matters as human rights, humanitarian interventions and military actions. On the other side, the conduct of individual states is subject to far more scrutiny and sovereign military intervention either multilaterally (United Nations) or unilaterally (purpose-built 'coalitions of the willing' led by the United States). Yet despite this apparent paradox in both domestic and international affairs, most influential social scientists would agree that sovereignty and nation-states are undergoing severe delimitation and mutation.

Perhaps this is at the core of the conundrum of the present. On the one hand, we have inherited the intellectual tools of a generation that told us that politics as they knew it was passing away, the social was dead, the nation-state was meaningless and the end of history was nigh. What was to replace all of this was the figure of a flatter, more participatory kind of ordering of human existence, 'governance', in which individuals and not social or national identity would matter, in which new forms of cosmopolitan identity and democracy would appear, and in which sovereignty would be transformed by notions of democracy and human rights. The paradox is not that this all proved to be false but that the very same discourses would be ready to authorize new forms of just war and military intervention abroad and new kinds of confinement and enforcement of obligation at home.

If the dense, episodic, eventful, cascading and hence already long history of the twenty-first century teaches us anything, it is that the dream of a post-political world dissolved by globalization into governance without government has passed and that we urgently need to rethink the meaning of the political today. Governing society might be about the construction and deployment of freedom, but it is also about the deployment of barbed wire in the construction of detention facilities (Diken and Lausten 2005: 41). It may be about the immanent principle of an ever-widening deliberative democracy; it is also about the treatment of refugees who sew their lips together in Australia's outback detention centres. This has implications for thinking about governing societies both as domestic and international projects.

Political projects

This political project of governing societies can be approached in its singular form or its plural form. It can concern the government of the internal or domestic affairs of a political unit, typically a nation-state. We are used to this idea and its association with the formal political institutions of the state. It can also concern the governing of a system or a number of such political units in the international domain by international law, international organizations or alliances. It could be argued that 'governing societies' is precisely what the United Nations, or the European Union, or even the parties to a free-trade agreement between two countries, tries to do. For some, governing society in the singular might concern the Earth as one society and the potential that institutions will develop which can effect such a world government or, to be more circumspect, global governance. In the plural, governing societies might be concerned with the common ways it is necessary to govern different societies, for example, governing with respect to universal human rights under the United Nations Charter or the introduction into diverse societies of World Bank-sponsored norms of 'good governance'. This is all quite straightforward.

Whether singular or plural, we can approach the project of 'governing society' as grand vision, an explicit and definite programme of government, as the largely routine and mundane activities of a national government or international agency, or as the loosely connected set of mobile aims and effects of various actors which constitute an overall strategic situation and which lock into place structures of domination. Grand visions of governing society over the last century can be found in sources as diverse as revolutionary socialist doctrines of the dictatorship of the proletariat, the racial theory and practices developed from eugenics, the fantasists' dreams found today in radical Islam and Christian fundamentalism, Keynesian macroeconomic policies or neo-liberal monetarism, ideals of a welfare state or good governance, notions of a strong nation or ideals of a cosmopolitan democracy.

Alongside such visions, we find more or less explicit programmes of governing society using particular techniques to serve diverse ends. Examples in modern American history would include the New Deal, the War on Poverty, and the Republicans' Contract with America which have aims as different as putting people to work again, empowering the poor and addressing the decline of virtue in the republic (Cruikshank 1998, 1999). We have had the Third Way experiment in the United Kingdom which was taken up by Labour politicians and their intellectual allies more broadly (Giddens 1998; Latham 1998). Intellectuals have propounded communitarianism (Etzioni 1995, 1996), the 'new paternalism' (Mead 1986, 1997) and associationism (Hirst 1993). A century ago there was the use of social insurance to establish solidarity among the population such as in the doctrine of *solidarisme* proposed by the French prime minister, Léon Bourgeois, in the Third Republic in France (Ewald 1991). Others include the use of public expenditure and investment to maintain full employment in the post-World War II Keynesian welfare state; or the reform of the public sector and social welfare to make institutions and individuals more efficient and globally competitive as in recent neoliberal policies. Such programmes can concern themselves with promoting harmony, tolerance and recognition about the members of a diverse population as, for example, in the official policy of multiculturalism practised in late twentieth-century Australia or the biculturalism of Canada or New Zealand. Not all the agencies of such programmes are national states. To cite again the example of the World Bank, one can view its use of 'conditionality' to establish protocols of good governance and anti-corruption as such a programme for governing societies.

These grand visions and definite programmes seek to define a specific role in governing society for business associations, corporations, churches, charities and trade unions, social movements and non-governmental organizations as well as for public bureaucracies, law courts and parliaments, for social welfare, healthcare and education systems, for economic and population planning, and for police and armed forces. Their ends are diverse and multiple: they might strive to ensure a stable settlement between classes and social groups, or to overthrow a certain class and to establish the reign of a previously oppressed one. They might seek to foster a public bureaucracy or to limit and control it to render it accountable. They might want to promote harmony, respect and tolerance among culturally diverse members or, conversely, to promote and engage in practices of 'ethnic cleansing' or the maintenance of racial purity. They might imagine a society that is based on multiple neighbourhoods, associations or communities or one composed simply of individuals or families. They might aim to foster patriotism or cosmopolitanism, to produce a nation or to integrate it with others, to define citizenship and human rights or establish obligations, to prescribe the forms of life as normal that characterize that nation or decide when the situation is no longer normal, to establish and defend what they understand as public peace, security and good order, or to say when they no longer obtain, to increase military capabilities and preparedness or to police populations and societies, and so forth.

Most of these programmes assume the existence of a constitutional sovereign government or a world of such governments. Many programmes for governing society, however, are effected through the design of governmental institutions such as doctrines for the separation of Church and State, the separation of executive, legislative and juridical branches of government, or forms of federalism, bi-cameral legislatures, representative voting, electoral colleges and so on. One version of this is the liberal concern, found both in David Hume and in the American Federalists, to extirpate the corrosive influence of faction and to ensure a sufficient distance between the people's representatives and the people themselves (Hindess 1997: 262–4). Thus part of the liberal-democratic project of governing society is to govern political action, to produce it in acceptable forms such as the cycle of regular elections and other civilized activities, and to make sure that the governed population does not interfere with the process of governing society itself. It is to make sure that the population does not get too political. The other side of such a liberal approach is the governing of governors, including politicians and public servants, themselves. At the core of this is the liberal problematic of corruption. Today the Holy Grail of the prevention of corruption is approached through the balancing effects of 'civil society organizations', institutional checks and balances, political accountability, public sector management, and a competitive private sector (Kaufmann 2005). Governing society then often means governing political actors to ensure that they do not interfere with the proper workings of government, whether those actors are among the general populations or they are governors themselves.

The phrase 'governing society' is also still commonly used to describe the routine and mundane activities of governments, that is, of the executive, legislative and juridical apparatuses of states. Many of these activities are undertaken through other non-state agencies of what is called 'civil society' or in response to the actions, regulations and programmes of international economic, diplomatic, legal, financial, philanthropic and non-governmental agencies. In this regard, governing society could be viewed less as the intended action of a particular agent (the government) on an object (society) but more as an overall strategic set of relations which are facilitated and coordinated by various regulatory agencies which for the most part remain under the auspices of the constitutional state in liberal-democratic societies. To speak of governing societies implies neither a unitary nor a single agent. It does not imply a subject with a definite intention or a fundamental effectiveness of policies and laws. It does, however, imply the political.

Meaning of the political

But what do we mean by political? The political concerns a specific kind of relationship of power. So we first need to specify what a relationship of power is. Michel Foucault argued that the fundamental relationship of power is 'a strategic game of liberties' (1988a: 19), a 'structure of actions upon the actions of others' (1982: 220). By this he meant that a power relationship is a relationship between any actors who seek to affect each other. Dialogue, conversations, friendship, intimate relationships can all be relations of power. Power relations are reciprocal, unstable and reversible. One of the innovations in this concept of power is the emphasis placed on the freedom of the protagonists to act in a plurality of ways. Relations of power are not simply forms of domination.

Foucault called such games between liberties 'agonistic', creating a word from the Greek *agonisma*, meaning 'a combat' as in a wrestling match. He distinguished between such a relationship and what he called 'states of domination' in which power relations have become relatively fixed, stable and hierarchical and 'technologies of government' which are instruments for the stabilization of power relations and the creation of states of domination (Foucault 1988a: 19). For Foucault what is fundamental is neither the system of stable institutions which are built out of these mobile relations of power or even the technologies they use in their struggles but the incessant cut and thrust of relationships of resistance and power. Power is thus more like a duel than a total system of subordination.

Further, Foucault himself suggested many times that his analytics of power takes as its point of departure the analysis of forms of resistance. This is why he gives as much weight to strategies of confrontation as to what he calls 'rationalities of government' which are embodied in various visions and programmes just discussed. While the latter seek to shape or guide the 'conduct' of one of the combatants of power, the former are strategies for the crystallization of 'counter-conducts' (Foucault 2004b: 199ff). The project of governing societies is involved in these power relations, in Foucault's sense, because it deploys ways of thinking, or rationalities, and ways of intervening, or technologies, to try to order, fix, stabilize or even disorder and reverse relationships of power and bring about the establishment or downfall of states of domination. This project can be undertaken by the agents of the political and juridical institutions of the national state, by an anti-globalization movement such as the World Social Forum, by globalist institutions such as the World Bank or the International Monetary Fund, by a group of partisan nationalist fighters or insurgents, by a revolutionary party, or a transnational terrorist network. It can have different concrete aims such as state security, social welfare, international competitiveness, economic efficiency, global governance protocols or bringing down the American Empire. Nevertheless, the task of governing society seeks to establish, contest, upset, transform or destroy a system of domination and form of order within a population, a collectivity, a territory or even the entire surface of the Earth.

Yet the project of governing a society or governing societies is also political in a very specific sense. Here Foucault is of only limited help. He has very little to say about the political and what political action might be as a species different from other kinds of agonistic action – from other kinds of power relationships. Following him, we could say that because all human interaction involves relations of power, everything is political. However, I think that evades the question that has concerned modern sociologists and political scientists since Max Weber's discussions of life orders (for example, [1918] 1972: 323–59), that is, what is different about the political from other kinds of human action including intimate, economic, religious and aesthetic action. All of these would involve relations of power in Foucault's sense but we need to be able to distinguish between, say, economic or religious orders and political ones, or to establish at what point the economic or religious becomes political.

Paul Hirst (1988: 274) once wrote a very simple answer to the question of what makes something political, which I believe is as good as any: 'That feature is struggle, and struggle means the reciprocal action of parties opposed to one another.' The political exists whenever power relations become adversarial, whenever human beings find themselves in a position of adversaries. A power relationship crosses the political threshold when it becomes mutually antagonistic, that is to say, when the existence of one side threatens the other. Political relations are no longer simply an 'agonistic game', as in the sporting analogy, but relations that contain the potential of an antagonistic confrontation. They are power relations that have passed the threshold of a certain intensity and their aims are to achieve a victory or to ensure that the opponent cannot threaten again. They are games that can become, quite literally, matters of life and death. For some, it is a testimony to what Norbert Elias (1978) called 'the civilizing process' that, in most liberal democracies, victory at a parliamentary election by an opposition means that one party voluntarily hands over the control of the enormous resources and powers of the state treasury, public bureaucracy, military and police without taking up arms. For others this may signal the high degree of depoliticization of contemporary liberal democracies with their professional politicians, party machines, polling techniques, spin doctors, campaign advertising and narrowing differences.

In any case it is this civilizing (or depoliticizing) of the political that makes it hard for citizens of contemporary liberal democracies to grasp what distinguishes the political from other forms of action. If power relations consist of 'agonism', the political emerges when that agonism gains a certain intensity which is manifest in its aims: to ensure victory, to vanquish the opponent, to ensure that he or she is no longer a threat, to use whatever means at one's disposal to get one's way. One of the sources of this intensity is when the resources of government are themselves the stakes in the contest. For Weber (1978: 54), social action is politically oriented when it 'aims to exert influence on the government of a political organization: especially at the appropriation, redistribution or allocation of the powers of government'. The reason that this is an intense struggle is not because people are power-hungry – and will do anything to usurp or hold onto power – but because those who are able to appropriate and use the organized resources of power are usually in a better position to stabilize relations of power in their favour. This is so due to another key feature of the political noted by Weber: that the political cannot be defined in terms of its many and disparate ends but in the means that are peculiar to it, the 'threat and application of physical force' (1978: 45). Relations of power, in Foucault's sense, become political when they pass a threshold of intensity and when the struggle is no longer the cut and thrust of words but over the means by which a settlement to a struggle can be forcibly imposed and when what is at stake are often matters of life and death.

All of these features were starkly illustrated early in 2005 in the controversy about the judicial orders that allowed the removal of a feeding tube from a woman, Terri Schiavo, in a 'permanent vegetative state'. The removal was accompanied by public demonstrations and acts of violence. At one point, the Florida Department Law Enforcement agents told local police they were coming to the hospice to remove the woman from the hospice to a hospital to resume feeding. According to the *Miami Herald* (Miller 2005), the local police told the state agents that they would not do it without the presence of a judge. The state agents withdrew on the brink of what could have been a constitutional crisis and armed conflict between two set of law enforcement authorities. The intensity of the antagonism between different groups, the use of force, and the matter at hand, make this a highly charged political contest. There is of course nothing necessarily political in the Schiavo case. Many people die from decisions regarding healthcare management in all sorts of jurisdictions but the publicity of this case, the decisions of high-profile politicians, especially the Bush siblings as Governor and President, and the wider context of US political theological dispute over end-of-life issues conspired to make this a media event.

In an unpublished manuscript, Foucault cites the controversial German legal thinker, Carl Schmitt,[3] and argues that while nothing is necessarily political, everything can become political (Senellart 2004: 409). In this text, Foucault agrees that the political concerns antagonism, combat and struggle between adversaries, which might result in an open confrontation between two political actors. Schmitt ([1932] 1996a) of course is famous for defining the political in terms of the friend/enemy distinction and finally restricting the use of the term to international relations between different states. We can agree that relationships of power, in Foucault's sense, can become friend/enemy relations, that is, relations of confrontation, but the identification of the public enemy, the *hostis publicus*, is neither the terminal nor most pristine form of power. These forms of confrontation generate new relationships of power that seek to convert public enmity into a stable state of domination whether within a state or between states, while such states of domination and mechanisms of power, in so far as they still contain the possibility of resistance, can also generate new forms of confrontation. Schmitt strikingly locates the essence of the political in an extreme and terminal situation: a war between states or a civil war. Foucault allows us to place the political in a field of power, resistance, strategy and confrontation. While the 'essence' of the political might be in antagonistic relations or what Schmitt called the friend/enemy relation, the practice of politics – whether domestic or international – is as much about transforming this antagonism into something else (treating insurgents or partisans as criminals), managing it (by international peacekeeping operations), deferring it and seeking its resolution (by mediation and diplomacy to resolve antagonisms between China and Taiwan), or by preventing it by positive measures (acceding to workers' demands for higher wages and better conditions). In the era of the Cold War, it was about avoiding nuclear direct confrontation between public enemies and their respective friends by the terror of mutually assured destruction (MAD) and deferring confrontation onto proxy third parties. The United States found itself supporting South American military dictatorships against democratic socialists, while the Soviet Union offered support for national liberation movements in Africa against colonial regimes or their successors. Schmitt's definition of the political as a radical antithesis appears to be coldly clear-eyed; it needs, however, to be corrected by a framework that can discuss its government.

Unlike Weber and Schmitt, it must be admitted that Foucault was not so concerned with defining the political. While they rightly draw our attention to the means of force and violence which define the political, Foucault, like, more recently, Giorgio Agamben (1998), shows how intense power relations can become when they concern matters of life and death – of euthanasia, abortion, genetic screening, notions of brain death and so on. Such practices often define political confrontation today and thus our task, like both these thinkers, is to address those political domains that draw their intensity in relation to powers of life and death: namely, 'biopolitics' and sovereignty. If we take seriously the political, we must take seriously these universal experiences of life and death and how they are linked to relationships of power. The debate over the removal of the feeding tube of Ms Schiavo in 2005 shows just how political such issues can get in the contemporary USA.

This is how we should view governing society. It concerns securing a particular form of life as something that is normal and, in doing so, deciding what is outside the limits to that life. It tries to stabilize relations of power, resistance and confrontation into states of domination that are accepted, whether for their wisdom or their naturalness, their taken-for-granted character or legality, as incontestable. It tries to create a certain minimum necessary level of homogeneity and identification among its members. It does this by forming bonds and creating solidarity among individuals and citizens, and establishing harmony between classes and groups. Yet, as we so often see, whether in contemporary Russia in Chechnya, with the USA and its allies and the War on Terror, on the Korean peninsular or between the Chinas, the formation of political units is still inextricably linked, if not defined, at least at an empirical level, with the potential of a confrontation with a public enemy. The project of governing society is thus two-sided. On one side, it seeks to reduce political action in Weber's sense within the space, boundaries or territory of a political unit; on the other, it is to form a collective into a unit capable of political action in relation to other such units.

Looked at in the plural, 'governing societies' is a project for establishing order among the collectivities produced in this way. The development of diplomacy, international law, the use or threat of military force and war, and even international commerce, are a part of the means of governing societies as a plurality, of governing a world divided into these units. It is in the international realm that these societies have ratcheted up relations of power into the most intensely political forms.

One can observe that those who, like Hobbes or Machiavelli, try to state the conditions of political action make few friends themselves. Those who seek to state, like Kant, how 'moral politicians' should act find themselves much better received, although Kant was far from naïve about politicians when he took their motto as 'Be ye therefore wise as serpents ... and harmless as doves' (1980: 116). In an era in which the moral politician acts in the service of a liberal-democratic pacific order, to point to the conditions of political action as mutual antagonism and reciprocal action between opposing parties is to risk being shunned as amoral. Yet in our time the moral politician is often indistinguishable from the 'political moralist' who, as Kant puts it, 'fashions his morality to suit his own advantage' (1980: 118). In the case of the 2003 invasion and subsequent occupation of Iraq, neither has proved 'harmless as doves'.

More fundamentally, at the edges of the liberal world we find Weber's concept of the political as the threat and use of physical force emerging again and again for all sorts of reasons: to provide security for the pacific order of commerce and trade, to root out and eliminate the terrorists who are beyond the boundaries of normal and civilized human existence, to keep the refugee at bay or locked in camps, to subdue the dictator and bring him to justice, to bring democracy and freedom to the populations of an unsettled region, to apprehend international drug and people traffickers and other criminals. We also find that the threat of force and sanctions are applied to those who stand outside normal frames of life within that liberal-democratic pacific space and its political and legal order: not only to the criminal but to greater sections of the population outside the habits and hierarchies of work and family, whether due to unemployment, poverty, single parentage, or even age and disability. Whether the project of governing societies takes the form of a vision, a programme, the practices of the routine and mundane government of the state, or a loosely coordinated set of strategic relations, it seeks to stabilize relations of power and confrontation and to impose a particular settlement on the one hand, and to resist other such settlements on the other. It is a strategy for forming collective actors and for dividing these actors from others. It is about making linkages and connections which form friends, citizens and allies. It is about drawing lines, dividing populations and marking others as outsiders, threats, outlaws and even enemies. The project of governing societies, and its political character, cannot be blotted out by the 'withering sun of globalization' or fade to grey in the drab world of governance.

This book

The primary context of this book has been shaped by an attempt to recast the immensely seductive narrative of the shift from hoary old ideas of politics and territorial states to a cultural and network form of governance. In the course of seeking to displace this narrative, I found the need to follow several broader initial injunctions.

Regard power relations as plural and heterogeneous

One key way of displacing this narrative of the shift from centralized and sovereign government to network forms of governance is to recover the ways in which power relations might take different and heterogeneous forms that enter into variable relations and recombinations with one another. Among those forms, zones or modalities of power are government or governance, and sovereignty and biopolitics. Such an approach, further, ought to prove useful to grasp the intelligibility of specific 'regimes of practices'.

Focus on 'dividing practices'

A closely related move is to shift the focus from general diagnosis of the *telos* of contemporary practices and institutions of rule to the way in which specific practices divide populations in order that they might be subject to different kinds of knowledge and different relations of power. While the headline value and proposed *telos* of liberalism is liberty, we should

examine the ways in which liberal practices of governing divide populations so that some can be governed by freedom, others by obligation and
sanction, and still others by sovereign force and coercion. We might also
examine that shifting division between state – or government in its formal
sense – and civil society constitutive of liberalism as a limited form of
government and the effects of the different versions of that division.

Think the exception

Within liberal ways of government, all forms of individualization and associated norms of living are accompanied by distinctive forms of pathology or
exception to these norms. We must examine such exceptions and their
relation to norms such as that of the cosmopolitan subject, or the life-planner,
or more broadly the norm of a liberal governing through the self-governing
or autonomous individual. Further, the notion of exception itself must be
approached in its multiplicity: the constitutional state of emergency or its
equivalents and the exceptionality of states within the international order
exist alongside these more quotidian instances of exceptions generated by the
expertise of the human and life sciences and the ideals of liberal autonomy.

Recover sovereignty

A part of the problem of this mainstream narrative is the way in which it
assigns sovereignty to a peripheral role as an outmoded or largely displaced
form of power. This book is premised on both the radical and urgent
necessity of rethinking sovereignty today and represents a partial contribution to such a task.

Investigate counter-narratives

A counter-narrative to the emergence of the norm of the life-planning or
cosmopolitan subject might adopt the perspective of the recent history of
the treatment of the welfare recipient or the refugee. The welfare recipient
is both the raw material and the limit of policies and practices destined to
produce a self-reflexive project of the self. The refugee is both the case
where national citizenship is shown to really matter for those who do not
have but seek the protection of nation-states, and the undoing of the idea
of citizenship based on birthright or nativity. Against a story of the decline
of sovereignty and the emergence of network forms of governance we
should take seriously Giorgio Agamben's provocation that the existence of
'the camp' is not an unhappy survival of a previous time in a cosmopolitan
age, but a permanent state of exception that reveals itself as the 'new biopolitical *nomos* of the planet' (Agamben 2000: 44). This does not mean, of
course, that we should find such a view unproblematic.

Foreground the limit case

As we shall see, there are clear limits to the move to a network and ethical
form of governance that displaces or diminishes the use of (an amoral, if not

immoral) sovereign power of states. By focusing on those limits in the form of questions of war and peace, the character of war (limited military intervention, pre-emptive strike, police action, virtuous war), its justification (for example, moral justification in terms of human rights violation), and the conception of enemy (as criminal or as terrorist network), a different type of intelligibility of power relations in the world today emerges which challenges those who would view those power relations as either benignly anarchic or a globalization without hegemony.

Repoliticize globalization

Simply, we must move from the fundamentally depoliticizing understanding of globalization that swings between economic and cultural explanations to the *political* question of world order. While these last two injunctions are taken up throughout this book, they await further occasions for their elaboration (see the commencement of this in Dean 2006a, 2006b).

The approach taken in this book is not a systematic study of the different ways in which we might talk about governing societies, but a response to an intellectual context in which the legitimacy of such a project or set of projects has been called into question. It is an attempt to render a displacement in various problematics, not only those of conventional social and political thought and but also studies of 'governmentality', by foregrounding rather than erasing the political. However, as I have indicated, this task is not so much one driven by internal intellectual concerns or paradigm shifts as one imposed by the urgency of the political scene of liberal democracies on a national and international scale today.

The book is divided into three parts. The first part, consisting of three chapters, sets up many of the *dilemmas* in contemporary thought concerning government, governance and state, and seeks to establish a distinctive approach in relation to what is an emergent mainstream of contemporary social and political science.

In Chapter 1 I examine the notion of governing societies and its historical preconditions and conceptual history. In Chapter 2, I offer an account of how the idea and project of governing society have fallen into disregard in contemporary social and political science. This entails an exploration of the re-emergence of the once nearly obsolete notion of 'governance' in different intellectual and disciplinary contexts. I then suggest reasons that we should resist the hegemonic view that governing societies is anachronistic and problematic.

Chapter 3 examines the themes of contemporary social and political sciences which have underpinned this rejection of the concept of governing societies. The argument that is contested here is that new kinds of (post-)political relations such as a post-sovereigntist governance − a 'culture-governance', as I call it, or governance of ethical culture – have emerged around the figure of the individual coincident with globalization. One version of this story is that of the emergence of the cosmopolitan individual and a cosmopolitan politics in a second age of modernity. I show why these kinds of narratives are incoherent and how we need to depart from their assumptions to rethink the political character of governing societies and what that might mean.

Part Two, consisting of the next two chapters, attempts to diagnose those dilemmas at the limits of the problematic of governmentality, whether by resituating governmentality studies within a broad conception of different zones of power or by showing how liberal forms of order are intrinsically dependent upon conservative and even authoritarian practices and rationalities. I am tempted to regard these chapters as undertaking a kind of *diagnostics* of both the liberal-democratic legal and political order and the capacity of established analyses to remain critical, or even thoughtful, in relation to it.

In Chapter 4 I take up the challenge left by Foucault to treat relationships of power as plural and heterogeneous and to seek to understand the different kinds of political power involved in biopolitics, or the power over life, and sovereignty, which entails a right of death, and the forms that these take today. I do this in a framework that is careful not to fall into the assumptions of current mainstream social and political science examined in the previous chapter or the closely related normative systems which seek to legitimize current liberal-democratic societies. I conclude that the description of how governing societies occurs today cannot be undertaken without a renewed sense of the powers of life and death as much as governance, the sovereign decision on the exception as much as choice, force as much as contract, discipline and obligation as much as empowerment, and enforcement as much as rights.

Chapter 5 continues the task of understanding liberal-democratic forms of governing outside their own normative or value framework by thinking through the ways liberal-democratic, including conservative, programmes and practices of governing society are linked to authoritarian measures. The latter are viewed as intrinsic, rather than external, to liberal-democratic practice and rest on a distinction between liberal government ('the state') and what lies outside it ('civil society'). The fostering of civil society was important to the aspirations of working-class and other popular organizations articulated through the emergent representative institutions. However, as I argue here, a liberal government of civil society also contains the potential of a liberal kind of authoritarianism. I conclude that 'authoritarian liberalism' is a distinctive and pervasive potentiality of advanced liberal government. This is a particularly interesting finding in light of the advocacy of a transnational civil society as an arena for deliberation by liberal cosmopolitans.

Part Three, consisting of the final three chapters, represents a set of theoretical and analytical *departures* which have grown out of recent more extensive engagements with the politics and history of the present and recent radical political theory, but which focus on quite traditional terms of political discourse such as sovereignty, legitimate violence, territory, exception, decision and security.

This part takes an engagement with the critical theory of sovereignty and the practice of sovereignty today as a departure from mainstream liberal and social science narratives of the present. Chapter 6 investigates the theoretical analysis of 'sovereignty' as both supreme power and a form of power bound to the exercise of violence. It is thus both an introduction to broad critical-theoretical perspectives and an elaboration of the thesis of the imbrication of sovereign power within the practices of liberal-democratic rule. It is a prelude to the major argument of Chapters 7 and 8 which move onto the specific question of the notion of sovereignty understood as the 'decision on the state of exception'. I start from the ideas of the Italian post-Marxist philosopher Giorgio Agamben, that the state of exception, once a temporary and emergency measure, has become a technique and paradigm of government in the contemporary world (in Chapter 7). I then explore the way in which the exception and decision-making occur within contemporary forms of rule and illustrate what is at stake by recent commentary and critique around the detention facility at Guantánamo Bay and related examples (Chapter 8). This allows me to make some broader suggestions about the role of the vocabulary of emergency, exception, crisis and necessity within contemporary 'authoritarian liberal' styles of rule. Rather than the camp being a *nomos* or paradigm of contemporary politics, or even the logic of contemporary society, it is illustrative of many features of contemporary liberal ways of governing and its exceptionalism.

The stance of the current book is to offer a critical analysis of contemporary liberal approaches to governing societies both in domestic and international affairs. Its focus on the question of sovereignty and related concepts is a part of an attempt to gain traction for an alternative, more measured kind of analysis rather than a full-scale 'counter-narrative'. The book does not offer an alternative normative framework. Its point is to show the continued salience of the projects(s) of governing societies and the relevance of a revamped political vocabulary around sovereignty and related terms, and to indicate the dangers of an uncritical conversion of liberal values into analytic tools. Its chapters consist of a series of related engagements taken over a period of several years which present at each stage provisional conclusions which then prepare the way for the next engagement. I include each of them as a component stage of this engagement with a theoretical mainstream which has appeared increasingly unable to speak to our political present and the problems confronting governing societies today.

Ultimately, then, this is not a polemical book that seeks to state a political or normative position. It is concerned rather with how we might think again about an old problem in new and revealing ways. Its concerns are analytical and diagnostic rather than polemical or normative although any description or redescription of the present must contain normative elements. If its chapters represent the unfinished explorations of a political history of the present, what connects them to the reader, I hope, are anticipatory routes of discovery.

PART ONE

Dilemmas

Zombie categories?

The title of this book is monstrous in two ways: it covers a very large terrain and it invokes certain figures recently thought to have been consigned to teratology (the study of monsters), state and society. They are, along with plenty of others, so we are told, 'zombie categories' (Beck and Beck-Gernsheim 2002: 203–4; Beck 2002: 47). One might suppose that this means putting the dead hand of old modernity on the new modernity of mobilities, virtualities, complexity and multiplicity, of cosmopolitan identities and politics, the world of networks and 'governance without government'. Perhaps regarding the state, at least, as a zombie is not so new. It echoes Nietzsche (2004: XI), for whom a state is 'called the coldest of all cold monsters. Coldly lieth it also; and this lie creepeth from its mouth: "I, the state, am the people".' For Hobbes, his image of the state was derived from the mythical sea-monster of the Book of Job, the Leviathan, who appears at once as an artificial man and a mortal god.[1]

Perhaps the zombie metaphor is linked to the recurrent description of the state as the 'body politic' and its nineteenth-century transformation into the social body (Neocleous 2003). No doubt such political metaphors contained extraordinary dangers which are partially at the root of the desire of today's theorists to dispense with them. The body politic is clearly aligned with medical metaphors of politics. Notions of the social body are associated with the attempt to eliminate dangerous pestilences and diseases from society which find their apogee in the 'racial hygiene' practices of the fascist state. My argument here is that to regard the categories of state and society as zombies is just as dangerous. This is because the denial of the currency of such categories is linked to the view that extraordinary measures will become necessary for a time which is, for many, a truly exceptional time, that is, one in which the reign of the state and its sovereignty has been drowned under the great oceanic flows and surfaces of globalization. It is to suppress the hard edge of politics, including the deployment of violence, conducted by certain states in relation to international and domestic opponents. It ignores the benefits that a state brings to its own populations by establishing a defensible legal order and public services, and the obligations it requires of them in many current governmental practices. We are discovering that the Leviathan, once a symbol of a terrestrial order derived from the sea-monster of the Book of Job, has a great capacity to survive and prosper under the great waves and surface of globalization.

Sea-monsters, like zombies, it must be said, have a strange way of catching up with us. They might lead us to do things we might otherwise not do. They frighten us into abridging our civil liberty to ensure security against terrorism. They might attack entities such as trade unions by restricting strikes and sidelining them in individual agreements.[2] Or they might come back to haunt us. Just when we thought that we inhabited a global world 'with no hegemonic power' we discover the greatest ever of such great men, a new American empire (Beck 2000b: 13, 2002: 49).

In this chapter I want to open up the notion of 'governing societies' and its current problematization in two ways, drawing upon different disciplines and working in several registers. I first provide an account of the broad historical conditions of how such an idea could become thinkable. I then elaborate upon its presuppositions as a concept. The task here is simply to clarify the presuppositions of the idea of governing societies in a present where we are told to dispense with it.

My broad view of notions of governing society, and the related vocabulary of state and nation, is broadly aligned to that of the governmentality perspective in so far as it undertakes a nominalist critique rooted in historical knowledge towards such notions as those of society and state (Foucault 1991b: 86). The outcome for political analysis is that what we call state and society should 'first of all be understood as a complex and mobile resultant of the discourses and techniques of rule' (Rose and Miller 1992: 178) and a key component of such discourses and techniques. This can be put in any number of ways. As Quentin Skinner would have it (cf. Tully 1988), we need to be attentive to the illocutionary force of statements, that is, what is being done when they are made, and thus, I would add, their consequences for those they affect. Or again, words such as governing, society and state 'are incomprehensible if one does not know exactly who is to be affected, combated, refuted, or negated by such a term' (Schmitt [1932] 1996a: 30–1). The observation that the state or society has no essential unity or functionality, made by Foucault (1979b: 20), thus does not free us from the obligation of examining the authoritative statements and projects of governing society which deploy notions of state and its related vocabulary. It does not free us from analysing the territorial state as an aspiration and, in some measure, a remarkable achievement of both discourses and techniques of rule with real consequences and effects, with benefits, risks and dangers. While acknowledging the usefulness of 'governmentality' and its analysis of the way we render our world thinkable and actionable, I agree with those who argue that we are not thereby absolved of the necessity of analysing social and political realities which are the contexts and conditions of discourses of rule and the consequences of such discourses (Stenson 2005).

Historical conditions of 'governing societies'

There is a complex history to the project of governing society. The conditions of possibility of such an idea are found in two divisions: the first between the government and its outside, namely society, and the second between one government–society unit and others. For governing societies to make any sense, we must have an agency which claims, with some efficacy, a monopoly of rule within a given territory. For that agency to take a sufficient measure of exclusive control over a territory there need to be demarcated divisions between territories. Up until the sixteenth and seventeenth centuries neither of these conditions existed because the territorial state as we know and narrate it did not exist.

Consider first the way in which the problem of governing society arose as an internal matter. This is where Michel Foucault's lectures (2004a, 2004b) have proved very useful. According to this view, governing society was first posed in European countries concerning the effectiveness of the rule of the territorial state in relation to what was called in the eighteenth century 'civil society' (Dean 1999: 113–30). A key component of the emergence of this idea of governing society was a liberal problematic of security in which the security of the state depended on securing the quasi-natural and necessary processes of civil society, including those of commerce and industry, the economy, the population and so forth. The relationship between security and liberty formed a significant field of problems. For instance, Adam Smith argued ([1752–4] 1978: 332–3) that the economic liberty of the manufacturing worker was the basis of the promotion of security because it was through liberty that the processes of civil society, especially those of the market, would come to operate. Jeremy Bentham, by contrast, would contend that 'a clear idea of liberty will lead us to regard it as a branch of security' while for Humboldt security was 'the legal assurance of freedom' (Neocleous 2000: 8–9).

This anchoring of security within civil society distinguishes aspects of modern rule from previous or other notions of governing such as seventeenth-century doctrines of 'sovereignty', 'reason of state', 'civil prudence' and even 'the science of police' or *Polizeiwissenshaft* (Oestreich 1982; Hunter 1998; Foucault 2001a, 2001b). These doctrines, at least from the perspective of their liberal critics, assumed a transparency of the objects of governing to the sovereign or statesman or other formal authorities and a kind of unlimited capacity on the part of these authorities. They envisaged the state or kingdom to be composed of households which were extensions and instruments of the royal house and its treasury (Dean 1999: 93–6). Security was a matter of defeating internal enemies, outlawing and punishing crimes of sedition, treason and regicide and relentlessly crushing uprisings and establishing order under the dominion of a single territorial ruler. By contrast, to conceive the object of government as securing society would be to imagine a sphere outside government having a history and a dynamism of its own which must be known and respected by anyone attempting to govern it. Civil society became an entity constituted by quasi-natural but relatively opaque processes of the economy, of population and of society itself. These processes, in turn, depended on the 'natural liberty' of individuals to pursue their own interests and better their own condition. Civil society could be known only through expert bodies of knowledge such as political economy and vital statistics, and later demography and the social and human sciences. In this new liberal problematic, the household and family, and the defence of the sovereign, were reconfigured rather than abandoned.

The focus on governing through civil society presented a limit to the 'domestic' extension of formal political rule in this liberal problematic. The focus on commercial freedom and individual responsibility, such as in the reform of the Corn and Poor Laws respectively in Britain, also left quite some scope for the development of a legitimate sphere of intervention of the liberal state and occasioned 'the nineteenth-century revolution in government' (see Polanyi 1957; Sutherland 1972). Later, the emergence of public education, hospitals and access to healthcare, workers' compensation, and unemployment, sickness and aged benefits arose from a definite historical complex. This included the expert knowledge of the diverse social, economic and industrial processes and the ills, problems and risks they posed and an appreciation of the limits of liberal political economy to solve such problems and provide for their solutions. It also included the actions of social, philanthropic, medical and educational movements and the organizations of the emergent working class and other popular associations. These practices, disciplines and actors helped establish political concerns for national well-being, prosperity, social solidarity and citizenship. A *social* domain was formed, and with it a social way of governing which combined collective responsibility and individual compensation for the ills or risks of the industrial economy (Donzelot 1979a; Ewald 1991; Rose 1999: 98–136). The ideal or project of a welfare state emerged in the mid-twentieth century, partially from the practices and institutions of governmental intervention in education, healthcare and social provision, and partially from the aspirations of mass movements and the programmes of mass parties within a widening electoral process. The liberal limitation of the sphere of government proved as enabling as it was restricting. Nevertheless, classic liberal and welfare states sought to maintain a distinction between a public sector bureaucracy and private domains of family and economic life which would be open to state interventions only in the case of knowable ills, problems or incapacities of self-government, or in the name of a greater good such as the security or prosperity of the nation.

It would be misleading to imagine that this social way of governing had a momentum that was not subject to alternative and in many ways more resilient rationalities of governing. The last quarter of the twentieth century saw a significant metamorphosis of the liberal project of governing societies in which the distinction that had emerged between public provision by means of state bureaucracy and private commercial activities came to be viewed as fundamentally problematic. A *neoliberal* way of governing emerged, first in the Anglo-Saxon countries, and only later, and in a much more limited way, in the states of Western and Northern Europe, which sought to breach this distinction by the marketization of public provision by a host of means and techniques, and a new rhetoric and integration of non-government organizations, particularly the private non-profit ones sometimes called the 'Third Sector'. One way of looking at this rupture would be that the collectivization of risks came to be viewed as a risk itself to the performance of the economy and hence risk had to be, at least to some extent, desocialized, individualized and privatized (O'Malley 1992).

From the beginning of the 1990s, the momentum of neoliberal 'reform', which might well have been fading, received a renewed impetus which could be summed up in one word: globalization. The concept of globalization tied transformations in politics, international law, culture, technology, trade and finance, to the evident growth of private corporations and international non-governmental and intergovernmental agencies. These organizations came to be conceived as *transnational* civil society (Held *et al.* 1999; Beck 2000b; Habermas 2001). This discovery of a civil society beyond the state, and the blending of diverse trajectories into the gargantuan concept of globalization, would rupture the older liberal problematic of security with which we commenced this exposition. An 'advanced' or neoliberal problematic of security would simultaneously argue that states have severely diminished capacities with regard to the management of their now 'unbound' national economies and demand that states reform as much of institutional and individual conduct as possible in order to make their performance competitive and efficient and hence attractive to the global capital and financial flows. It is this dual attitude that is at the core of the view that the project of governing society has diminished in importance. Security has become unbound from the governance of civil society within the territorial state and has grown to encompass, among other things, the environment, economy, politics, terrorism, food and health within a global arena (Neocleous 2000). To use another image, the markings, boundaries and hierarchies of the territorial state amount to nothing under the massive, smooth surface of the great global sea which envelops them.

This 'governmentality' account of governing societies is one concerning domestic affairs and needs to be complemented by an account of the conditions of emergence of territorial states themselves (Schmitt [1950] 2003: 128–9; Hirst 2005: 26–38). On the one hand, the emergence of such a view of government meant the emergence of a political unity, the state, which was capable of putting an end to religious and civil conflicts within its territory (Hunter 1998). This process began in Europe in the sixteenth and seventeenth centuries and most particularly, at least in the grounding narrative of international relations, with the Treaty of Westphalia of 1648 concluded at the end of the Thirty Years' War (Zacher 1993; Krasner 2000). The key principle of that treaty was the non-interference of external powers in the religious conflicts within states (Hirst 2005: 35). The principle was summed up as *cujus regio, ejus religio* (whose is the territory, his is the religion), a tenet enunciated earlier in the Peace of Augsburg of 1555. The population would henceforth follow the religion of the prince and the prince could not change his faith without forfeiting his territory. The consequence of this was that rulers were able to take control over their territories without undue anxiety about the savage destruction of life committed in the name of doctrinal differences by bands of militia and mercenaries. In the process, they could begin to form societies. They could start to build a stable identity of the population based on common religious identity, and muster this loyalty to discipline populations to turn their aggression away from internal civil war towards other states.

Second, the territorial state had to gain exclusive control over a territory. Political power was not always coincident with 'a given spatially and culturally coherent territory', as Paul Hirst reminds us (2005: 27). Ancient Greece knew only the small territory of the city-state, which was unable to develop a coherent political unity at a higher level and hence doomed once it met an enemy that had achieved that political unity in Macedon. The Roman Empire had ever-expanding frontiers which knew no legal and cultural limits thus giving it a politically inactive and militarily demobilized population, leaving it open to civil war and vulnerable to barbarian incursions deeper into its heartlands. In late medieval Europe, rule was undertaken by a multiplicity of powers which '. . . competed to control the same spaces, claiming forms of territorial and functional rule that are ill-defined in their scope and rights' (Hirst 2005: 31). Much of what Jean Bodin distinguished as the various marks of sovereignty in his *Six Livres de la République* ([1576] 1955: 40–9), to give orders but not to receive them, to make laws, to administer justice, to coin money, to tax, to raise armies, and to deal with other rulers, was distributed across a wide variety of other agencies. These included leagues of cities such as the Hanseatic League, monastic military orders, city-states, prince bishoprics, and mercenary forces (Hirst 2005: 33). It was the great achievement of the development of European thought and law that all of this would be sought to be put under a single centralized jurisdiction, legislation and administration of the territorial state.

The third aspect of the development of the territorial state was that states had to mutually recognize one another within a common legal framework, to form what some have called a 'society of states' (Bull 1977; Held *et al.* 1999: 37–9). The central plank of this recognition is the principle of non-interference which allows states to get on with the task of unifying their own populations and homogenizing them to form societies. All of this formed a comprehensive European spatial order based on the territorial state summed up by the most vigorous statist of the twentieth century in the following terms:

> First, it created clear internal jurisdictions by placing feudal, territorial, estate, and church rights under the centralized legislation, administration and judiciary of a territorial ruler. Second, it ended the European civil war of churches and religious parties, and thereby neutralized creedal conflicts with the state through a centralized political unity … Third, on the basis of the internal political unity achieved *vis-à-vis* other political unities, it constituted within and of itself a closed area with fixed borders, allowing a specific type of foreign relations with other similarly territorial orders.
>
> (Schmitt [1950] 2003: 128–9)

If the 'internal' outside of government came to be society or civil society in eighteenth-century Europe, the 'external' outside of the state was first a world of other such states bound by interstate law and offering mutual recognition to one. This was first found in the seventeenth century. A condition for this mutual recognition was the existence of a clearly demarcated and mutually recognized frontier between two such states, which enclosed them against one another. The idea of a border that could be mapped and defended as a clear line between states is itself coincident with the territorial state system and is only an episode in the history of geographical boundaries. Just as the territorial state replaced the tangled web of overlapping jurisdictions in late medieval Europe, so the border replaces other kinds of political boundaries. We mention the march and the *limes* to make this point.

The march, exemplified by the Anglo-Celtic and Anglo-Gaelic marches, is a kind of neutral 'interzone' between different powers, a place of interaction and assimilation between peoples and cultures (Walters 2004: 683–4). In a geopolitical sense, the march has a long history of association with Central and Eastern Europe, so that the meaning of the word Ukraine is 'march' or border area. The *limes*, by contrast, is more like the edge, fringe or limit. It divides a world and its outside, the Empire and barbarians, the cosmos and chaos, a house from a non-house, a pacified order from a quarrelsome disorder, an enclosure from the wilderness (Schmitt [1950] 2003: 52; Walters 2004: 690–1). It is discontinuous and mobile but more permanent than a march, which can act as a changing 'buffer zone'. Often it is marked by a wall, such as Hadrian's Wall and other Roman fortifications and the Great Wall of China. While there is an acknowledgement of the danger and even the enemies beyond the *limes*, there is no formal recognition of other political units. The *limes* is less a definite marker of territorial boundaries than a system of management, channelling movements of population with the help of rivers and mountain ranges, and providing early warning and detection against possible incursions (Hirst 2005: 62). While the eighteenth-century European border was both an enclosure and a mutual recognition of the sovereign territory of one's neighbours, the *limes* marked a radical exclusion of that which lay beyond civilization and the march an interzone between powers and cultures.

The comprehensive European spatial order based on the territorial state thus gave rise to the notion of a world constituted by mutually recognizing territorial states. As Foucault notes (2004b: 303–13), the relation between these European states would be made by new diplomatic and military techniques after the Treaty of Westphalia which put an end to the dream of the reconstitution of the Roman Empire. These would include the very idea of Europe itself as a plurality of different sovereigns, supreme in their own domain and recognizing each other, new diplomatic models around the notion of a 'balance' between such states and their spheres of influence, new permanent military apparatuses including standing armies and the professionalization of the 'man of war', and new concepts of war for reason of state. These new international legal relations crystallized into a system of European interstate law (called the *jus publicum Europaeum*), which would regard war as a kind of duel between two sovereign persons, two *magni homines*, and would reject the *bellum ex justa causa* (war from just causes) of medieval Christendom (the *respublica Christiana*) and the chaos of confessional conflict typified in the Thirty Years' War (Schmitt [1950] 2003: 126–30). War between European sovereigns would be a formally declared war between two mutually recognized sovereigns, *une guerre en forme*, war in form, which limited and to a certain extent humanized and civilized war in contrast to the religious civil wars and feudal feuds (Schmitt [1950] 2003: 141).

This spatial order, however, also included a conception of parts of the world not occupied by such states and within which European states would be able to engage in conquest and competition outside the normal structures of European law. The discovery and occupation of the New World was integral to this distinction between European and non-European parts of the globe and between those parts of the world in which European law held and those parts beyond European law. The earliest examples of this kind of consciousness followed almost immediately the discovery of the New World (Schmitt [1950] 2003: 89–99). Pope Alexander VI famously drew a line from the North Pole to the South Pole one hundred miles west of the Azores and Cape Verde meridian. The *rayas* drawn by Spain and Portugal divided the world among the two Catholic powers still operating as a part of a common Christian empire. These were followed by the 'amity lines', which belonged more to the age of religious wars and consisted of defining the limits of application of treaties between Catholic and Protestant powers. What emerges alongside a notion of European interstate law is a specification of the zones in which this law did not hold, which belonged 'beyond the line'. These were zones of contestation between European powers, of conquest and colonization. They were zones in which Europeans no longer felt bound by their own treaties and concepts of war and aligned themselves with heretics and pirates, freebooters and buccaneers of all sorts, against one another. The absence of European legal jurisdiction, and the absence of recognition of the sovereignty of those 'beyond the line', provided the means of the great land-appropriation of the New World, and the expropriation of its indigenous peoples, and the later subjugation of local populations in the acquired colonies in Asia and Africa. Following the work of Hugo Grotius, the world would be divided along a fundamental antithesis of firm land and the free sea, *terra firma* and *mare libre* (Schmitt [1950] 2003: 172–3). By 1713, after the Treaty of Utrecht, the global consciousness of Europeans not only distinguished between land and sea but between the various 'soil statuses' including state territory, colony, protectorate, free occupiable land and exotic countries with European extraterritoriality, and the notion of territorial waters (Schmitt [1950] 2003: 179–84).

The security of the territorial states of this European system was gained by this process of the mutual recognition within a common framework of law. While some contemporary commentators (Held *et al.* 1999: 38) argue that this international law was composed of minimal rules of coexistence with 'virtually no legal fetters to curb the resort to force', this would seem at least contestable. *The* Nomos *of the Earth* (Schmitt [1950] 2003), first published in 1950, shows European public law to have been a highly regulated system of military, commercial and diplomatic relations between states with a global outlook which contributed significantly to the limitation and humanization of war, at least on the European continent. It also evinced a global spatial consciousness which was capable of discovering and occupying much of the globe, colonizing it, and finally making its own state–system universal. This system created the terror of colonial wars, the extirpation, mass murder and enslavement of indigenous populations, and a legacy of economic exploitation and cultural subordination, a point that Schmitt underplays. For him, the great tragedies of the twentieth century, including the two world wars, were the result of the disarray of this international legal system. These tragedies were also, we might add in response, a part of the key legacy of that international system – the territorial nation-state.

Given these relatively pacified and secure territorial boundaries, the development of national culture and social provision also sought to complete the internal pacification of states by forming them as 'imagined communities', in the famous phrase of Benedict Anderson (1983), spaces in which individuals would feel primary identification with the nation and thus could be mobilized for purposes such as military preparedness and defence, for the colonization of other parts of the globe, and for economic competition. The identification of state with nation could be viewed as a way of achieving internal homogeneity (that is the minimum necessary degree of commonality among the population) and fostering capacities for effective external economic competition, military conflict and the conquests of empire. As Foucault (2003) showed, this 'homogenization' of the population was sometimes achieved by the identification of nation with a biologized conception of race in new forms of state racism.

One of the reasons that this European international order persisted so long until World War I was that the system of sovereign states fostered trade and commerce around the globe on a scale not reached again until recent years (Hirst 2005: 38–41). Under the new political principle of commercial liberalism, and under British hegemonic naval and commercial control of the seas, the liberal constitutional state was committed to enforcing definite international norms of the freedom of trade. The long nineteenth century of 1815–1914 and its pacific international order were based on a world free-trading system and the mass migrations of European populations to the New World. The territorial state and the state-system that made it possible, together with the maritime *Pax Britannica*, were the twin conditions of what in retrospect was the first great global era of liberal commerce.

The twentieth century saw the – in retrospect – inevitable mutation of this system of European-based interstate law with the recognition of nation-states in the New World and the Orient in organizations such as the International Telegraph Union of 1864 and the Universal Postal Union of 1874, particularly the United States of America, and in Asia, Siam, Japan and China. International law would attempt to take a universal rather than European perspective in first the League of Nations and then the United Nations. Crucial to this move from a European world outlook to a 'spaceless universalism' would be the rise of the United States of America and the idea of a Western Hemisphere. This idea was enunciated as early as the Monroe Doctrine of 1823 which sought to annex the Americas from the interference of the powers of the now Old World of Europe. After the catastrophes of the new 'Thirty Years' War' in Europe from 1914 to 1945, and the genocides which would have their most horrific exemplar in the Holocaust committed upon the Jews and other peoples by the Nazis, aggressive war for national purposes would be criminalized, notions of crimes against humanity and peace would emerge, and doctrines of universal human rights would come to dominate the discussion and practice of international affairs. This first World War saw the collapse of the old international order and British hegemony and the emergence of a range of authoritarian nationalist and state socialist regimes which sought to base their alternatives on enforced large-scale economic and social control over citizens and their movements. After 1945, and particularly after 1989, the United States would take on the role once held by Britain of establishing the rules for a new international trading order and enforcing existing territorial borders. As Admiral Alfred Thayer Mahan (1894) had predicted in his case for an Anglo-American reunion, the USA would assume the role of the bi-oceanic continental 'larger island' which Britain, now grown too small, had to forfeit, and act as guarantor of world trade through its global maritime (and air) power.

The high point of welfare-state doctrines and of confidence in the capacity to govern societies occurred in Western nation-states during the thirty years after the end of World War II. Now the internal balance of European states and their empires gave way to the balance of mutually assured destruction (MAD) made possible by massive nuclear arsenals with intercontinental delivery systems. The Cold War promoted a security balance between a capitalist and a communist world, West and East. In effect, the Cold War acted as a proxy international system. In the West, the nation-state was protected in a system of financial and currency controls, after the Bretton Woods agreement of 1944, including semi-fixed exchange rates, one-off devaluations, insulation of domestic money markets, and the use of International Monetary Fund loans. All of this 'was designed to ensure that domestic economic objectives were not subordinated to global financial disciplines but, on the contrary, took precedence over them' (Held *et al.* 1999: 200).

The Cold War stand-off started to see the emergence of a new domain of superpower contestation in the process of decolonization of the former colonies which had been the products of the older European state system. A 'Third World' emerged between the authoritarian land-based socialist empire and a liberal trading sea-empire. Paradoxically the model of the territorial state would be claimed by or extended to those former colonies without the capabilities of the management of their own population, not to mention the defence of their own territory, which had been the hallmark of the classical European concept of the state after the Treaty of Westphalia. The extension of the number of states that were clearly not capable of acting like such a model, together with the growth of non-state international organizations and the criminalization of acts of aggression under international law, has led to a situation in which the state is no longer viewed as a political entity that can secure its own position within the international order and becomes, in large parts of the world, simply those forces that are most likely to maintain a minimum of political and social order.

If the nineteenth-century revolution in government marks the first flowering of the task of governing societies first enunciated in the eighteenth century, the post-World War II welfare state marks its full summer bloom and was only possible, in retrospect, in these very particular historical conditions. The welfare state was underpinned by a specific regulation of international finance which created a secure space to enable domestic macro-economic policies such as Keynesian demand management by manipulating levels of public expenditure and investment. Externally, the Western liberal democracies were confronted with an authoritarian alternative with command economies, enforced trade and military cooperation between socialist blocs, and control of their population, activities and movements.

One key context for the problematization of the idea of governing societies, then, was the neoliberal critique of the domestic capacities of the state mentioned above. At the heart of those critiques was the view that the welfare state, high wages involving collective bargaining with trade unions, and high levels of public investment in education, healthcare and infrastructure were all brakes on the competitiveness and productivity of the economy. The aggressive neoliberalism was first adopted in the Anglophonic parts of the West, led by Margaret Thatcher and Ronald Reagan. These leaders also adopted tougher stances toward the Soviet alternative, which was collapsing under the weight of its own inefficiencies, lack of domestic legitimacy, and inability to compete militarily with the West. The neoliberal critiques, combined with the collapse of this alternative, prepared the way for the invocation of globalization, at its core meaning intensified flows of trade and investment between parts of the world, as a standing reason for the conduct of neoliberal policies. Liberal intellectuals in the West pronounced the inevitable spread of the liberal capitalist system across the globe, summed up in Fukuyama's 'end of history' (1992) and globalization as the 'One Big Thing' (Friedman 2000). All, except ultra-conservatives in the United States, dubbed 'neocons', who controversially came to incumbency after a pro-globalist decade, seemed unprepared for the resistance to the end of history and globalization as American hegemony. The conjuncture witnessed the unexpected strengthening of authoritarian and semi-authoritarian regimes across Central and East Asia, the stalling of the democratization in Russia, the persistence of rogue states and regimes as enemies of the proclaimed cosmopolitan order, sometimes basing their resistance on religious and national fundamentalism, and new forms of war and struggle including global terrorism and its response, which seemed to lie outside the law of war and its twentieth-century codifications in the Geneva Conventions.

To return to the longer-term picture, a territorially bound state, with an effective central government, in a world of other such states, which would trade with one another, form alliances and rivalries, and potentially find themselves at war with one another, was a condition for the emergence of a notion of governing societies. The system of such territorial states was a key postulate, aspiration and achievement of myriad practices and discourses of domestic and international rule from early modern times. The problematization of the pertinence of such a world order, and the place of the bounded entity of the state within it, is the immediate reason for our current sense that the idea of governing societies has been eclipsed. As we have seen from the already long history of the twenty-first century, we might wish to revisit what now appears in retrospect to have been a rather too hasty conclusion. The events of 9/11 and the War on Terror, the treatment and internment of refugees and 'unlawful enemy combatants', the proliferation of security concerns including the protection of 'homeland', the scandals of the prisons of Abu Ghraib and Guantánamo Bay, and the desire to enforce obligation and hierarchy amongst domestic populations in, for example, 'workfare' policies and practices, could not be made thinkable and actionable without a vocabulary of sovereignty, territory, society and central government.

I shall take up aspects of this narrative of governing societies at later stages in more detail. The above, however, is a description of the conditions of existence of the government of society, and its relation to the legal governance and regulation of the society of states, which came to establish the relationship between state and civil society in the eighteenth century and which lasted for the next two centuries. It was largely on the basis of this liberal government that the notion of governing societies acquired the taken-for-granted meanings that are under suspicion today in social and political theory.

Having sought to understand the general historical conditions of the concept of governing societies, I now turn to the concept itself.

The concept of 'governing societies'

At its most basic, this classical liberal idea of governing societies assumes a relationship between an agency of political rule and administration, commonly called government, and a sphere external to that realm, society or civil society, and a set of purposes and means for the action of one upon the other. This is encapsulated in Jeremy Bentham's view ([1789] 1996: 74) that the 'business of government is to promote the happiness of the society, by punishing and rewarding'.[3] While few today would agree that the means of governing are limited to punishments and rewards, or with his calculus of happiness, Bentham's statement does presuppose an action of a political agency ('government') upon a unified entity ('society') for a distinctive purpose – happiness. In a more recent version, we might talk about the role of government in securing the welfare of the citizens of nation. Yet it is precisely all of this that is called into question in much of the contemporary social and political sciences because it eschews a paradigm in which governing can be understood as the existence of a relatively centralized body acting within a unified area or territory with particular jurisdiction.

Before we move onto that, I want to show what the term presupposes, drawing upon sociological, legal and philological points of view. I am interested in the force of the term, what is intended by it, how it condenses important features of the worlds we inhabit and the effects of the ordering of those worlds.

Let us start with the idea of governing. This is fairly easy to deal with since, conveniently, Thomas Hobbes provides us with two classic and contrasting senses of the term. In his *Leviathan* ([1651] 1996: 185) he uses the term in a very familiar sense: 'If the Soveraign of one Common-wealth, subdue a people that have lived under other written Lawes, and afterwards govern them by the same Lawes, by which they were governed before; yet those Lawes are the Civill Lawes of the Victor, and not of the Vanquished Common-wealth'. Here the sense of the term 'to govern' is to rule with authority, that is, to rule with some basis, in this case, in law. This I take to be the still extant primary sense of the term and the one we usually intend when we speak of governing societies.

In his *Behemoth* ([1679] 1840: 347), however, Hobbes uses the term 'govern' in a somewhat different sense during a discussion of the attitude of Parliament to the supposed virtues of university life: 'Some others were sent thither [to the university] by their Parents, to save themselves the trouble of governing them at home, during that time wherein Children are least governable'. Here, govern is used in a much broader sense of any practice that more or less deliberately seeks to direct, guide or control others, for example, children, subjects, wives, a congregation, even live-stock, and so forth. This latter use of the term 'to govern' is largely obsolete although it is clearly related to the sense of the term Foucault sought to revive in his lectures on governmentality in which one can speak of the government of a vast group of heterogeneous persons and things: children, families, households, livestock, congregations and souls, as well as of a domain, a principality, and a state (cf. Foucault 1997b: 68). The 'gov-ernmentality' problematic, concerned with the rationalities and techniques of the direction of conduct of different social and political actors by a variety of agencies and authorities, relies heavily on this second sense of the term.

On the other hand, the notion of governing as authoritative rule is found every day in newspapers, on television and in our conversations. Moreover, it is usually associated with a particular kind of authority, that of the sovereign state as a site of command and lawmaking. As the *Oxford English Dictionary* so succinctly puts it, to govern in this sense means 'to rule with authority, especially with the authority of a sovereign; to direct and control the actions and affairs of (a people, a state or its members), whether despotically or constitutionally ...'.[4] Now, I would contend, it is this sovereign-based action that is at least one primary meaning of discussions of 'governing societies', which I shall come back to. More limited discussions of governing, such as 'governing a corporation' or 'governing a university', do not, however, entail the action of a sovereign, although they certainly take care to be done in a manner consistent with law and governmental policy or risk disfavour or punishment for not doing so.

Sociologists, following Weber, have spent much effort in discussing questions of authority and particularly legitimate authority, that is, the basis on which the authority of rule is justified. Weber ([1918] 1972: 78–9) himself distinguished three different 'types' of legitimation – 'the authority of "eternal yesterday"' or traditional authority, 'the authority of extra-ordinary and personal *gift of grace*' or charisma, and 'domination by "virtue of legality"' or legal authority. These 'types' are fairly straightforward and easily recognizable (without getting into the question of their methodo-logical status). It was Weber's contention that rule 'by virtue of legality' became the predominant form in modern societies. We might now wish to add the authority of expertise. If we were today to discuss governing children, for instance, we could easily find examples where the justification and direction of what we were doing would be found in manuals on child psychology and childhood education and in expert practices of family therapy, counselling and social work.

It is not specious, therefore, to say that much contemporary governing in this second sense above relies on the 'authority of expertise'. The legitimacy of that expertise, moreover, is found not in the unquestioned specialist training and access to knowledge of medical, psychological or other experts, or the unquestioned hierarchy of doctor and patient, but in the promise of that expertise to help individuals help themselves, and lead happy and satisfying lives as individuals, as well as in families and communities and at school and work. Governing in this sense has found its own justification in its powers to unleash the inner capacities of individuals, to allow those who are governed to govern and to fulfil themselves, to overcome the experiences and obstacles of victimhood, exclusion and dependency, and thus to empower themselves and finally to make themselves more truly free. In this respect, Foucault (1982) is right to argue that the problematic of rule in such instances is neither primarily a question of sovereignty and violence nor of law and legitimacy but of government in the second sense above, government as the 'conduct of conduct', as the more or less calculated shaping of the needs, desires and aspirations of individuals and populations for various ends. His followers, too, have been right to stress the importance of government by means of this expertise. Given that the notion of 'society' is an object and domain of knowledge, and will give rise to various bodies of expertise, I shall argue below that one sense of the term governing societies is precisely governing through a specific kind of expertise.

However, much of what we call government and the activity of governing are activities that operate by virtue of legality, as Weber had already noted. We do not need to get into the niceties of an argument about whether we should pose questions in terms of legitimacy, or the relationship between legality and legitimacy, to note that much of governing entails the machine-like production of law. In liberal democracies, much of the effort of executive government, as well as the legislative and juridical institutions of the national, regional and local state, is devoted to the production, interpretation and enforcement of law. The actions of office holders within the public service, university administrations, companies and philanthropic bodies, and indeed anyone managing workplaces, are prescribed in law or in the rules and regulations that are attached to them. Thus the idea of governing society presupposes a body that makes, negotiates or imposes laws. To use Weber's language again, the legitimacy of the governor 'to give commands rests upon rules that are rationally established by enactment, by agreement, or by imposition' ([1918] 1972: 294). This body can be centralized or federal, monarchical or republican, liberal or authoritarian or both, a representative government or a military or populist dictatorship. It can even cede aspects of its authority to other such bodies and create an association of states such as in the European Union with functionally specific, common governmental institutions. The fact that practices of governing, in the first restricted sense above, can make reference to more than one body, or that certain laws and regulations (for instance, the European Convention on Human Rights) can be used to countermand and override those of another (say, as in recent British High Court judgments concerning control orders of terrorist suspects), does not mean that this kind of authority 'by virtue of legality' has ceased to exist. If anything it is proliferating and becoming more complex. Like security, legality with its machine-like production of laws, has come to assume even more significance.

If one wanted to push this to a further, more basic, level, the idea of governing (as a system of authority) justified by virtue of 'legality' pre-supposes a system of lawmaking and a 'jurisdiction', that is, the domain that defines the extent or range of validity of those laws. While there can be multiple and overlapping jurisdictions, they are usually applied to a geo-graphically delimited area or territory. Thus the laws of New South Wales, the Australian state in which I am writing, have as their jurisdiction a geographically delimited area. They do not apply to the neighbouring Australian state of Victoria or the faraway nations of Botswana and Bel-gium, for instance. This does not mean that other lawmaking bodies are excluded from having their jurisdiction across the same geographical area (the Commonwealth of Australia, for instance), or activities within that area (various UN treaties to which the Australian government is a signa-tory, the recently signed Free Trade Agreement with the United States of America, and so forth). It does not stop the Australian government from cooperating with Indonesian authorities on border patrol, immigration controls and other security issues in the seas between them. Thus even a relatively isolated and sea-bounded territorial state such as Australia can have multiple and overlapping jurisdictions and institutions of government.

The concept of jurisdiction does not preclude cooperation between different agencies and authorities at local, national and international levels. William Walters (2004: 677–80) has argued that the removal of border controls between nation-states within the European Union under the Schengen Agreement is accompanied by other kinds of regulation including cross-border police cooperation, mobile surveillance teams operating within an extended strip, information exchange, common visas, common migration policy and common standards of management. He calls this 'the network non-border'. The EU also employs strategies akin to the march and the *limes*, particularly on its eastern and southern frontiers. These strategies address new security concerns such as drug smuggling, people trafficking, terrorism, arms dealing and asylum seeking. More broadly, Walters suggests (2004: 678), we should see different kinds of borders as 'geo-strategies', following Michel Foucher (2001), which involve '. . . the instrumentalisation of territory for the purposes of governing one or more of these new security issues'.

In different territorial states today we witness the coexistence of different geo-strategies which render the notion of a fixed, fortified border as but one form of frontier between states. The different frontiers can make territorial states more or less 'porous' for different reasons, and more or less connected to other states. North Korea is quite a deal less porous in this sense than Denmark, for instance. While people on both sides of the Korean border have been separated from each other and from their families since the Korean War, people who live in or near Malmö in Sweden can commute to work in Copenhagen each day on the local rail network. For the Danes the more relevant frontiers might be not the imaginary line in the sound (the Oresund) dividing it from Sweden but the eastern frontier the Baltic States have with Russia after the accession of these states to the European Union in 2004 or those parts of the Copenhagen international airport that accept arrivals from outside the EU. Borders are still something that can be defended and protected; but they can be something that can facilitate relationships and cooperation, and provide benefits. In all cases, however, borders delimit territories and utilize them in various ways to define what is inside and outside, and to address different types of threat and problems. Since early modern Europe, to speak of governing the state is to speak of a project or an aspiration to control the activities within a given space, to be able to know and locate the edges of that space, and to define the population that inhabits that space. That this remains simply an aspiration can be evidenced by the admission of the United States President's address on immigration on 15 March 2006 that 'for decades, the United States has not been in complete control of its borders' and that as a result it 'must secure its borders' as 'a basic responsibility of a sovereign nation' and 'urgent requirement of our national security' (Bush 2006). In this speech, immigration policy blends with border control policy in the aspiration to be able to control both the borders and those who belong to the body of the sovereign nation.

It is clear that the conventional understanding of a border as a line of separation and fortification between two discrete territories is only one way of utilizing territory and that 'borders' are best thought of as resultants of different strategies. Nevertheless, each of these strategies engages in 'territorialization', that is, 'any movement which striates, draws lines, fixes, orders, localises and segments' (Walters 2004: 681), and thus presupposes territory and an attempt to govern it. If governing implies law and law entails jurisdiction, then jurisdiction relies on the existence of territory. It is the strength of territorial jurisdiction that is a condition of multiple, overlapping, shared and even networked arrangements such as those obtaining today in Europe.

Consider now notions of society. Our notion of society has as its historical condition the system of states described above and the emergence of nations. It is probable that the Ancient Greeks did not have a word for society given that they only knew city-states and their hinterlands. Twentieth-century translations of Aristotle, however, attribute to him the view that, while human beings come together for the sake of merely living, or to secure and protect their lives, the 'good life is the chief aim of society' (1957: 201). Here, however anachronistically, society is indeed a project. Yet it is a particular kind of project involving the coming together of human beings. The English word 'society' is derived from Latin, *societas* and *socius*, meaning companionship, companion, friend or associate. Society thus implies some coming together of human beings in friendship. For Hobbes, society still entails all of this except that it must occur under the protection afforded by the strength of the Leviathan, the state. For the pre-political state of nature is not only 'solitary, poore, nasty, brutish and short' but also with 'no ... Industry ... no Culture of the Earth ... no Navigation ... no commodious Building ... no account of Time; no Arts; no Letters, no Society; and which is worst of all, continuall feare, and danger of violent death' ([1651] 1996: 89). For Hobbes, the formation of the state is thus the proper and necessary project for governing society.

Hobbes's notion of society is still enwrapped in a discourse on friendship and association. His notion of society is but one example of the early modern vision of society as a covenant, compact or contact, that is as an outcome of a political agreement of free persons (usually men), an 'assemblie and consent of many in one' as the author of *Mirrour of Policie* put it in 1599.[5] Later versions of society, such as those of the eighteenth-century Scottish Enlightenment (Adam Ferguson, David Hume, Adam Smith), adopt a separation between state and society and in some sense break their identity. To these thinkers, society ceases to be a kind of relationship and becomes more the quasi-natural, non-political sphere in which humans are found. Yet the opposition between state and civil society was still programmatic. This was because for these thinkers the state must be trained to respect the autonomy of civil society and to base its mode of government in the knowledge of the processes, laws and tendencies of civil society. The latter might include the development of nations, the laws of commerce, the tendencies of populations, and the customs of peoples. If society had become quasi-naturalized, it was still as an artefact of liberal political programmes and arrangements.

During the nineteenth and early twentieth centuries, society came to be considered a whole or a totality which was separate from the individuals who composed it and within which government might be viewed as a specific set of institutions. It acquired organic and evolutionary metaphors derived from advances in biology and from Darwinian theory. It became the object of a science, sociology. Later, many thinkers rejected the idea of both such organicism and even the idea of totality and preferred to focus on such things as social action, social interaction, social institutions and social classes. Marxists wanted to retain the notion of the whole or totality but tended to use terms such as mode of production or social formation to designate it. Despite the views of specialists, society has survived in commonplace usage. In it, like specialist knowledge, the adjective 'social' tends to invoke the quality of processes that are thought to have their origin in society, such as in notions of social inclusion and exclusion.

The notion of society still retains many happy connotations of human association, sociability and so on. Adam Smith ([1759] 2002) noted a fundamental 'sympathy' or 'fellow-feeling' which bound individuals together. Emile Durkheim ([1893] 1997), two centuries later, analysed different forms of social solidarity consequent on different forms of the division of labour. Indeed, the latter notion was also linked to a political doctrine of governing society, *solidarisme*. However, to understand that notion of society, which concerns the drawing of human beings into common identification or bonds, is also to acknowledge that it draws geographic and other lines between territories and populations. Thus notions of society contain an idea not simply of space but of place. Societies exist in distinctive locales. These locales could be of the city, the pathways of nomads, or defined by the boundaries of national states or even of an alliance or other grouping of states. They could be places to be defended from various groups: from the illegal immigrant or the internal partisan or insurgent to external hostile forces.

Thus, if society implies identification and fellow-feeling among friends or citizens, it also implies at least the potential for enmity. This enmity might take the form of defeating insurgents within a society or trying to reconcile partisans to the existing order. The history of the struggles of the Basque separatists in Spain or Irish nationalists in Northern Ireland reminds us that civil war, insurgency and attempts to overcome them are still characteristic of the liberal democracies of Europe. While the enemy within must be persuaded either to give up his or her enmity or to be defeated conclusively in order to prevent or halt civil war, the idea of a society also draws a line to its outside and contains the potential of an external enemy which threatens the security and way of life of a particular society. In the traditional legal system of European states, the public enemy was the just enemy (*justus hostis*), another sovereign state. In the present international order, the public enemy is more likely to be one on whom a new form of just war has been declared. This can be a 'rogue state' acting outside international covenants on, say, the production of nuclear weapons or led by a dictator engaged in gross human rights violations. It can be a non-state actor such as a terrorist network, an international criminal organization which smuggles people and drugs, or even one engaged in piracy, whether maritime, industrial or virtual. Even a perfectly cosmo-politan society would be open to enemies: for example, political parties seeking to maintain national identities and build national states (Beck 2000a: 98) or those who seek to destroy such a society because it appears to promote various kinds of immorality. There have always been changing ways in which lines are drawn between friends and enemies but we should not be led to believe that such lines are no longer relevant and that the project of defining and dividing societies does not entail such fundamental political constructions.

Conclusion

This chapter has investigated both the historical conditions under which governing societies became thinkable and actionable and the conceptual distinctions through which this became possible. The former was found first in the ways in which, after the pacification of their internal territories and centralization of administration, judiciary and rule, governing developed as a domestic art concerned with establishing its own proper limits. This took the form of limiting the role of the state in relation to a sphere of civil society and the security of the processes constitutive of it, particularly the economy. It was found secondly in the emergence of a comprehensive, Eurocentric spatial order founded on the mutual recognition of these states as sovereign moral persons in an interstate sphere.

From the perspective of conceptual history, the emergence of this idea of governing societies rests upon a displacing of diverse meanings of the word 'govern' onto the centralized system of legitimate and law-based authority of *the* government and on the gradual identification of the notion of society with the territorial nation-state. Society retains a notion of identification, amity and fellow-feeling among its members and often, as we have seen, forms of enmity and exclusion of outsiders.

We have thus argued that 'governing societies' thus rests on two key conceptual distinctions: the first, within the territorial state, between society and state; the second, between the state and its outside, whether conceived as a society of states, the international community or a Hobbesian state of nature. The first distinction gives rise to strategies that employ forms of knowledge or expertise of domains external to the formal institutions of government but within that territory to pursue specific goals. The second distinction gives rise to attempts by international agencies to govern aspects of particular state-societies (for example, the World Bank with its protocols of 'conditionality' of loans), by different state-societies to cooperate, for example, in policing, security, asylum and immigration issues, and by international agencies to set up ground rules for the entire system of state-societies (the United Nations' Security Council and General Assembly).

The frontiers of and between these societies can change over time through war, acquisition and international agreement. Even more basically, the notion of a fixed, fortified border is only one historical form of a frontier between states. The different frontier forms can make societies more or less 'porous' for different reasons, and more or less connected to other societies.

No doubt the European Union is a particular case: it is neither a unitary territorial state nor quite a federation of such states; it results from a series of treaties but is not simply a treaty organization; it receives input from member governments but is more than an intergovernmental organization (Hirst 2005: 14). It does, however, seem less like a new global project and political–juridical discourse (like the *jus publicum Europeaum*) than an arrangement led, sometimes falteringly, by a core of strong territorial states to gain the benefits of economic cooperation and to prevent the blood-baths and other excesses of territorial sovereignty of the last century. For large parts of the world, particularly in Africa, Central Asia and the urban poor in Latin America, the territorial state and the government of society it permits is still only a distant prospect or project. For others, particularly the already multicultural federations of the USA, Canada and Australia, the European project seeks to achieve a different route to what they have achieved by federalism and mass migration: continental wide spheres of relatively peaceful cooperation of diverse peoples. For others still, from China and Russia to Israel and Iran, borders, the sovereign autonomy within them and the right to defend them with whatever means they deem necessary still override any story of the emergence of a cosmopolitan democracy or multilayered governance on the face of the planet. As a one-time famous advocate of globalization put it in relation to Israel's bombardment of Lebanon in response to Hezbollah's guerrilla actions in mid-2006, this war 'is about some of the most basic foundations of the international order − borders and sovereignty − and the erosion of those foundations would spell disaster for the quality of life all across the globe' (Friedman 2006).

This notion of governing societies becomes acute when we consider the considerable historical and contemporary effort put into the work of controlling and defending borders, asserting sovereignty, defining populations and cultivating their attributes. Given that much of this kind of work is still in evidence, then, we might ask, how is it that this idea of governing societies has come into such disrepute? If the certainty that Foucault's lectures sought to confront was the substantiality of the state, the certainty we must now contest is a form of liberalism so assured it drowns the concepts of state and society in the great tsunami of globalization under the grey skies of global cosmopolitan governance.

Ungoverning societies

Having explored the historical conditions and concept of the idea of governing societies in the previous chapter, we now trace the trajectory of some key problematizations of the idea of governing society and examine the idea of post-societal governance.

From ungovernability to governance

It is no doubt possible to offer many accounts of diverse sources of the current problematization of the idea of governing societies. Let us consider and explore a few such sources without making any claims that this is definitive or exhaustive.

First, there is the literature on *the crisis of governability* diagnosed in the 1970s. Various theorists, from different political perspectives, began to talk about the ungovernability of liberal-democratic and capitalist societies (see Stehr and Ericson 2000). From one side, they diagnosed the problem as a crisis of democracy or rather an excess of democracy (Crozier *et al.* 1975). Here Western liberal-democratic societies begin to suffer bureaucratic 'overload' and a civic irresponsibility, both of which can be traced to structural changes and trends present from the 1960s, including mass higher education forming a new class and an 'adversary culture' among the intelligentsia (Crozier *et al.* 1975: 6–7). At the same time, a new post-materialist ethic of aesthetic self-fulfilment is found particularly among the younger generation. Such value changes and new strata, themselves a product of democratic processes and the bureaucratic administration of liberal societies, spawn social movements which place new demands upon the political system. This in turn led to a kind of overload on the political system in which there was a disparity between the claims that are directed towards government and the ability of government to deliver on these claims. The root cause of the crisis of governability of democracies was thus democracy itself. The democratic process had led to a breakdown of traditional social control, a delegitimation of authority of all kinds and an overload of demands upon government.

From another perspective, there was the problem of the crises and contradictions of capitalism (O'Connor 1973; Offe 1984). Here, the capitalist economy seeks to displace labour power in its drive for capital accumulation and profitability, and because it relies on a healthy and skilled working class, it generates needs to be met by the state in the form of the alleviation and relief of poverty and unemployment, and in the provision of adequate healthcare and education. However, as these needs, articulated as demands, increase, the state is progressively unable to establish the fiscal basis on which to meet them. Moreover, due to the pressures of the electoral cycle, it often finds itself committed to limiting if not reducing taxation. The extension of public provision itself thus works against the profitability of capital, resulting in further economic problems. Viewed in this way the irreconcilable contradictions of capitalism lead to a fiscal crisis of the state and a crisis of the welfare state. Thus both the fiscal crisis approach and the excess of democracy thesis lead to the view that the state is unable to develop and implement policies in an effective manner. The limitation in the effectiveness of the state itself leads, or at least is linked in a circular manner, to a 'crisis of legitimation' (Habermas 1975). In any case, whether from a conservative liberalism or from socialist political economy, the problem of ungovernability is a problem of governments' or states' effectivity.

Another, perhaps more theoretical and technicist, version of the ungovernability thesis can be found in systems theory, and particularly in the work of Niklas Luhmann (1997). For Luhmann, the model of a political system acting upon other systems assumes an action perspective in which the state is conceived as a kind of subject capable of 'steering' the economy or other subsystems. Such a view, however rooted in the history of Western political thought, is misplaced because it fails to recognize the process of modernization as one in which society is increasingly functionally differentiated into communicative subsystems, each of which is closed to the other and is constructed according to its own binary code. Subsystems are thus 'autopoietically closed'. This means that information cannot be transferred from, say, the political system to the economic system because each operates according to different codes. The only kind of steering that can occur is the self-steering of subsystems, and the most that the political subsystem can do is to influence the self-steering of the economy by taking into account how the other system operates. In perhaps the most radical formulation of the rejection of what is implicit in the idea of governing societies, Luhmann (1997: 49–50) concludes that 'there is, in the strict sense of the word, no self-steering of society on the level of the entire system'.

Such problematizations of governability are realist in that they argue that the nature of contemporary social forces and political institutions or even the entire process of modernization render the aspirations of governing society impossible. They have a parallel in the theoretical problematizations of the explanatory capacity of the concept of the state and the related architecture of ideas which occurred during the late 1970s and 1980s. Let me give some by no means exhaustive examples. The ungovernability of society is accompanied by the *dethroning of the idea of the state*.

In the history of political thought, the state becomes a completely historicized concept. Quentin Skinner (1989: 116) maintains that the concept of the state only emerges fully with those 'theorists whose aspirations included a desire to legitimize the more absolutist forms of government that began to develop in Western Europe in the early part of the seventeenth century'. The key point here is that the modern idea of the state is inherited from a particular political project in debate with a range of different positions. This modern idea includes the idea that citizens owed their allegiance to a unitary sovereign authority rather than a range of different jurisdictions, and local, municipal and ecclesiastical authorities. But this allegiance was owed to something that was 'doubly impersonal' (Skinner 1989: 112). Against divine right thinkers who sought to obliterate the distinction between office and office holder, Hobbes, Bodin, Hugo Grotius and others insisted that citizens owe their allegiance to the office, not the person of the sovereign. Against republican thinkers, on the other hand, however, they argued that this unified and supreme power should not be viewed as identical to the powers of the citizens who contract into the state. By this, Skinner means that this modern sense of state distinguishes it from both the governors and magistrates who are entrusted with its authority and with the body of citizens or whole society over which its powers are exercised. While Skinner's account might be contested by other historians, what is interesting for our purposes is that a once unquestioned master concept of political thought is now located within a particular context and political project in early modern Europe. Skinner's intention might have been to give the concept of state greater weight than it hitherto had possessed. The effect of the demonstration, however, is to show that it is discursively constructed in the service of absolutism. If the state is thus a construction of a particular political discourse, then it loses all self-evidence. Today, we could extrapolate, political analysis might have no need for the state and the term could indeed be an obstacle to analysis.

This is the conclusion reached by a range of French theorists in the 1970s and 1980s. It is found in the political thought of Michel Foucault and other theorists of power such as Callon and Latour (1981). Where Foucault (1980: 121) seeks 'to cut off the King's head' in political theory, Callon and Latour request that we 'unscrew the big Leviathan' in sociology and its studies of science and technology. They present an agenda for the analysis of power in terms of networks and the translations between different human and non–human actors. For Foucault, the idea of the state

belongs to the 'juridical-political theory of sovereignty', again fundamentally bequeathed to us from early modern thought, and particularly
Hobbes (Foucault 1980: 102–3). The notion of the state, and the related
vocabulary of sovereignty, of right and of legitimacy, acts as a kind of
obstacle to the analysis of power.

The central problems with this language for Foucault are threefold.
Firstly, it focuses attention on the question of the sovereign, of who or
what holds power, and whether and how that power-holder is legitimate.
This is counterposed to Foucault's own concern for the multiple and local
relations of power and domination exercised throughout the social body.
Secondly, the image of the state raises the question of how the ruled obey
such a form of power and this is reflected in questions of legitimacy,
consent and ideology. Against this, Foucault insists that the exercise of
power works neither through the commands backed by the actuality or
threat of violence, nor mechanisms for the generation of consensus or
compliance, but through heterogeneous mechanisms that act in different
ways on possible actions (for example, Foucault 1982). A third problem
with the notion of the state for Foucault is that as an image it acts as a kind
of epistemological obstacle. He criticizes the lyrical and affective image of
the *monstre froid* confronting us, encapsulated in Hobbes's image of the
Leviathan, and the paradoxical reduction by Marxist political economy of
the state to reproducing the relations of production, which turns the state
into the privileged target for political action (Foucault 1991a: 103). In the
effort to think beyond such an obstacle and the language of the juridical
theory of sovereignty, Foucault himself turned to the idea of 'government'.
While Foucault would not have bought into the discourses of the ungovernability of contemporary liberal democracy, his theoretical trajectory
suggests a parallel displacement of the focus on the state by a conception of
the plural and heterogeneous mechanisms by which the conduct of individuals and collectives are governed. His work on government as the
'conduct of conduct' could thus be viewed as in part anticipating the shift
of analysis from the state and its functions to what would more commonly
be called governance.

A third set of problematizations of governing society, then, have their
source in *the emergence and proliferation of the concept of governance*. It would
simply be impossible to map all the uses of the term or to offer a general
explanation of its multiplying uses. It certainly has a source in attempts to
define the limits of state action and thus could be viewed as a positive
recasting of the problem of state effectivity revealed by the crisis of governability theorists. This is closely related to the rise of the 'new public
management', encapsulated in the phrase 'less government and more
governance' (Osborne and Gaebler 1993). Governance here is a way of
thinking about the relation of a limited public sector to the individuals,
communities and organizations which lie external to it but which are
necessary to the achievement of its aims and purposes. Linked to this is the
idea of governance as 'steering'. The debate over steering in Germany takes

a theoretical form about the efficacy of interventions within self-steering subsystems such as the economy and thus contests Luhmann's positions (Mayntz 1993). In the United States, the idea of steering is used to advocate an approach to public organization as one that 'steers rather than rows'. Government, in this view, must not attempt to provide all the services and fulfil all the needs of its citizens. It must facilitate citizens, neighbourhoods and communities in the project of establishing their own forms of organization to achieve their self-defined goals and satisfy their self-defined needs. A related use of the term, then, is the idea of governance as self-organizing networks or policy networks of different organizations, individuals, communities (Rhodes 1994, 1996). In this respect, governance comes to mean a kind of organization and form of regulation which is distinguished from both the hierarchical and bureaucratic form of the state and the anarchical form of market organization. In the international relations literature, the concept of global governance is linked to the decline or limitation of the 'sovereignty' of nation states and the idea that governance occurs through a multiplicity of agencies at supranational, subnational and cross-national levels, as well as requiring the cooperation of national states (Rosenau and Czempiel 1992; Held and McGrew 2002).

In general the story of the rise of governance, whether in domestic or international contexts, is linked, as we shall see, to the narrative of the decline of the national state and its capacities. There are discussions of global governance and advocacy by agencies such as the World Bank as to what constitutes 'good governance'. One can now talk of corporate governance, the governance of the economy, or of schools, of the social security system, of local administration and so on. Given that governance in this respect is tied to specific spatial locales (communities, neighbourhoods, regions, sectors and so on), it is possible to talk of attempts to mesh the visions, objectives and outcomes of these instances, and thus to discuss a 'governance of governance' or meta-governance (Jessop 1998) or perhaps even a 'reflexive governance' (Ashenden 1996; Dean 1999: 188–97).

Within this literature it is possible to make certain analytical distinctions. For Jessop (1998: 29), governance refers to 'any mode of coordination of independent activities', and thus to the 'anarchy of exchange' typified by markets, organizational hierarchy typified by bureaucratic bodies, and 'self-organizing "heterarchy"'. In a more restricted sense, he argues, governance has become identified with the third meaning. Here the forms of governance 'include self-organizing interpersonal networks, negotiated inter-organizational coordination, and decentred, context-mediated inter-systemic steering'. Governance is thus viewed as the missing third term in the traditional dichotomies around the opposition of state and market. It is presented as a solution to the problems of ungovernability we have mentioned. It is a solution both to the failure of the hierarchical organization of the state with its rigidity and inefficiencies and to problems of the anarchical organization of the market with its disregard for equality, justice and social consequences. In this formulation, 'meta-governance' lies beyond the decentred forms of self-organization and interpersonal, inter-organizational and intersystemic networks. Meta-governance concerns the organization of these self-organizing networks, the institutional design to facilitate self-organization in different fields and the coordination of objectives, actions, temporal and spatial horizons, and outcomes (Jessop 1998: 42). A kind of paradox is thus present. While governance in this restricted sense is presented as a solution to failures of states and markets, states still occupy a central role in the exercise of meta–governance. They organize dialogue, they provide a regulatory order, they attempt to make subsystems cohere, and form 'the sovereign power responsible "in the last resort" for compensatory action where other systems fail'. The activities of governance thus remain entangled in the shadow of the hierarchical structures of state and sovereignty.

The rejection of the notion of the state and related concepts as master explanatory devices in political and social thought and the problem of governability might not directly explain the explosion of governance paradigms since circa 1990 but they provide something of its context and conditions of possibility. However, we can see that they explicitly address both normative problems of how we should govern and explanatory ones of how best to describe changes in areas such as public policy and management. Many of the governance approaches are explicitly normative in that they seek to offer practical solutions to the problems of governability. A visit to the World Bank Institute's website on Governance and Anti-Corruption (http://info.worldbank.org/governance) will show how good or bad governance can be measured by a set of factors such as:

- 'voice and accountability', including citizen participation in government selection;
- 'political stability and absence of violence', measuring likelihood of government destabilization;
- 'government effectiveness', combining quality and independence of the bureaucracy and public servants with the credibility of the government's commitment to policies;
- 'regulatory quality', including perception of 'market-unfriendly policies' and excessive regulation;
- rule of law; and
- control of corruption, the latter defined as 'the exercise of public power for private gain'.

The point of this is to inform the World Bank's criteria of 'conditionality' on its loans by which borrowing countries would need to show active measures on policies to address poor performance in these areas. In advanced liberal democracies, governance in this normative sense might be linked to the minimal state, to the advocacy of public–private partnerships and to various forms of the 'new public management'. These approaches thus ask: what does good governance consist of? What objectives should it seek? What characteristics does it have?

On the other hand, there are a group of approaches that address the problem of the effectiveness of governing descriptively. These ask the question of how governance operates within national states and across them in the international domain and how it displaces conventional images of states as political actors. Such approaches might seek an explanation of governance as complex socio–political relations (Kooiman 1993, 2003), as self–organizing policy networks of heterogeneous and plural actors and associations (Rhodes 1997), as forms of political communication (Bang 2003), as modes of coordination, steering, and so on.

It is not easy to draw an easy line between these two. The notion of steering, for example, can become part of a normative discussion of governing in the idea of steering rather than rowing, and, at the same time, be part of a German debate of how governance can affect the role of the self-steering mechanisms of social and political systems. There is a deeper question here of whether an explanation or description can be entirely divorced from normative values. Indeed, one might ask whether the emphasis on governance implies a set of prescriptions in favour of a narrative of the rise of network forms of organization and around the decline of state capacities.

Some have posited a third position around Foucault's concept of government (Rose 1999: 17–19). Foucault's position clearly differs from the more realist conception of governance in that government has no substantive content and concerns the ways in which we think about governing – hence the term, govern*mentality*. Further, advocates claim that this position is neither descriptive nor normative but 'analytical and diagnostic'. They claim that governmentality rejects the realism of the description of governing networks in order to understand those 'vectors of thought, will and invention' that seek to problematize and reform, within a contested domain, how we govern. However, there is a sense in which this approach remains descriptive. It is descriptive not of the real networks or socio-political relations but of the ways in which we think about and imagine governing and the instruments of reform to which such imaginings are linked. Rather than normative, such an approach presents itself as diagnostic, which means showing how we have come to think about governing in a given situation and to deprive those ways of their obviousness, their naturalness and their self-evidence. The problem that this diagnostic raises, however, is that the injunction to shake up the ways in which we think about governing is itself a normative one. Governmentality is thus an analytical framework to describe second-order statements about governing which comprise 'rationalities of government' (for example, 'good governance means proper accounting standards') and the techniques and technologies to which they are linked. It also enjoins us in a normative sense to problematize or call into question and to make strange the rationalities by which we make these first-order statements, including for our purposes those that have allowed us to speak of 'governing societies'. It is my contention here that, however useful such a stance has proved to be, it is limited unless combined with a set of minimal presuppositions about the nature of the political and the project for governing society. Otherwise, the study of governmentality will tend to be captured by its own privileged object, the governmental discourses found in liberal democracy, as we shall see in the next chapter.

A further issue, found in the governmentality and governance literatures, is the absence of a sustained reflection on how 'the state' and related concepts are formed within a political imagination and poetics in such a way as to help make certain problems amenable to governing. One of the limits, as well as strengths, of the governmentality literature is indeed its insistence on *rationalities* of government; more or less consistent ways of thinking about governing. However, in discussions of state, society, sovereignty and world order, many projects and political stances are condensed into symbolism, myth, imagery (Neocleous 2003) or even simply a sharp turn of phrase. In political theory, we can observe that the myth and symbolism provided by Hobbes's Leviathan as monster, impersonal machine, huge man and 'mortal god' provide plenty of ammunition for those who would fight the monster, unscrew the machine, decapitate the huge man, and announce that the secular god, too, is dead. Foucault, like Nietzsche, has called the nation-state the *monstre froid* and Beck has called it a 'zombie' category. We can also see how myth, poetics and symbolism make the political world actionable, most famously for conservatives such as Fukuyama (1992) and Huntington (1996), liberals such as Thomas Friedman (2000, 2005), or radicals such as Hardt and Negri (2000, 2004) and Agamben (1998). In these kinds of discussions the camp becomes emblematic of the current world order and the failure of sovereignty, the Empire faces the Multitude, the world is flat, history comes to an end and civilizations clash.

In the relatively prosaic world of English studies of public administration, the images of the state over the last three or four decades have decisively changed from the 'overloaded states' of the 1970s, to the 'hollowed-out state' of the 1990s (Rhodes 1994) and, more recently, to the 'congested state' (Skelcher 2000). Moreover, the apparent paradigm shift to governance can be summed up in a few catchphrases as 'government beyond the state', 'government at a distance' (Miller and Rose 1990), 'governing without government' (Rhodes 1996), 'governance without government' (Rosenau and Czempiel 1992), 'more governance, less government', 'governing beyond the centre' (Marinetto 2003), and so on. And what is supposed to have emerged from the ungoverning of society can be summed up in a few key words, such as networks, partnerships, self-organization, complexity, and so on.

Leaving the reflection on the non-rationalities of government to one side, there are two basic problems with this scenario of the incoherencies and outmoded character of the notion of governing societies. First, the very development of notions of government, state and society reveal that the project for governing society, both in liberal and in corporatist and authoritarian forms, has been, since the eighteenth century, a project of governing through multiple sites and institutions (households, families, churches, firms, and so forth), more formal political associations (local, urban and municipal government, unions, business associations, political parties) and forces within society (factions and political disruptive elements, social movements, commercial activities, population growth). Both liberal and non-liberal kinds of governing seek to operate through the existence of a multiplicity of sites and forces beyond the direct control of formal political authorities. Most critics of the project of governing society attack something of a straw man in the supposed relations between state and society and certainly do not understand that project as an aspiration, a vector of thought, will and invention. Secondly, and perhaps even more importantly, the idea of governing societies already presupposes the existence of a system of international government and interstate law which recognizes and attempts to regulate the economic, diplomatic and military relations between such societies. The definition of sovereignty as a supreme power over a territory implies a geopolitical order in which territory is distributed to sovereigns. The idea of distinct states, which would later be viewed as distinct national societies, is an artefact of a European international law and order that arose about the beginning of the seventeenth century to put an end to what amounted to bloody religious civil wars. Far from being isolated political atoms, states were from the start conceived as components of a system of international and interstate relationships or at least as ideal components of how such a system might function.

The crisis of governability, the dethroning of the idea of the state, and the emergence and proliferation of the concept of governance are among the preconditions for the problematization of classical conceptions of governing societies. I shall now turn to the contemporary status of the idea.

Post-societal governance

In the previous chapter, we investigated the historical conditions and concept of governing societies. In this chapter, we have examined some of the preconditions for its current status of being called into question. At base, as we have seen, to govern society implies a supreme body within a territory (state, the government) exercising authority within the relatively bounded sphere of society which is distinguished from that of other societies. Today both sides of the state/society couplet are being called into question. I again consider them in turn.

When we consider the state, we are immediately confronted with the prospect that the operation of rule and the ordering of social and political life is something that is no longer the sole prerogative of the political, legal and administrative systems of the territorial state. Classical conceptions of the state emphasized the state's sovereignty, that is, the idea that the state is the supreme power or authority within its own territory. Sovereignty here is understood in terms of Jean Bodin's ([1576] 1955: 25) definition as 'that absolute and perpetual power vested in a commonwealth'. Many international relations thinkers date modern notions of state sovereignty from the agreements that followed the Peace of Westphalia and which view the state as having both 'autonomy' and 'territoriality' (Zacher 1993; Krasner 2000: 124). Autonomy here means the capacity to exercise independent action and territoriality means that the state's authority is exercised over a defined geographic space. Around the time of Westphalia the ideal of the state emerged as 'spatially self-contained, impermeable, unburdened with the problem of estate, ecclesiastical and creedal wars' (Schmitt [1950] 2003: 129). The state itself was sovereign and relationship between states was imagined as a relationship between sovereigns as moral persons.

The state – according to most recent accounts – today finds itself something more like an 'enslaved sovereign'. Its autonomy is compromised. Internally, it must rely on relationship to other 'non-state' forms of organization such as businesses, charities and local organizations to implement policies and achieve its goals. Externally, it must attract the attention of large corporations and flows of investment. It is beset with obligations to international governmental organizations (for example, the United Nations or the International Monetary Fund) and subject to scrutiny by non-governmental agencies (Amnesty International, Greenpeace). It is undermined by impersonal forces beyond its control, principally those of technology and a world market which integrates the decisions of transnational corporations and of private enterprise in finance, industry and trade (Strange 2000). Legally it cannot do what it pleases. It is bound by international covenants and treaties, such as those prohibiting the proliferation of nuclear, biological and chemical weapons or those concerning the human rights of its subjects or citizens (Held 2000, 2004a).

The state's territoriality is also called into question. Many, if not most, of the nearly two hundred states of the world today have only a very limited capacity to defend themselves against conventional attack and no capacity to defend themselves against nuclear attack. This has been exacerbated by the threat of terrorist attacks and the proliferation of 'weapons of mass destruction' among states and non-state actors. Even the United States has proven unable to secure itself against terrorist attacks on its embassies, its military, and above all its own territory. If 'sovereignty' means something like the undisputed capacity to make and enforce laws within its own territory and to protect that territory from attacks by other states and forces, then, according to this argument, the nation-state has been undermined by the relentless forces of economic globalization and by new forms of international conflict involving new non-state actors and new weaponry. Indeed, globalization defined as the processes 'through which sovereign national states are criss-crossed and undermined by transnational actors with varying prospects of power, orientations, identities and networks'

(Beck 2000b: 11) is the very keyword for the process of displacement of the state and state sovereignty. The outcome of these processes is summed up by Susan Strange this way (2000: 154): 'The diffusion of authority away from national governments has left a yawning hole of non-authority, ungovernance it might be called'.

In this discourse on the decline of state sovereignty, there is a kind of mutual constitution and circularity between 'globalization' and 'governance'. Globalization is held to explain the demise of older conceptions of national states and their sovereignty and hence requires us to rethink diverse forms of authority under the rubric of governance. Governance already indicates the penetration of the image of the state with sub-, inter- and transnational forces, actors and networks revealed by the postulate of globalization. Indeed, from the perspective of what has probably become the mainstream, it is far more sensible to discuss 'governing globalization' than governing societies (for example, Held and McGrew 2002).

On the one side, then, we have the widespread perception of the diminution or transmutation of state power and sovereignty. But what of society, the element in which political authority was to be exercised?

Professionally suicidal as it may seem, many sociologists seem very keen to give up on the notion of society. In 1987, Mrs Thatcher famously announced that 'there is no such thing as society'. Whatever else might be said about that statement, she was at least consistent with much of contemporary social theory. Before her, Jean Baudrillard had already announced the 'end of the social', by which he meant the effacement of all political meaning generated through society by its simulation in opinion polls, mass media and the like (1983). Regarding sociology, Baudrillard (1983: 4) believed that the 'hypothesis of the death of the social is also that of its own death'. Since that time there has been no shortage of attempts to show that 'society' in any of its myriad forms must be given up and that, contrary to Baudrillard, sociology can live perfectly well without it. Following his theory of risk society, Ulrich Beck (2000b: 23) believes that the concept of society belongs to the first age of modernity when the world was represented in the image of the nation-state. He argues that states can no longer act to secure themselves against the incalculable risks they face from economic integration, environmental catastrophe and global terrorism. He thus comes to reject 'the container theory of society' in which society was bound by national borders and which he argues all the famous classical sociologists assumed. John Urry (2000) has set out a manifesto for a post-societal sociology rejecting the image of the 'nation-state-society' in favour of a study of mobilities of people and their social and cultural products. Others have suggested that the idea of a bounded society has lost its self-evidence and that we are witnessing, at least from the perspective of rationales of governing, something of a 'death of the social' in which, as a result, sociology experiences an identity crisis (Rose 1996). If it is to recover from such a crisis, one supposes, sociology will be about networks, spaces and flows, and about identities and life-politics. Its objects will be mobilities, communities, transnational social spaces, and even political rationalities and technologies, but not, except as reanimated zombie, society.

Of course, certain quarters within the social, cultural and political sciences have millenarian tendencies. This means that to get noticed and to achieve a public presence in a period of low interest they need to emphasize that we live in a time unlike any other, a new epoch, or moment of rupture or cleavage. However, the best of this recent literature is cautious about the claims around globalization and governance and admits that nation-states do make important differences by good economic management, their health and welfare systems, effective leadership, and the promotion of education and learning, and that countries that have strong traditions and social compacts can dampen inequality and affect the impact of economic liberalization (Held 2004b). It is also noticeable how the events of the five years following 11 September 2001, and the terrorist attacks on the United States, have led to a muting of some of the most blanket claims about the death of the nation-state, the absence of hegemonic power on a global scale, and the irrelevance of sovereignty.

Nevertheless, what is at issue is even more basic than allowing the recognition that the nation-state can make a difference to more fundamental processes or that the United States still operates within a paradigm of sovereignty, security and its own hegemony. First, most accounts of the decline of state capacities with respect to governing society assume a legal and political paradigm of state capacities within early modern Europe as a fully accomplished reality. They have failed to grasp the extent to which the state was an extraordinary accomplishment in the face of internal and external conflicts, civil and religious war and foreign predators, and to grasp it as an *ideal*. To imagine that the territorial state is anything less than an aspiration and a fragile and precarious achievement since it first emerged in seventeenth-century Europe is to take an ongoing and changeable political construct for a permanent ontological category. Whatever ontological status is attributed, the state is linked to its *claim* to a sufficient monopoly of violence within its territory to defeat other forces and to the legal regulation of the deployment of that violence both by international and domestic law.

The second point is that many of the ideas of society concern the best way to maintain that problematic and fragile achievement. In the eighteenth and early nineteenth centuries in Western Europe, following from the prescriptions of Adam Smith and the Scottish Enlightenment, this was first done by seeking to better the conditions of life for the population by knowing how to properly govern the economic processes of industry and commerce which exist in civil society and by fostering international trade. Later, in the late nineteenth and most of the twentieth centuries, inspired by new social disciplines and building upon innovations and reforms, others sought to overcome the fractious character of the groups and classes in civil society, to limit the bounds of economic inequality, to ensure a minimum quality and standard of life for all, and to bind them in solidarity and national identity. If society is very much a particular political construct, it is one that might allow authorities to act in such a way as to bring security and order domestically, that is, within the boundaries of state territory, and to cooperate, compete and survive in a world of other such entities.

Central to my argument here is the view that discussions of society are better thought of as programmatic or strategic, as framed within and framing of political action, but also as less than completely accidental in the trajectory of liberal-capitalist societies. As Giovanni Procacci (1998) has argued, social citizenship might be seen as a solution to the problem of how to reconcile inequality and poverty with a society of equals. However uninteresting it might be to those captured by current culturalist tendencies of 'signs, speed and spectacles', as Foucault brilliantly summed it up (Gordon 1986: 81), or to those who bundle together diverse trajectories to invest globalization with the force of teleology, to ignore this project, or its multiplicity of strategies, is to miss much of what is characteristic of contemporary liberal democracies. It is to miss what accounts for the benefits the state/society relation has offered to citizens to allow them to go about their business, to exercise political freedoms and participate in a pacified environment, to support them in their vulnerabilities and to manage their risks. It is also to miss the threats and forms of domination, coercion and highly rationalized violence the state can bring to citizens and non-citizens alike. Finally, it is to evacuate the very possibility of analysing the implications of the discourse on globalization for the balance between the enabling, rights-granting and coercive, obligations-enforcing dimensions of the liberal-democratic territorial state.

The notion of governance unbundled authority and order from notions of state, sovereignty and hierarchy, and thus promises a kind of multiple and grassroots empowerment of communities, regions, neighbourhoods, and so on. However, the bundling together of transformations into the new monster of globalization, the One Big Thing of the new world order as Thomas Friedman (2000) put it, would seem to foreclose on these forces of multiplicity and hybridity. Nevertheless, governance and globalization might be said to be the two 'G-spots' of the *fin de siècle* social and political sciences. The more optimistic stories of them pose the new world order as one of exciting potentiality and opportunity, as one in which 'the world is flat' (Friedman 2005).

Others present a world in which insecurity is endemic – a world of 'ontological insecurity' (Giddens 1994). It is one in which the capacity of states to manage risks has largely faltered – a 'world risk society' as Beck puts it (1999, 2002). Such a society stands in contrast to the management of risks in the first age of modernity. Then, the state management of risks, in the form of private and public insurance, was part of a social compact against industrially produced hazards. The risks of industrial production, however devastating to certain populations and individuals, were limited, calculable, and amenable to compensation (Beck 1992a: 100–2). Security was at least theoretically possible within the nation-state and the welfare state could be viewed as a way of managing risk in order to steer or govern society.

In contemporary modernity, by contrast, environmental, economic, technological, health and latter security threats have become unbounded and escape the limits of the national state. The management of catastrophic global risks – from financial meltdowns such as the Asian Financial Crisis to pandemics such as SARS (Severe Acute Respiratory Syndrome), BSE (Bovine Spongiform Encephalopathy) and avian flu, to global climate change, to terrorist attacks on Western capitals and holiday resorts – can only be undertaken by transnational agreement, cooperation and organization. This necessity for cooperation to manage catastrophic risk is one central imperative for a cosmopolitan society. In such a framework, the argument continues, the attempt to inscribe all sorts of problems within the discourses of sovereignty and security amounts to a kind of reactive response or an 'archaic excess' (Spence 2005: 291). Whatever view we take on the putatively ruptural character of the experience of risk in contemporary life, there does seem an alternative and rather more plausible hypothesis than the disintegration of sovereign state in the face of unbounded risk. In this account, the management of risk and uncertainty is a component of the transformation of sovereignties and their place in the contemporary world order rather than a marker of their decline. Just as one widespread response to the experience of ontological insecurity is the reassertion of order and hierarchy found in religious fundamentalism, so the knowledge of risk can come to be embedded in state sovereignties (for example, in the management of crime) and in the international order of which they are a part (in the doctrine of pre-emptive military intervention in cases where the international community is at risk from a rogue state developing weapons of mass destruction).

Yet even the idea of a 'world risk society' does not capture the simple danger and violence of the contemporary moment. Nor does it capture the strategies by which nation-states have responded to threats. The postulated decline of the nation-state does not necessarily lead to a pacific and cosmopolitan paradise of cooperation. It can and does lead to the violent disintegration of former federations and bloody civil wars – witness the decline of the Soviet Union, Yugoslavia and the loosening of central control over parts of Indonesia. Those places without effectively functioning states are among the most miserable in the world and failed or failing states have come to represent threats to the rest of the world (such as the Taliban in Afghanistan). They constitute what one senior British diplomat has called a zone of chaos and a new *terra nullius* (Cooper 2003: 17–18). While some celebrate the decline of a primary identification with a particular national society, and call for a cosmopolitan citizenship (Beck 1998; Habermas 2001; Held 2004b), those without national citizenship or residency papers within such societies find themselves in a precarious position in which they face arrest, detention, deportation, internment in camps and a life of illegality. Consider also that places without effectively functioning states can be those where international interventions are most difficult and are the locale of the most recent genocides, such as Rwanda in 1994 (Carlsson *et al.* 1999).

Furthermore, the apparent or proclaimed decline in national sovereignty has not meant a decline in war as an instrument of international relations for even well-developed states. War is justified in new and different ways, as a War against Terror, or a pre-emptive strike against rogue states with 'weapons of mass destruction', or as a virtuous quest to protect the human rights of distant others such as the intervention in Kosovo. Certain nations, or coalitions of nations, led by the United States, are willing to take military action without the agreement of international bodies, for example in Iraq in 2003. The framework of sovereignty and security has been renewed rather than effaced in the post-9/11 world. Consider the establishment of the Department of Homeland Security in the United States and the Patriot Act and the similar moves to abridge civil freedoms in the face of security measures justified with reference to terrorism in many countries. The use of torture, and more fundamentally the juridical redefinition of torture, and the use of arbitrary detention of those suspected of involvement in terrorism, attest to the emergence of a new kind of security state. The detention of 'enemy combatants' in Guantánamo Bay, and of refugees in 'detention centres', gives some credibility to Giorgio Agamben's (1998, 2005) thesis of the camp as the 'bio-political *nomos* of modernity' and that the state of exception or state of emergency has become the generalized norm. In contrast to the celebration of new mobilities, travelling across the frontiers of liberal-democratic societies, including the edges of the EU established by the Schengen Agreement, has become at best an irritating and potentially very treacherous business. Sovereignty does not appear to have vanished, but to have taken new, different and freshly virulent forms. The concern for security has not disappeared in a 'networked' world; it has increased and multiplied. Can sovereignty and security simply be the archaic excess of a worn-out form of politics? Are such concerns but the reactive, symbolic and nostalgic response of a zombie category?

At the very least, there is enough to suggest that the various narratives of governance and globalization, and of world risk society, need some revision of their more sanguine versions. They have underestimated the persistence and in some cases extension of forms of political power concerning security, sovereignty and the use and threat of physical force and violence. The latter would appear to be more than the 'the residue of founding violence', or 'an archaic form of rationality' that lives like a virus in the DNA of the political (Spence 2005: 291). There is enough then to suggest that the obituaries of State and Society have been a little premature. Either that or the 'undead' are doing a good job at unnerving the living. The Leviathan was always two-sided. On the one side, it was the cold monster we needed to control by establishing the rights of the citizen against it. On the other, as Hobbes suggested, the Leviathan offered us protection in a dangerous world and built up our collective identity, our standard and quality of life, and our participatory rights. By focusing on the first side, we have perhaps come to make the state into a kind of auto-maton, a Frankenstein's creature, which – far from offering protection against economic liberalization – itself might become the main threat. But not far behind this threat is another monster. Like the original Leviathan, it is perhaps a sea-monster. Under the global system, we try to navigate storms and reefs in little lifeboats as our recently evacuated 'ships of state' sink below the waves.

Conclusion

In this chapter we have explored diverse sources for the contemporary problematization of the idea of governing societies. Among these sources are the literature on the crisis of governability found on both the Right and Left in the 1970s, the dethroning of the idea of the state in English intellectual history and in French 'poststructuralist' political thought in the 1980s, and the emergence of a notion of governance in public adminis-tration, political science and sociology. Contemporary contributions to this narrative unfold in discussions of current international organization and law, in the meta-theory of globalization and in the widespread rejection of notions of society in current social theory and analysis. I have argued that such views underestimate the extent to which the 'state' was always a fragile and precarious achievement and that the domain of society was constituted from projects and strategies for the establishment and main-tenance of political order and stability. I have also suggested that the proliferation of security concerns, the experience of ontological insecurity, and the existence of risks not bound by the territorial state presages a reconfiguring of the sovereign state and the international system of which it is a part as much as its demise.

────────(3)

Individualization

◯──────────────────────────────

Identity is becoming the main, and sometimes the only, source of
meaning in an historical period characterized by widespread
destructuring of organizations, delegitimation of institutions, fading
away of social movements, and ephemeral cultural expressions ... *Our
societies are increasingly structured around a bipolar opposition between the Net
and the self.*

(Castells 2000a: 3, original emphasis)

There is a not so hidden complicity between the focus on governance and
certain kinds of claims around individualization in the contemporary
world. This is the argument I make in this chapter. Here I examine
authoritative social science literature which, in a number of different
variations, and with varying degrees of criticism, offers a diagnosis of the
present as one in which global transformations have led to a new emphasis
on the individual and its self-governing capacities, on the one hand, and
new forms of organization, variously described as 'networks' or 'communities', on the other. This thesis, illustrated by the epigraph, has
implications for how we can think about democracy and politics today.
After giving an exposition of the thesis I suggest a number of criticisms that
help us undo the dangerous simplifications of the relation between governing and individuals. I instead argue that contemporary discourses on
individualization are themselves tethered to certain power relations and the
'dividing practices' of liberal-democratic societies.

There are a whole host of themes in recent, what might be called
'progressive' social and political thought of a new politics that links the
individual to issues of its governance and self-governance: the 'politics of
identity/difference', 'individualization', a 'life politics', 'cosmopolitanism',
and so on. The effects of such themes is to suggest that there has been a

displacement of politics from a struggle, contest or even combat over the appropriation of resources and power to a concern about identity and recognizing different or particular identities, and that the nature of the political has changed with a new focus on a kind of self-governing individual. Such discourses are also at the heart of the suggestion that it is not possible to talk about society as an object of analysis because cosmopolitan self-making individuals no longer make a primary identification with nations.

At some distance from, but related to these themes stand a number of theoretico-political programmes which contain views of the roles and responsibilities, capacities and obligations of the citizen as a governable and self-governing individual in a contemporary liberal democracy. These are located within a wide political spectrum. They include such formations as 'neoliberalism' (Hayek 1979), the 'new paternalism' (Mead 1997), the 'third way' (Giddens 1998), 'communitarianism' (Etzioni 1995) and even the 'compassionate conservatism' (Olasky 2000) associated with the domestic policies of President George W. Bush and his 'Faith-based and Community Initiatives'.[1] While the sociological narratives stress the sense in which individuals are becoming authors of their own lives and identities, these more practical political philosophies and programmes proclaim the need to require or oblige individuals to become such authors. Governing through freedom, choice and agency is thus linked to a governing that tries to make people responsible and which might view ethical self-governance, moral character building or even a religious faith as a means to do so. Responsibility for one's actions and their future consequences might be called 'obligation', which is a keyword in the lexicon of many of these programmes.[2] Part of the displacement of politics is a move towards viewing formerly political matters such as the provision of social assistance as entailing a specific moral or ethical reformation of the character of the individual. This displacement drives the political toward a concern for personal ethics in its liberal and secular versions and toward religious faith in its most conservative version.

No doubt there are very large divergences between these theories and diagnoses, on the one hand, and moral programmes on the other. Common to many of them, however, I believe there stands a barely articulated thesis I would like to call 'culture-governance' or governance through the ethical culture or cultivation of the individual. This is the view that rule in contemporary liberal democracies increasingly operates through capacities for self-government and thus needs to act upon, reform and utilize individual and collective conduct so that it might be amenable to such rule. Related to this is a very specific conception of the individual subject as one involved in existential self-problematization. Within this self-problematization, all ascribed and received identities of nation, class, sexuality, gender and ethnicity might be called into question, leaving the individual in a position of choice with regard to his or her identi-fications. This idea of a set of conditions that lead to the necessary self-problematization of the individual can be open to apparently opposed colonizations by different normative or value frameworks. Neoliberals will find this an occasion to stress the need for a self that forms itself through its own enterprise. Liberal and social-democratic internationalists will see in this individual the possibility of a primary identification with the whole of humanity, a cosmopolitan self. Yet, as compassionate conservatives will know, such self-problematization, particularly among the vulnerable, may, under the right conditions, result in discovering a new, born-again religious identity.

This culture-governance has quite a long recent history as an objective of rule. It was first perhaps applied to the poor and is still today writ large in 'welfare-reform' talk. From the 'cycle of dependency' and notions of the underclass to remedies for social exclusion, poverty was only partly viewed as structural. Another part of it was cultural and, because of this, its remedy was to be found in moral and personal transformation. 'Culture' here means something quite specific: the cultivation of the capacities of the individual. Just as 'physical culture' concerns the development of the physical capabilities, so 'ethical culture' concerns practices of moral development, guidance and government. There is no clear political locus or value of the notions and techniques of ethical culture. One source was the Community Action Programs which were a part of the War on Poverty in the USA in the 1960s and introduced the language of empowerment (Cruikshank 1999). While the practices of empowerment were taken up and carried by feminism and new social movements, concerns around the low 'self-esteem' of various groups (teenaged mums, those dependent on drugs and alcohol) and in various personal and more public relations became a governmental concern in California and elsewhere in the 1980s and 1990s. While culture-governance can be found in the writings of the free-market Right such as in the later writings of Hayek (1979), the idea of fostering enterprising individuals in an 'enterprise culture' and later an 'enterprise community' was raised to an objective of the government of the state in the UK in both the Thatcher and Blair years (Young 1992). From an explicitly conservative point of view, the undermining of the virtues of the citizenry by inappropriate or big government was a component of both the Republicans' Contract with America of the 1990s and George W. Bush's promotion of notions of 'compassionate conservatism' (Olasky 2000). During this whole period, welfare reform shifted welfare state measures away from a discussion of entitlement and rights towards one of the need to 'activate' welfare beneficiaries by various measures or to fulfil their obligations to the communities that support them (Peck 2001).

All of these movements, practices and styles of political thought seem to manifest a common intuition in the claim that the reform and governance of institutions and practices must then be articulated within a particular discursive modality. This is neither the fundamentally suspect and anyway outmoded modality of the formal political sphere, tied as it is to a fading nation and state and to adversarial politics, nor the discredited domain of 'the social', connected to the rigidities of the welfare state and the homogenizing ideals of solidarity. Finally, it cannot be economic, in the sense that the mantra of economic globalization is tied to a vision of the decline of Keynesian macro-economic management with its core belief that nations can or should seek to enhance their 'comparative advantage' in international trade (Hindess 1998). The modality will be cultural, and ethical, in which the governance of institutions will be tied to the attributes and capacities of individuals and the transformation and self-transformation of their conduct (Dean 1995, 1998a). This entails various 'ethical projects', by which we mean projects in which individuals are asked to work on themselves and their conduct and to transform themselves with the help of experts, training and services. In one version, such a reform will act in the name of a cultural pluralism constituted through a generous recognition of the 'agonism' of culturally constituted differences within the public sphere – a kind of tough multiculturalism (Connolly 1999). In another, such reform will target those who cannot help themselves, are unable to act in their own best interests, and need to have others paternalistically put their lives in order for them (Mead 1986, 1997). All sides, however, argue that democracy, of course differently conceived, inheres in a form of everyday life that depends on the capacities of individuals for deliberation and participation and the respect for common values of law, others' rights, and one's own personal responsibilities. Democracy, and a way of life necessary for democracy, thus depends on the constitution of individuals as self-reflexive authors of their own life-plans and accepting the obligations that citizenship entails of them. While there are clearly different political choices and emphases here, if the memory of the welfare state belongs to the Left, and the nostalgia for the nation to the Right, this thesis of governance of ethical culture is perhaps less 'beyond Left and Right' than found across the pervasive conservativism of the contemporary liberal-democratic political spectrum (Giddens 1994).

Individualization and modernity

Our types of society, we are told in many authoritative and undoubtedly progressive social narratives, are ones that have undergone a fundamental transformation, even if somewhat behind our backs. The variants of this narrative tell the story of a continuation, completion or transcendence of the story of modernity. Hence there is a proliferation of diagnoses of the present all relating to 'modernity' as the dominant term: postmodernity, an 'incomplete modernity' (Habermas 1985), 'late modernity' (Giddens 1991), or most recently the 'second age of modernity' (Beck 2000b). What is common to these accounts can be approached by what they view as in decline. First, there is the relativization of the authority of the legitimating truths of an earlier phase of modernity. The meta-narratives of reason and progress that accompanied the early stages of modernization begin to fail, instanced by the loss of an unquestioned faith in the benefits of science, of economic growth and industrial production. Truth is contested within the public spaces provided by social movements (Greens, those against genetically modified food) and the news and information media. This occasions a new awareness of risk, so much so that contemporary modernization is organized around the production and distribution of risk as much as wealth (Beck 1989: 86–7). Secondly, the role of the national economy and actors tied to it such as organized labour has been bypassed by the effects of 'globalization', a term that principally refers to the flows of financial capital through electronic information and communication technological networks, the movement to interconnected economies and flexible production, and the cultural consequences of new transnational media (Castells 2000b). Together with the emergence of trans- and international political associations, and international non-government organizations, there is, thirdly, a parallel decline of structures of national state sovereignty (Rosenau 2000). Fourthly, the institutions of these states such as welfare, income support, state expenditure and industrial relations legislation 'melt under the withering sun of globalization' (Beck 2000b: 1). We thus have a fundamental theoretical delegitimation of bureaucratic and welfarist forms of rule so that within and outside the borders of the territorial national state we witness the emergence of an authoritative order which is best described as 'governance without government', one in which states 'steer' but do not 'row'. There is a sense in which the 'authority of authority' has come into question. Science has lost its monopoly on truth. The state has lost its monopoly of legitimate power over a given territory. The nation has lost the monopoly of its claim on the identity of its citizens. Bureaucratic organization has lost its monopoly on the welfare of the population. Truth has been relativized, power deterritorialized, identity pluralized, welfare individualized.

According to our now largely accepted narrative, these economic and political developments undermine the old solidarities based on class. So too the (post-, contemporary, or late) modern fragmenting, mixing and invention of cultures and identities, the new information and communication networks, the global cultural industries and the patterns of consumption they foster break down solidarities and dependencies of neighbourhood, community, locality and even family (Beck 2000a). There is thus an undoing of the stable identities of class, gender, sexuality, ethnicity and nation. From a more critical perspective, what emerges has been called the 'naked individual' (Hardt and Negri 2000: 203–4), which can be diagnosed as a new merging of political life with 'bare life' (Agamben 1998). This 'do-it-yourself' individual is nevertheless institutionally mediated and needs to invent itself to give itself some kind of identity in the face of the uncertainty of these changes (Beck and Beck-Gernsheim 2002). Put in a more sophisticated way, the subject is always in a process of ethico-political becoming through arts of existence (Connolly 1999: 143–53). As Ulrich Beck puts it, '(c)hoosing, deciding, shaping individuals who aspire to be the authors of their lives, the creators of their identities, are the central characters of our time' (1998: 28). He goes on:

> Let's be clear what individualism means. It is not Thatcherism, not market-individualism, not atomisation. On the contrary, it means 'institutionalised individualism'. Most of the rights and entitlements of the welfare state, for example, are designed for individuals rather than for families. In many cases they presuppose employment. Employment in turn implies education, and both of these presuppose mobility. By all these requirements people are invited to constitute themselves as individuals: to plan, understand, design themselves as individuals and, should they fail, to blame themselves. Individualization thus implies, paradoxically, a collective lifestyle.[3]
>
> (Beck 1998: 28)

The story of the second age of modernity is one of the coming into being of this individual stripped naked of all received attributes involved in a constant and institutionally provoked self-problematization. An individual whose social determinations are subject to 'reflexive' questioning is hence a cosmopolitan one, open to the AIDS crisis in Africa, global environmental destruction, and so on. Cosmopolitan individuals make their own lifestyle and will come to realize themselves as a part of a world democracy in which they have rights as individuals and are obligated to the defence of the rights of other such individuals wherever they might be violated. Thus: 'living alone means living socially' (Beck 1998: 28). The cosmopolitan individual can also be viewed as an institutionally mediated one with ever higher levels of interconnecting layers of global governance ensuring that there is no automatic identification of the individual with national society and requiring further institutional reform to guarantee a multi-layered world citizenship (Beck 2000a; Held 2004b).

But there is also a darker side to this individualization. As we have already noted, the progressive sociological narrative speaks of a second age of modernity organized as much around the production and distribution of risk as much as wealth (Beck 1989: 86–7). It thus brings a proliferation of frequently incalculable industrial and technological hazards. While distributed differentially among populations and subject to constant attempts at risk assessment and monitoring, these are nonetheless global in that they no longer respect the borders between nations. Contemporary modernity is thus a 'risk society' marked by an increasing publicity of, and indeed contestation around, the threats posed by the application of techno-science, and its application in the energy, biotechnology and chemical sectors (Beck 1992a: 101–6). Individuals are left in the fateful situation of attempting to control their own proneness to risk by the use of expert knowledge that has been deprived of intrinsic authority. Indeed, 'risk society' is something of a misnomer. Not only has expertise lost its intrinsic authority, but the kind of risks that we face today are ones that often cannot be limited, are unpredictable, incapable of compensation and finally incalculable (Dean 1999: 182–3), for example, the effects of a nuclear accident, or the consequences of genetically modified organisms (GMOs), or again the risk of being subjected to a terrorist attack. The more we attempt to calculate and manage our risk, the more we realize that we live in a kind of perpetual uncertainty.

The impact of risk culture on individual and collective conduct raises questions of trust in abstract systems and expertise and calls into question individual and collective security in ways that resonate with other general features of the second age of modernity. The relentless tide of globalization and the undoing of traditional, familial, communal and even societal bonds leaves the individual in a perpetual state of 'ontological insecurity' (Giddens 1991), no longer able to take confidence in gender, class or national identities. He or she is forced to choose among the multiplicity of forms of life and consciously adopted lifestyles and to navigate him- or herself through the world in which he or she lives. The result is not simply a postmodern one in which identities are decentred, dislocated, fragmented and placed in crisis (Hall 1992). Rather, the condition of ontological insecurity produces 'existential anxiety'. On the one hand, the search for authentic forms of life becomes refracted through the commodified lifestyle provided by the mass media and advertising that leaves genuine needs in a permanent state of dissatisfaction. On the other, ontological insecurity leads to an attempt to construct the self, turning it into coherent narrative and autobiography, with the help of the multiplying numbers of therapists, counsellors, writers of self-help manuals and other experts. The self becomes a 'reflexive project'. Traditional politics is displaced by a 'life-politics' geared to self-actualization rather than emancipation. This politics is practised first of all by ethnic and sexual minorities, feminists, Greens and others.

All of this has an impact upon how we must conceive of political and social organization and can be hooked up with what I have called the thesis of culture-governance. Wherever one looks, it is claimed, authority, the hierarchy and chain of command it entails, has lost its justification with the decline of the moral, legal, religious and even epistemological foundations of its legitimacy. Even more broadly, under the onslaught of the relentless forces of globalization and the emergence of the polycentric 'steering mechanisms' inside and outside nation-states, power has lost its centre and notions of state and its sovereignty have lost their purchase on contemporary political realities. One rather extreme version of this has been put forward by James Rosenau:

> It might well be observed that a new form of anarchy has evolved in the current period – one that involves not only the absence of a highest authority, but that also encompasses such an extensive disaggregation of authority as to allow for a much greater flexibility,

innovation and experimentation in the development and application of new control mechanisms.

(Rosenau 2000: 184)

These interdependent and proliferating mechanisms at subnational and supranational levels constitute a form of 'governance without government' (Rosenau 2000: 182). Here the account of global transformation mirrors the new 'sociology of governance' that is applied to the multiple organization and associations that operate in and across various social and political spaces (Kooiman 1993). In place of a centralized sovereign power of the state, we witness a heterogeneity and pluralization of relevant actors (public, private and non-government). Rather than hierarchy and structure, these actors enter into relations of interdependency, create networks, undertake exchanges and enter multiple relations of reciprocity. Instead of systems of command passed down from authoritative actors, governance is effected through the outcome of all these relationships.

Inside and outside thus begin to disappear. The implication for the attempt to 'govern society' is that society is revealed to be the artefact of the state it always was. The state was the container for society (Beck 2000b: 23–6). But just as the image of a sovereign state that exercised ultimate power over a particularly territory is dispersed, divided and shackled in the new stage of globalization, so too is it nonsense to talk about society at least in the sense of a national society. The project of governing society, if by that we mean an attempt to use the existing sovereign institutions of liberal democracies to make policy to benefit the welfare of those populations that reside within the territorial boundaries of the national state, is impossible. The search for contemporary social theory to help us understand the task of governing society meets with the dramatic response – that 'what you are doing is fundamentally nonsense'.

If power is to be exercised, this story continues, it must and will be exercised in such a way that it is consistent with the freedom, values and choices of individuals and the communities and collectivities in which they live. Sometimes, this freedom is something that is immediately found in the capacities of certain types of motivated and enterprising individuals and communities. At other times, subjects need to be 'empowered' to exercise such freedom by therapeutic or other means. Individualism is not pure: it is something constructed with the help of experts and has an institutional face. Arrangements need to be made through which those choices and that freedom can be shaped or constructed in some way, for example by the construction of quasi-markets or market-like arrangements for the delivery of services to customers, or the tailoring of public services to individualized needs. What is crucial is that according to much of what is now almost taken for granted in contemporary social thought, we are leaving behind a sovereign power that is hierarchical, totalizing, territorialized, centred on nation and states, exclusionary, and operating through commands and law. We are witnessing the emergence in its place of the thesis and techniques of a culture–governance, which works through networks and flows rather than structures and hierarchies. It is inclusive, individualizing, deterritorializing and polycentric, operating to include through choice and agency and the transformations of identity and difference. The consequence of such a position is that the idea of a coherent project of governing society has fallen into disrepute as an archaism based on authority structures now undergoing transformation.

I have tried to summarize the changing vocabulary of analysis in Table 3.1. The principal narrative of transformation is towards those on the 'governance' side of the table. However, such a narrative would also appear to open up the possibility of a narrative that shows how those categories on the 'sovereign government' side of the table still operate or are transformed in terms of this shift.

Table 3.1 Displacement of the language of analysis of governing society

Sovereign government	$\longrightarrow$	Governance
	$\leftarrow$	
1. Hierarchies		1. Networks and flows
2. Totalizing		2. Individualizing
3. Territorializing (the state)		3. Deterritorializing
4. Borders		4. Erases borders
5. Centralized		5. Polycentric
6. Exclusionary		6. Inclusive
7. Commands and law		7. Choice and agency
8. State		8. Heterogeneous actors
9. Nation		9. Transnational civil society
10. Citizen		10. Cosmopolitan individual (self-governing actor)
11. Society		11. Communities/regions

The thesis presented in this table is that there is an authoritative sociological narrative of individualization which connects with meta-themes of globalization and of governance. It can be summarized in the following form: the present is the time of a new ('late', 'post-', 'second', 'modern') form of individuality, a self-reflexive one, capable of making and remaking itself, which relativizes the taken-for-granted character of traditional modern identities of class, gender, sexuality, race and ethnicity and, importantly, nation. The self-becoming individual thus raises the possibility of a new cosmopolitan identity beyond the boundaries of national citizenship, and a new sub-politics of identification beneath and across nation-states. This new form of individuality is, further, linked to transformations in how individuals are to be governed and to govern. They are to govern and be governed no longer through hierarchical systems of command but through their own capacities of self-government, even if we should recognize that these capacities are institutionally formed. They are to be governed no longer through traditional and modern ascribed identities and forms of legitimation but through their own (acquired) capacities for deliberation and participation. Traditional and (early) modern forms of authority are thus displaced by new, more participatory and democratic forms of social relations characterized by flatter structures, inclusivity, networks and communities, and above all the choice and agency of participants. The vocabulary of the political must be fundamentally changed: from emancipation to fulfilment, from identity to identifications, from society to networks and communities, from sovereign states to heterogeneous and interdependent agents, from government to governance. The new language of politics will stress the management of uncertainty, risk and insecurity, as much as the construction and maintenance of social and political order. The discourse of security will increasingly replace the discourse of sovereignty.

Criticizing individualization

One of the key problems with the progressive sociological and governance narrative of individualization is that it is clearly teleological, that is, it presupposes a set of outcomes that are already inscribed in the processes it postulates. For even if we accept the processes of globalization and individualization it supposes, there is no guarantee that it will deliver the outcomes it promises. Take the view that the fundamental process of the detraditionalization of identity leads to a self-problematizing individual with cosmopolitan proclivities. This view reveals itself to be at one with deep-seated sociological assumptions that modernity equals secularism and that any transformation is along an axis of secularization. As we know, however, the contestation of the authority of the truth of scientific knowledge can and does just as easily take the form of creationists challenging the teaching of the theory of evolution in many parts of the USA by the idea of Intelligent Design as it does German Greens calling GMOs to account. Indeed, Islamic fundamentalism is a pervasive feature of present-day political and social life. If, moreover, we are in a situation of existential anxiety occasioned by the tearing away of fixed identities, then there is no reason to be surprised at the attempt to deal with insecurity by recourse to religious faith or obsessive nationalism. Indeed, the outcome of self-problematization might be the process of being 'born again' as much as remaking oneself with the use of therapists. A life politics (or an 'ethopolitics', Rose 2001) is played out not only by those who imagine themselves to be therapeutically self-actualized human individuals but by religious fundamentalists of different stripes, right-to-life anti-abortionists, traditional Roman Catholics, and those who support what George W. Bush called the 'culture of life'. Indeed, these groups engage in life-politics with a ferocity that the cosmopolitan individual could never imagine, let alone muster.

Moreover, the sociological story tells us of the way in which truth enters into a public space of contestation provided by the international and national news media. However, what we witness is the continued production of truths – and falsehoods – and the sidelining of their investigation, at least until it no longer matters anyway. Think here of the role of quite liberal (*New York Times*) as much as conservative (Fox News) news outlets in establishing evidence for weapons of mass destruction in Saddam Hussein's Iraq prior to the invasion and occupation of that country in 2003. This case is paradigmatic: the 'half-life' of truth might be a lot less than in former periods but it fulfils a function – to legitimize a military invasion or occupation, to get leaders re-elected – and then it no longer matters and can be 'contested' and even repudiated.

As we have noted above, the domain of culture-governance is occupied not only by sanguine internationalists promoting a cosmopolitan identity but also neoliberals hoping it will deliver a more entrepreneurial self, and conservatives and religious organizations as an opportunity to recruit born-again Christians. We might reflect that techniques such as self-narration and self-confession are not simply the province of therapists and psychologists but the stock-in-trade of pastoral forms of government found in the history of Christian religions, whether Catholic or Protestant, liberal or evangelical. If the sociological narrative of the late-modern self can be used to justify the discipline and rigours of the life-planning required of the welfare recipient by contemporary welfare reform, it can also be used to justify the need for religious values and faith to navigate the reefs of contemporary life and its risks. Paradoxically perhaps, the Christian fundamentalist lobby in the USA – unlike the progressivist teleologies we have explored here – does not systematically underestimate the importance of technologies of government, including especially the very arrangements of the national government of society, for the attempted construction of various kinds of identity. This is why at the heart of President G. W. Bush's compassion agenda is a very long list of legal and regulatory changes which permit 'faith-based' organizations to have access to US federal funding often to engage in activity such as the training of ministers and priests.

We can also note one further teleological feature of the sociological narrative. It proposes that individuals in contemporary modernity are subject to underlying processes of globalization, on the one hand, and arrives at the conclusion that the most likely form of subject of this modernity is a truly globalized one who identifies with the whole of humanity, that is, a cosmopolitan one. While we have shown that there is no guarantee of such an outcome, even if this was the outcome there is a deeply paradoxical character of this kind of subject that is not apparent to its advocates. The cosmopolitan subject only or primarily identifies with the whole of humanity and is presumably tolerant of diversity and plurality. Yet the sociological narrative stresses the calling into question of all particular characteristics and the formation of a kind of universal subject. In this view, the rainbow-coloured path of cultural pluralism leads to a monochrome world in which all tend toward a universal subject.

I have elsewhere offered the framework of a genealogy which calls into question the basic assumptions of the sociological narrative: the newness and prolific character of individualization, its millenarianism, its generality, its analysis of power, and ignorance of the political construction of forms of individuality (Dean 2003a). Here I simply note two examples of the weakness of the thesis of displacement and sidelining of sovereign power.

First, there is the instructive history of 'welfare reform' over the last three decades in many liberal democracies. Here we have witnessed various combinations of quasi-therapeutic and pedagogic tactics for empowering, facilitating and activating the individual – rendering the unemployed a 'jobseeker', for example – and 'sovereign' and coercive techniques. The latter involve the restriction or cutting off of social benefits, and the use of workfare or welfare-to-work schemes in an effort to combat welfare dependency, social exclusion, demoralization and so forth (Schram 1995, 2000; Peck 1998, 2001; Theodore and Peck 1999).

The history of welfare reform reveals that while the transformation of the self can take a liberal and pluralist form of working through the self-governing capacities of individuals, this does not preclude the use of sovereign kinds of rule in local contexts that link governing through self-governing and self-becoming with the enforcement of obligation. This example thus demonstrates another key limit of the thesis of culture-governance. Far from emerging at the point of the decline of sovereignty and sovereign powers, the attempt to govern through the freedom of the individual in a process of becoming links arms with the enforcement and closure of a particular kind of 'positive' freedom by sovereign (in this case, legal and/or coercive) means. Except that sovereign power is today often delegated onto a range of 'private' authorities, the production of a positive form of life which is nominally regarded as freedom is consistent with Isaiah Berlin's famous scenario of the totalitarian uses of positive concep-tions of liberty ([1958] 1997).

Sovereign powers still play a key role in state-administered asceticism for the poor and unemployed, and dictate to them what shall constitute freedom; they are also exercised, sometimes with a certain amount of impunity, and often in the name of freedom, on the international stage. The view that the human rights regime vitiates sovereignty needs to be considered in this light. The argument here is that the precedence of international law over human rights has been reversed and that gross violations of human rights such as genocide can thus occasion military interventions in the affairs of sovereign states (Beck 2000a; Habermas 2000). Such interventions, it is claimed, thus show the emergence of a cosmopolitan world which will no longer be based on unrestricted respect for the rights of nation-states. Such a view comes up against some very simple questions. When are human rights violations recognized as such? When is genocide recognized as genocide? Who and what decides where and when violations take place of sufficient magnitude to warrant a right of military intervention, whether or not it is authorized by international bodies? While state sovereignty might no longer be the sacred principle of international law and international relations it once was, it is clear that some bodies and agencies (the United States, European states such as the UK, France and Germany, the allies of NATO, the United Nations Security Council, China) claim on different occasions, more or less successfully, to be able to decide under what conditions military interventions are appropriate and necessary. On the one side we have the appeal to human rights violation as one among several reasons to sanction the virtuous use of military force; on the other we have a system of disorganized sovereignty in which today's versions of the Great Powers, particularly the United States, can prevail depending on threats to their vital interests, domestic political considerations and the orientation of the incumbent administration. The idea that human rights represent anything like an enforceable set of rights parallel to national citizenship rights in the current circumstances is laughable.

Mainstream social and political science tells us a story of the production of contemporary political identities as a result of globalization and the triumph of the principle of human rights over national sovereignty. Yet being cosmopolitan should not be treated differently from other forms of ethical comportment and political identity. The shaping and self-shaping of individuals occurs through singular practices of the regulation of conduct from school and military discipline to the cultivation of manners and civility, from therapy to established and new religious practices. For our purposes, such ethical practices and forms of moral government are routinely used in programmes for governing society and are often components of the disciplining and training of populations. In this respect, rather than a universal attribute presaging a universal equality of rights, cosmopolitanism might be viewed as a form of moral self-government practised and encouraged by certain political and diplomatic circles and the executives and staff of large corporations or those in parts of organizations such as universities engaged in international activities. In this sense, cosmopolitanism is a form of comportment of certain elites who become exemplary beings. It is, as Weber would have recognized, an ideal of cultivation rooted in the social personae of prestigious social groups ((Weber [1918] 1972: 426–7; Hunter 1990: 397). Such prestigious personae are the ideal of cultivation of a specific social stratum. They enter into the political as repertoires of conduct which mark one group as superior and one as inferior, one worthy of ruling and another in need of being ruled. Political struggle can take the form of a struggle over various forms of prestigious personality, for example the cosmopolitan versus the national or parochial. These struggles, we should not forget, however much framed as cultural identities and ethical dispositions, concern the appropriation, development and distribution of material and symbolic resources, of space and of territory.

Dividing practices: truth, norms and power

In the preceding section I have sought to raise a series of questions that allow us to identify some crucial moves of a discourse that is composed of the story of globalization and individualization, on the one hand, and what I have called the thesis of culture-governance, on the other. This discourse is premised upon a certain hubris – that of the newness of the present and its ruptural characteristics. It claims to discover this newness in the thematic of a prolific individualization that gives us the general form of a deterritorialized cosmopolitan subject (or naked individual, that is, the individual stripped bare of necessary social, political or cultural determination). This subject is held to be the outcome of a reflexive project and its processes of self-narration and self-construction, possibly conducted with the help of experts. The individual is a DIY (do-it-yourself) artefact. It is also a subject of risk, of the attempt to navigate the reefs found in its voyage of security. Strangely, however, while the individual might confront power structures in a life-politics in order to achieve 'self-actualization', its formation is divorced from power relations, from programmes of rule, practices of government and self-government and their effects, and indeed from the political itself. In part this is because the story of the cosmopolitan individual presupposes the story of the (ongoing) emancipation of the subject from older systems of domination of class, of gender, ethnicity, community and nationality. It is thus a subject that is freed from power relations and from political structures rather than fabricated through them and within them. In part, this emancipation of the individual is the story of the decline of the state and its sovereign powers, and the rise of the sovereignty of the individual over its own life. It is hence a story of depoliticization.

The self-reflexive, cosmopolitan individual is thus held to be the single figure of the second-age modern self, the most prestigious persona one can take in an age of globalization. It corresponds to a deterritorialized political sphere and a detraditionalized social sphere. Thus the story of this contemporary self is the effect of a fairly simple dialectical overcoming of the dominated individual and dominating state and society. The first stage of modernity liberates individuals from traditional and feudal statuses and dependencies. However, it blocks their full development as self-governing individuals in a process of becoming by reinscribing them within the territorial dominations of the state and the 'traditional' structures and cultural identities of modernity and nation. It is only with emergent globality, undermining the very concept of a national society, and the displacement of state sovereignty with networks of governance, that full individualization can occur. Because the exercise of authority will now be forced to route itself through the agency of the free individual, then the political logic of state and sovereignty structures, with all its 'demonic' potential (Foucault 2001b: 311), will re-emerge fully exorcised in a multilayered governance that has to draw upon the cultural resources of individuals and use that culture as its means and agency.

What are we to make of this story? How are we to analyse it? It would be easy to dismiss it as mere mythology of the intellectual mandarins of new global elites. However, as I have suggested, the 'cosmopolitan self' is a kind of prestigious identity that is based on the social persona of certain strata engaged in international political, diplomatic and business affairs. Political and social theorists are thus working to make the components of the cosmopolitan persona clearer and providing justification for education in this prestigious personality, as evidenced by the current fashion for 'international studies'. It is not the only kind of prestigious personality that is current. The clear-eyed patriot who can identify the enemies of freedom might well be another that is in conflict with it, and there are a range of others to be cultivated among the poor and other populations in liberal-democratic societies. The self-reflexive global individual is one that might appeal most to multilateralist and often social democratic intellectuals in North America and Europe who value human rights, inclusiveness and ethnic and cultural diversity. However, in so far as it values globalism over localism, it links these 'progressive' impulses to the dismantling of protection of the national working class and the welfare state. Further, the other side of its insistence on universal human rights is to convert the latter into a kind of 'just cause' threshold for military interventions. The cosmopolitan self has a rather ambiguous political valency.

If we return to the broader, globalization–individualization, narrative, we can see it provides a distinctive governmental rationality, a kind of 'theory-programme', as Jacques Donzelot once put it (1979b: 77), with limited and local impacts. These latter are on the research and analyses of intellectuals, the ways they imagine themselves and others' being in the world, the ways in which problems are constructed, practices described and redescribed and invested with purposes, the kinds of solutions offered, and the types of politics they authorize. As such, this narrative acts as conditions of acceptability of certain practices and politics, codifying and reforming them. Let us concentrate on three such effects: a truth effect, a norm effect, and a power effect.

One of its major truth effects is to erase the sphere of contestation, appropriation and domination from the twin forces of globalization and individualization. It is to make what might be contested appear as inevitable or necessary, whether we like it or not. Whether it is given a triumphalist or critical modulation, its truth effect is to 'black-box' certain practices and to render them immune to inspection. An apparently neutral description or analysis of this kind acts as a 'condition of acceptability' for certain practices, which it only dimly acknowledges (Foucault 1981). Thus despite his view that globalization is to be subject to political moulding, Beck (2000b: 1, original emphasis) can tell us that its consequences are that

the premises of the welfare state and the pension system, of income support, local government and infrastructural policies, the power of organized labour, industry-wide free collective bargaining, state expenditure, the fiscal system and 'fair taxation' – all this melts under the withering sun of globalization and becomes susceptible to demands for political moulding. Every social actor must respond in one way or another and the typical responses do *not* fit in the old left–right schema of political action.

Thus this narrative provides the conditions of acceptability for certain practices and approaches to governing societies that seek and demand the reform of public sector organization, taxation and industrial relations systems, and so on. It also provides a language of reform, one increasingly couched in terms of security. Here ontological insecurity and the incalculability of risk mean that a key problem becomes the security of just about everything – the wealth–poverty divide, global environmental concerns, food, health, personal and community life, the institutions of national governments and of civil society, and so forth (Neocleous 2000). 'Societies', once the grand ocean liners of domestic or national security, become leaky refugees' boats with faulty engines navigating the reefs of a 'world risk society' on an open sea of perpetual insecurity and uncertainty. Only the cosmopolitan, able to self-interrogate, question and overcome all their old, partial and shop-worn identities of class, gender and nation, can accommodate to this situation.

While there is no necessary form in which practices of reform should operate, and security be attained, the necessity of reform is not doubted. *How* reform will proceed links the truth effects with the norm effects.

The thesis of individualization presents us with a sociological *fait accompli* that institutions, policy makers and indeed national and international organizations need to respond to. On the one hand, as we have seen, the thesis presents a description of how people of the second age of modernity will behave. They will turn their lives into a 'planning project' (Beck-Gernsheim 1996). 'In the individualized society, the individual must learn, on pain of permanent disadvantage, to conceive of himself or herself as the centre of activity, as the planning office with respect to his or her own biography, abilities, orientations, relationships and so on' (Beck 1992b: 135). Whether we like it or not, there is a 'tendency towards *planning and rationalization in conduct of life*, which is increasingly becoming the task of individuals' (Beck-Gernsheim 1996: 139, original emphasis). On the other, this description is capable of generating a set of norms that might govern the reform of institutions. For Giddens (1998: 36–7):

> If institutional individualism is not the same as egoism, it poses less of a threat to social solidarity, but it does imply that we have to look for new means of producing that solidarity. We have to make our lives in a more active way than was true of previous generations, and we need more actively to accept responsibilities of the consequences of what we do and the lifestyle habits we adopt. The theme of responsibility, or mutual obligation, was there in old style social democracy but was

dormant, since it was submerged within the concept of collective provision. We have to find a new balance between individual and collective responsibilities today.

Thus this discourse is capable of not only codifying the operation of practices and providing authoritative descriptions and justifications for them. It is also capable of converting its authoritative descriptions into normative judgements, and thus of producing personae that can be learnt, imitated or taught. It is thus able to generate a kind of programme for reform of the operation of institutions and institutional practices and orienting them to a new set of ends such as making individuals the 'head office' of their own lives. A perfunctory familiarity with welfare reform over the last two decades, as noted previously, would show that these norms and the kinds of programmes of reform they might justify are hardly novel or inventive. What we might conclude, then, is that that if cosmopolitanism is the persona of the well-travelled business and intellectual strata, the active life-planner in its many versions (the prudential subject, the active citizen, the enterprising individual) will be fitted out for the poor and the welfare recipient.

These norms are ones of inclusion and difference, rather than exclusion and stratification. The active and enterprising life-planner and the cosmopolitan personality are two sides of a kind of norm that works to include by combating those attributes and orientations that leave individuals and populations in a condition of what is conceived of as 'social exclusion' and 'dependency' or lost in their particularities, their uncritical attachments and conduct, their nationalism and patriotism. These norms also actively combat those identities and affiliations that would form the basis of political struggle. If there are capacities, expectations and attitudes derived from 'traditional' class, gender, ethnic or national identities, these are reconfigured as obstacles and forces of resistance to be overcome. Once these are up for negotiation, the individual is left only with depoliticized cultural differences that are put into play as the agencies and energies that are to be transformed by proper moral self-government. These differences, shorn of the possibility of forming solidarities that can form counter-conducts, provide opportunities for enterprise and business, and for mass events and consumption.

Yet it is not possible to have a programme that claims to include and respect and use differences without generating new forms of exclusion and indeed new enemies. On the one hand there are the old enemies: the proletariat and capitalist classes whose children's sandpit had been bulldozed as they knock over each other's sandcastles (Beck 2000a: 89). On the other there are the new enemies: a programme for the production of a cosmopolitan identity generates its own forms of exclusion which come back to haunt it as a kind of resistant medium, counterforce or 'counterconduct'. Patriotism and all types of ethnic and national self-identification would be cast in this role. So too are various fundamentalisms, whether religious, communal (football 'hooliganism') or sexual ('real men', 'women who want to be women', veiled women). Internationally, the main enemies are those cultures and nations that refuse contemporary Western-style universal political and economic modernity, and foment groups engaged in violent action against it, including amongst migrant groups in cosmopolitan democracies. Domestically, the enemy is the underclass and the welfare dependant, and all who refuse the buoyant regime of the cycle of production and consumption, and those who are unable to make themselves the chief executive of their own life as enterprise. The identification of these norms, and examples of exceptions to them, allows us to follow the loop back to relations of power.

The story of culture-governance is a dialectical one. The opposition between nation-state and individual is overcome by the new, multilayered, polycentric network 'governance' that needs to become 'cultural' because it must work through, shape and be shaped by the agency and energies of the self-governing individual and the communities they might form. The 'positive' power effects of this programme are to authorize certain kinds of practices which seek to produce certain kinds of responsible, orderly, self-managing subjects. But they also make it difficult to ask certain kinds of questions and render invisible specific kinds of forces. We might want to ask when, in what contexts, how, and for which individuals and groups, 'governance' conducted with the aim of 'activating' individuals comes to place obligations above freedom, and use sanctions and coercive measures in the establishment of a particular form of life? Is it a case of governing through freedom for some (the consumer of services, the businessperson using his or her laptop in business class above the North Atlantic), obligation for others (the welfare dependant), and sovereign force for still others (the illegal immigrant)? How is the diagram of a polycentric, individualizing, enabling and networking form of governance laid upon a centralized, totalizing, commanding and hierarchical form of territorial power (and the international order made up of relations between such powers)? In other words, how is culture-governance connected to new figurations of disciplinary and sovereign forms of power, and new forms of territorialization? These are the types of questions the dialectical narrative precludes or downplays in relation to the emergence of governance through self-governing individuals and its promise of the coming of the cosmopolitan world citizen. It may be, for example, that, rather than a movement from state-centric sovereignty to polycentric governance, we have transformations and interlacings of the sovereign and the governmental and a new kind of language of politics.

Conclusion

This chapter has shown that the narratives of globalization and the decline of the nation-state presuppose another story, that of the individual and his or her self-governing capacities. It examines the progressive sociological narrative of individualization with its twin imagined outcomes of the cosmopolitan individual and the individual as life-planner. It argues that this individualization thesis echoes many programmes across the political spectrum today. In them reform often comes packaged as cultural or ethical projects in which social and political reform is replaced by the transformation of the individual and individual conduct. These reforms are based on a series of assumptions I have sought to sum up in the term 'culture-governance', that is, the attempt to govern the individual through his or her ethical culture. They work through diverse ethical orientations and capacities such as those of freedom and agency, or self-responsibility and moral obligation. They might advocate a self-reflexive relation to given and ascribed identities of class, gender and nation; or they might demand the reinscription of individuals within the regularities, routines and expectations of work, family and community. While these projects of reform rest on the supposition that contemporary modernity leaves individuals in a naked state without the security of earlier attributes of gender, class, tradition, nation, and so on, they often point in very different directions. Even contemporary social democrats can hold both that welfare reform should reinscribe the poor and workshy within the habits and hierarchies of work and that we must come to accept and indeed celebrate a cosmopolitan identity which emerges from the collapse of the nation and its authority.

What I have sought to show is that the narrative of individualization is largely incoherent and is based on a kind of teleology in which the outcomes are already present in its premises. It cannot account for the field of contestation within contemporary politics over ethics, identity and culture, and the way the mechanisms of the governing of individual conduct can be taken up by different groups with different aims. It cannot provide an account of why fundamentalism is as much a feature of the contemporary landscape as cosmopolitanism. Even its own advocacy of cosmopolitanism fails to notice the problem of the celebration of diverse identities and the recommendation of a single universal one. We need, I have suggested, to understand how identities are formed as ideals for certain social strata engaged in particular social and political practices and come to act as educative mechanisms for others – both the life-planner and the cosmopolitan individual are fitted out for different social groups and purposes. We need further to link such authoritative discourses to the deployment of various sovereign, disciplinary and governmental powers which divide populations and seek to fabricate specific forms of individuality, to the production of self-evident truths for public policy and governmental practices, and to the normalization of particular ways of life embedded in a particular social and political order.

PART TWO

Diagnostics

Life and death

The narrative of globalization, the decline of sovereignty and the displacement of the nation-state by multilayered governance and by the ethical culture of the self-governing individual is shared among much contemporary social and political science. There is a certain resonance of such themes with the Foucauldian literature of governmentality, particularly with its treatment of contemporary liberal forms of rule. In this chapter, I concentrate on two dangers of this Foucauldian literature. The first is to regard liberalism, understood as a way of governing through freedom, as providing safeguards against the despotic potentials of biopower and sovereignty. The second is to view governmentality as subsuming or reinscribing these heterogeneous powers of life and death. I first discuss the ways in which these dangers are manifest with particular attention to their relation to the social science themes of governance and globalization. I then propose that the task of governing societies needs to be rethought within a field of heterogeneous and sometimes 'indistinct' powers and that we need to come to an intelligibility of contemporary governing outside the normativity (that is, the value system) of liberalism. In so doing, our understanding of the ethos of liberal governing is transformed. In a final section I show how that ethos links governing through freedom to the powers of life and death, the exercise of choice to the sovereign decision, the contract to violence, economic citizenship to moral discipline, individual obligation and political order, and rights and liberty to enforcement.

Governmentality

Of all the themes concerning power in the work of Michel Foucault, the theme of governmentality would appear to have given rise to the most sustained body of empirical political and social analysis, not only in France but also in several other countries, including Australia and the United Kingdom (Barry *et al.* 1996; Dean and Hindess 1998a).[1] Foucault conceives government as a way of reposing the question of power outside the apparent antimonies of coercive violence and legitimate consent. As he puts it in the 'The subject and power' (2001d), he approaches power through neither the model of war, with its language of repression, violence and coercion nor through the juridical theory of sovereignty which discusses power in terms of its legitimacy and the ways in which consent is secured. Foucault is placed, rather, in a tradition of Hannah Arendt and Talcott Parsons which emphasizes the productive and creative nature of power. He assumes a constitutive relation between power and freedom, describing 'relationships of power' as 'strategic games between liberties' distinguishable both from 'states of domination' and 'governmental technologies' (Foucault 1988a: 19). Relationships of power as such always entail opponents who are the loci of free action, that is, those who can act in a number of ways. Power is thus a 'mode of action on the action of others' and the 'exercise of power is a "conduct of conducts" and a management of possibilities' (Foucault 2001d: 341).

For Foucault, the exercise of power is a question of 'government' understood in its sixteenth-century sense in which one could speak, to draw upon the *Oxford English Dictionary Online* (hhtp://dictionary. oed.com/), of a 'government of cattel' (1587), even of hemp (1660) or disease (1612), or the government of women (1559) or particular persons. Indeed, government might almost be a synonym for conduct and most particularly becoming conduct, as in: 'How did the university applaud Thy government, behaviour, learning, speech' (John Ford's *'Tis a Pity Shees a Whore*, 1633). For Foucault, conduct is used here as a noun and a verb. As a verb, to conduct means to lead, to guide and to direct. As a noun, conduct could be viewed as roughly equivalent to behaviour, action, comportment, and may give rise to the embodied repertoire of such that sociologists call *habitus* (Mauss 1979; Bourdieu 1990; Elias 1997). Government is given the very broad definition of the deliberate shaping of the way we act. It covers 'not only the legitimately constituted forms of political or economic subjection but also modes of action, more or less considered and calculated, that were destined to act upon the possibilities of action of other people' (Foucault 2001d: 341). Foucault's use of the term would be one familiar to Hobbes, as we saw in Chapter 1.

Elsewhere I have shown how this notion of government gives rise to an analytic of government which focuses on the rationalities and technologies of rule and the way a practice of government is invested with an *ethos* and seeks an end or goal, a *telos* (Dean 1999, 2002b). All this is something like what Clifford Geertz (1973) might wish to call a 'thick description' of aspects of government. That is, the point of the analysis is first and foremost an effort of understanding attained by a detailed description and analysis of the rationalities, techniques, goals and identities formed in the practices that seek to guide the conduct of oneself or others.

Yet there is also the possibility of another, *critical*, side to these analyses which arises from such thick descriptions or analysis. I want to emphasize this here because I believe it has not received enough attention from followers of Foucault. This critical side first emerges when analysis reveals points of disjunction between the more or less explicit rationalities of government, both in their theoretical and their programmatic forms, and the operation of 'regimes of practices' which '... possess up to a point their own specific regularities, logic, strategy, self-evidence and "reason"' (Foucault 1991b: 75). To put this another way, these analyses reveal the immanent disjunction and dissonance between the 'programmer's view' and the logic of practices, their real effects.[2] The domain of effects cannot be read off the programmes of government themselves. Explicit theoretical and programmatic rationality thus enters practices and may be deciphered within them, but it never exhausts them.

Barbara Cruikshank's (1999) work on empowerment is a case in point. The programmatic rationality of empowerment views the world as dichotomized into the powerful and powerless, and claims to be an external means of effecting a quantitative increase in the power of the latter. The logic or effects of practices of empowerment are quite different: they entail technologies that seek to qualitatively transform subjectivity; they deploy and extend powers of self-government; and they exist within a specific set of relations of power between various agents (bureaucrats, activists, politicians, the poor). To show that rationalities of empowerment exist within this wider field of effects is to have the critical consequence of calling into question the claims of the rationality of empowerment itself. This disjunction between programmatic rationality and the logic or basic intelligibility of governmental practices is, I believe, absolutely crucial.

The study of government, governance and governmentality is thus not simply about philosophies, mentalities, or theories, and the ways in which these come to use technologies and techniques for specific ends. While it studies rationalities, it does not assume a rational model of governing. Contrary to recent arguments (Dupont and Pearce 2001), an analytics of government does not claim that the intelligibility of political and social practices can be read off the writings of governors, policy writers and advisers. When applied to the contemporary government of the state, as we shall do here, it concerns not simply liberalism, conservatism, authoritarianism, managerialism, and so on, but also and principally liberal, conservative and authoritarian ways of governing. Theories, ideologies and philosophies of the state or even approaches to management undoubtedly play a role in how we govern and are governed but we should not exaggerate that role. For so too do handbooks and textbooks, manuals and memorandums, statistics and maps, flowcharts, graphs and diagrams and all sorts of practical forms of knowledge concerned with 'how-to' and 'know-how'. Philosophical reflection on the arts of government has a place amidst the myriad and heterogeneous elements that constitute a regime of practices but it remains one possible and contingent element, not necessarily and rarely ever a defining one. While it is possible to talk of a liberal (or neoliberal) manner of governing, for example, what we are confronted with is a complex and often dissonant relationship between a theory of limited government underpinned by a universal moral philosophy of freedom and rights *and* singular logics of liberal practices of governing particular problems (cf. Dean 1991: 13).

Normative and analytical dilemmas

In this section, I outline the intertwined problems of analytical confusions of different kinds of power relations and of veering toward a soft kind of liberal normativity which views liberalism as protecting us against the despotic powers of unlimited sovereignty and biopower. I shall also highlight potential areas of similarity between studies of governmentality and the thesis of culture-governance outlined in Chapter 3.

In the context of the emergence and coming to prominence of 'neo-liberal' – or small state conservative – approaches to the government of the state, much of the governmentality literature has focused on liberal and neoliberal techniques and rationalities of government (for example, Barry *et al.* 1996). It has thus emphasized indirect forms of government. In this respect, it seeks analytically to bypass the nation-state as the context for thinking about governing societies in a move that is common to various 'governance' schools and which we have seen follows from the postulate of globalization. In fact, the special emphasis of governmentality thinking has been on those mutations in our techniques and rationalities of governing that have made the contriving and shaping of freedom into a means of achieving of governmental objectives. Government is characterized as facilitative and preventive rather than directive and distributive.

In this respect, the notion of government comes to be viewed as exemplifying a key feature of power in general which Foucault sought to stress after 1976, its operation through freedom (1988a). For these analytics of contemporary government, Foucault's characterisations of power (1982) as 'a structure of actions upon the actions of others' is nowhere better exemplified than in contemporary forms of liberal rule. These forms of rule activate what Nikolas Rose (1999) has succinctly summed up as 'powers of freedom'.

Neither Foucault nor this ensuing literature, however, would wish to reduce the entire field of power and rule to the issue of governing as 'conducting conduct' or the 'liberal governing through freedom', or even 'action upon the action of others'. Foucault's concepts of government were situated in a much more complex topography of rule. His work attempts to locate government within a general conceptual terrain of 'relations of power' and 'states of domination' (Foucault 1988a; Hindess 1996). It also locates government as a singular historical formation on a field traversed by zones of power relations covered by 'sovereignty', 'biopolitics', 'pastoral power', 'discipline' and the like (Dean 1999, 2001). The latter set of concepts give names to fields, zones or clusters of power relations within the historical trajectory of particular societies, most prominently those that call themselves 'Western' and those whose political culture has been formed in colonial and postcolonial interaction with these societies. The critical issue is, given the emergent governmental form of power, what are the relations between it and the other modalities just mentioned?

Indeed, in one of his best known lectures on 'political rationality', Foucault argues (1981, 2001b) that modern states have the potential to become 'really demonic'. They do this because they contain elements of political power derived from what he calls 'the city-citizen' game with those of a pastoral care of life and the living found within the 'shepherd-flock' game. What is dangerous about the states of the twentieth century, according to this statement, is the way in which they combine, articulate or reinscribe aspects of two trajectories of rule sourced from the Hebraic and the Greek parts of Western political traditions. These are the powers of a self-governing political community, later understood as deductive sovereign right of death and the productive biopolitical powers of life and the living. Foucault himself returned to the theme of the emergence of a politics of life and death several times, particularly where he sought to discuss state racism, national and state socialism, the Holocaust, genocide, and the development of total war. 'Massacres have become vital', he wrote (Foucault 1979a: 137; see also 2003: 239–64).

If what is dangerous about certain states is the way in which they combine forms and discourses of rule, it follows that there might be less dangerous, or even benign, combinations of these discourses and practices of rule in other states. In this context, consider the discussion of liberalism by Foucault. It is interesting that when he turned to that discussion, it was in a lecture course called 'The birth of biopolitics' (Foucault 1997a: 73–9, 2004a). Perhaps he was stuck with an old title. But, nevertheless, if we refer to the course summary, there liberalism enters into the picture as the framework of political rationality in which problems of the biopolitics of the population began, as he puts it, to have the 'look of a challenge'. 'In a system anxious to have the respect of legal subjects and to ensure the free enterprise of individuals', he asks (Foucault 1997a: 74), 'how can the "population" phenomenon be taken into account?'

On this account, liberal and democratic forms of governing are a relatively benign version of the combination I have just spoken about. Biopower is tempered by liberal economic freedoms and democratized sovereignty. Liberalism criticizes, reviews and rationalizes powers of life and death by governing through the liberties and rights of subjects, that is, by the employment of the powers of freedom.

According to this view, a 'system of natural liberty' is first found in those different spheres external to government, such as those of commercial society or the market, by the empirical philosophies of the Scottish Enlightenment. Here, liberalism suspects that 'one is always governing too much'. In contrast to the German police science – *Polizeiwissenschaft* – of the seventeenth and eighteenth centuries which is always worried whether there is disorder and insufficient regulation, 'economic' liberalism does not dare to exercise governmentality 'without a "critique" far more radical than the test of optimization' (Foucault 1997a: 74).

On the other hand, we have witnessed what might be called a 'demo-cratization of sovereignty' with the development of parliamentary insti-tutions. This is a delegation of sovereign powers onto representative institutions that make it possible both to identify the exercise of sovereign powers with the 'will of the people' and to regulate the participation of those who comprise the people. Part of the problem of representative democracy is how to govern the participation of individuals and factions in government. It is how to keep governors and governed separate, or how to ensure that the exercise of freedom by individuals does not undermine the security of governmental institutions either by the over-enthusiasm for politics of the governed or the corruption of public officials and politicians (Hindess 1997).

There is undoubtedly a kind of radical undecidability about Foucault's relation to liberalism. It is apparent that he approaches the discussion of liberalism and neoliberalism with an openness and generosity in regard to their capacity for political and social invention. On the other hand, it is precisely those countries that would adopt liberal constitutional forms of state from the nineteenth century which are responsible for massive ela-boration of disciplinary and biopolitical techniques charted by Foucault and the forms of domination and despotism with which they are associated.

The view that liberal–democratic forms of rule offer safeguards against aspects of sovereign and biopolitical powers of life and death is found on occasion in the literature of governmentality. Nikolas Rose (1999) has undoubtedly provided a most complete account of the mentalities and technologies of rule in contemporary liberal–democratic societies. How-ever, even given his willingness to analyse explicit programmes of 'control' in these societies, there is still a sense of the protection afforded by liberal arrangements. Rose appears to endorse the relatively benign character of liberalism. Thus, he argues in relation to biological technologies and their development in Nazi Germany that '. . . without the controls exercised by liberal concerns with limited government and individual freedoms, the despotism of the state that is always an immanent presence in all govern-mentalities is manifest in all its bloody rationality' (Rose 1999: 23). In this regard, there is a narrowing of the relationship between the normativity of liberal conception of government and the analysis offered by govern-mentality studies. Other thinkers in this field take a more explicitly liberal normative stance. Thus, Kevin Stenson (1998), in a paper that importantly reinstates the significance of sovereignty, argues that the explicit normative commitments of studies of governmentality should be focused on liberalism as a form of critique.

If there is an undecidability about Foucault's relation to liberal government, much of the literature on governmentality appears less so even if it would reject a resounding endorsement of the normative claims of contemporary liberal-democratic forms of rule. At times, however, it can appear to view liberalism as offering a prophylaxis against the less savoury aspects of biopolitics or of sovereign powers and even to connect the critical function of liberalism with the critical impulses of governmentality. This tacit endorsement of liberal government over the powers of life and death of sovereignty and biopolitics parallels the way US liberal internationalists such as Joseph Nye favour 'soft power', defined as 'the ability to shape the preferences of others' or as 'getting others to want the outcomes you want' and thus coopting them rather than using coercion (2004: 5).

Let us call this danger within governmentality studies, the danger of a kind of soft liberal normativism. It is connected to another possible danger, which I shall call the 'reinscription thesis'. Here, these other domains of power might be treated as having been reinscribed and in some sense made subordinate to the contemporary liberal framework of governmentality. In liberal regimes of power, continues Rose, 'the thematics of sovereignty, of discipline and of biopower are all relocated within the field of governmentality' (1999: 23). In such a view, heterogeneous powers such as sovereignty, discipline and biopower are all repositioned within the space of governmentality. The richness of empirical possibility of an analytics of power and government thus leads to a downgrading of the importance of theoretical questions of the relations between these power formations. In my view, it is vital to consider these theoretical questions in relation to the government of the state more broadly and liberal government more specifically.

There are a number of possible interpretations of this idea that other modalities and trajectories of power relations are relocated or reinscribed within governmentality. *First*, this view could simply mean that sovereign, disciplinary and biopower undergo their own transformations which, in part, are affected by the proliferation of techniques for the direction of the conduct of individuals and collectives. They now must be analysed in their singular and contingent relations to governmental technologies and rationalities and, conversely, governmental practices should be understood in their relations to other forms of power. This is the view argued in this chapter. From a normative perspective, there is always an open question about whether a liberal practice of government augments or protects us from the unsavoury aspects of forms of power. *Second*, this view could suggest a subsumption of these other forms of power under the coming to dominance of governmental power. If we take the latter approach, I would contend, this problematic starts to veer toward the sociological narrative sketched in Chapter 3 in one key respect. It could be taken as proposing a narrative of the decline of earlier and sovereign kinds of authority and power relations in favour of one that proposes to govern through the self-governing individual, a project that has fundamentally displaced the aspiration of governing society.[3]

Governing without society?

An apparent similarity between the sociological narrative of culture-governance and the governmentality literature concerns the fate of the notion of society. We shall deal more closely with Foucault's own conception of liberal governing as finding its object and justification in the idea of society, or civil society, and not the state, in Chapter 5. Broadly, however, for the governmentality literature the notion of society is regarded as an artefact of liberal ways of governing through a specific domain, the social. The early work of Jacques Donzelot (1979a) regards the formation of the 'social' or of social government as a component of the liberal problem of the state which was concerned in the nineteenth century to authorize interventions into family or economic life without completely dissolving the shifting boundaries between the liberal state and those spheres formally understood as private. As Deleuze (1979) points out, rather than being understood as a general feature of human existence, coextensive with sociality, the social is a 'particular sector' within certain societies, an historically and geographically limited sector of problems, cases, institutions and personnel. It is, moreover, a way of thinking and acting undertaken by a particular set of authorities of all types. It gives rise to and is codified and stabilized by particular forms of knowledge and particular disciplines such as social statistics, sociology, welfare economics, criminology, and so on. And it becomes a component in diverse sets of political demands and rationalities. Through a complex history, these diverse and multiple social concerns give rise in the early twentieth century to the formation of society as the object of government *par excellence*. Ewald (1991), for example, has shown how the relationship between the development of social insurance techniques in the Third Republic in France was connected to the development of political doctrines of *solidarisme* and the problematic of the solidarity between individualized subjects found in Emile Durkheim's idea of society. With the development of a form of rule animated by the ethos of the welfare state, the object of government becomes, in the first half of the twentieth century, the welfare of society. At a theoretical level, society is the most general and abstract condition in which social relations, institutions and processes can be observed. As a governmental object, however, society is now conceived as the totality of the population inhabiting the territory that defines the nation-state. In both current sociology and in the diagnosis of governmental rationality, it is this notion of society as a unified domain that is rendered highly problematic. Sociologists view the irresistible forces of globalization as undermining the boundaries that define that territory, and thus the integrity of their own previously taken-for-granted object, and hence decry, as we have seen, the 'container theory' of society. The governmentality approach views the displacement of conceptions of national economy, and the techniques and forms of expertise by which the economy is knowable, as one aspect of the transformation or mutation of social government which places the object of 'society' in crisis.

Aligned with this mutation is the thesis of 'the birth of community', that is, the view that the decline of the social as a key domain of government is accompanied by the discovery of the multiple field of community (Rose 1996). The birth of community can first be approached descriptively in noting the proliferation of new languages around community, from multiculturalism to gay politics; new vocabularies of administration, from community care to community consultation; the formation of risk and lifestyle communities, and so forth. Here we find political languages that problematize issues in terms of communities, devise programmes to act upon communities, reconfigure the imagined territory of government, and specify subjects as members of communities.

Examined more analytically, the birth of community, however, actively undoes the features of the social. Where the social indicates a form of governmental territorialization delimiting a nation and the conditions of its solidarity, community is a symptom of its 'detotalization'. Against the unitary spatialization of the social, there are a plurality of communities, some occupying specific geographic locale, others located in non-geographic or 'virtual' spaces, and still others traversing real time and space. Community also marks a transformation in the character of ethics. The social, an order of collective being and collective responsibilities and obligations, is displaced by the self-responsible subject tied to others by bonds of affinity. Finally, the 'socially identified' citizen gives way to the multiple, overlapping allegiances the individual makes with various communities and which he or she is helped to make with specialists of various sorts. Communities are understood both as 'natural' and something that require a labour of construction to be brought into a particular form.

In contrast to the culture-governance thesis, it is not the 'real' effects of globalization that have undermined the notion of a national society but the rationalities and techniques of economic governance and the new imaginaries, vocabularies, problematizations and identifications of community. Thus, '... it seems as if we are seeing the emergence of a range of rationalities and techniques that seek to govern without governing *society*, to govern through regulated choices made by discrete and autonomous actors in the context of their particular commitments to families and communities' (Rose 1996: 328, original emphasis). Our dilemma of how to render the analysis of 'governing society' into a thinkable, analytical project in a sense has increased with these insights. Whether we deal with first-order statements about the real (sociology), or second-order statements about how we understand and act on the real (an analytics of governmental rationalities and technologies), we find all the same themes. We have the emergence of a polycentric governance without sovereign government, the apparent displacement of the classical themes of state, nation, territory and citizen in favour of a language of plurality, hetero-geneity, networks, flows, and so on. In place of the citizen who identifies with a nation-state, we witness the emergence of the self-governing actor. And in place of the notion of society coincident with a population living within a particular territory, we have the polymorphous language of community.

It is important to emphasize that the focus on the self-governing indi-vidual is not antithetical to that of community. They are complementary. It is the self-governing individual who identifies with plural and overlapping communities. And it is because individuals can no longer rely on their identities as social citizens, or social roles ascribed to them, to ensure their support that they need the values, organizations and support of commu-nities. The virtue of the governmentality approach is that it starts to give us detail of the mechanisms and rationalities by which the task of culture-governance is to be accomplished. The risk is that its thick descriptions begin to render that task a taken-for-granted component of contemporary governing.

We are thus becoming clearer, I hope, on how the individualization thesis is related to the governing without society theme. The knowledge of society, and the attempt to govern it, can be viewed as an artefact of a world divided into separate sovereign states. Society is thus equivalent to the national populations that exist within the frontiers of these states. But because the problematic of society is always one of solidarity and order, it also presupposes the capacity of the state-container to elicit the identifi-cation of individuals in the name of society. If we presuppose a diminishing capacity of the container in the form of a decline of its authority, then we presuppose a decline in its capacities to require identification. If, on the other hand, individuals are now the masters and mistresses of their own fates and identities, then there can be no privilege given to national identity. They will identify with whatever collectives they choose, using and mobilizing this identification however they might. Individualization in Beck's sense presupposes the capacity of individuals to identify with the plural communities found in contemporary rationalities of government. Individualism and communitarianism no longer appear as opposite. While Mrs Thatcher might be viewed by communitarians (Etzioni 1996: 11) as far too individualistic and in need of correction, it is clear that she already understood governing without society in terms consistent with commu-nitarian logic. She claimed to have meant by her famous phrase 'there is no such thing as society' that 'society was not an abstraction ... but a living structure of individuals, families, neighbours and voluntary associations' (1993: 626).

It seems to me that studies of governmentality have picked up very well the kind of underlying transformations that have occurred in authoritative descriptions of the real found in political thought and social theory. But that creates a dilemma. Doesn't the study of rationalities of contemporary liberal government wish to move beyond the claims of such authoritative discourses to a different kind of intelligibility located within the practices of contemporary governing and their effects? Can it offer another kind of analysis of the assemblages of rule we find today? Can it help us think differently about governing society?

I want here to propose some key arguments in contrast to this exegesis. These points are crucial if we are to understand contemporary transformations of liberal-democratic rule. The first is a kind of methodological point on these domains and zones of power. The second concerns this tendency toward acquiescence to the normativity of contemporary liberalism. These points need to be accepted before we can begin to characterize the contemporary metamorphosis of the liberal government of the state. That government, I shall suggest, is multiform, arising as much from powers of life and death as forms of 'government' in Foucault's sense. Biopolitics and sovereignty might be being rewritten in the language of governmental expertise in the multiple, negotiated contracts by which conduct is to be shaped. But powers of life and death remain in the premises of such contracts. The ethos of liberal government today – indeed, as ever – is as much about life (and death) as liberty, responsibility as freedom, obligation as rights, decision as choice, and violence as much as contract. And while there are rationalities which downplay the capacities of the formal political sphere, which reformulate the rights and obligations of individuals outside the idea of social citizenship, and which deny the salience of governing society, it would be a mistake to underestimate the continued, if reconfigured, importance of the themes of territory, of society and nation, and the role of the formal political system and its use of sovereign powers, within contemporary forms of power and rule.

Heterogeneous and indistinct powers

My first counter-premise, then, is the following. If we take seriously the postulate that power is heterogeneous and multiform, then the field of power relations cannot be reduced to an analytics of 'government', where the latter is understood as the 'conduct of conducts'. While there is no doubt that this analytics can help us understand the practices concerned with the direction of conduct for various ends, it is important not to telescope contemporary politics and power into questions of government. Transformations of governmentality need to be placed against contingent transformations of the exercise of sovereign and biopolitical powers of life and death. They also need to be balanced against the forms of resistance, the 'counter-conducts', to which they are opposed.

The work on governmentality is thus of a limited region within modern power relations, politics and forms of rule. The analytics of government, conceived as the multidimensional analysis of the different ways in which our conduct is guided and directed, and for various ends, exists within a broader field. This is a complex field of overlapping powers which has been partially mapped by Foucault.

This field includes the powers of death, of punishment and of coercion that are usually associated with the idea of sovereignty. Sovereignty is indeed a complex of powers unto itself. Its territoriality and its claims to a monopoly of legitimate violence were noticed by Weber ([1918] 1972: 77–8). Its 'decisionistic' character is emphasized in the early work of Schmitt's treatment of the sovereign ([1922] 1985b). Its deductive character, grounded in the spectacular of the right of death, is analysed by Foucault (for example, in 1979a: 135–59). To speak of sovereignty does not amount to a project of 'bringing the state back in'. Indeed, sovereign powers could today be as dispersed as governmental powers, as we shall see in Part Three of this book.

One of the features of sovereignty is that it has been a delegated power, or at least a power capable of delegation. As we have seen in Chapter 1, the development of European international law from the sixteenth century assumed that the civilized world was made up of territorial states that acted according to established rules of conduct as sovereign persons toward one another. To discuss sovereignty, at least since the beginnings of the European state-system, is to discuss a system in which sovereignty is delegated to the rulers of European states. This sovereignty is delegated by interstate law to such rulers not only over internal territories but also certain forms of extra-territoriality – colonies, protectorates, and so forth. The first point to make about sovereignty is that it assumes a plurality of formally, equal and mutually recognizing sovereigns and that these sovereigns exist within a system that is greater than each of them but formed through their agreement. One could say that as a precondition for a domestic or national government of society, it was first necessary to have an international system of governing societies which was founded on the delegation of sovereignty to territorial states.

Within certain of these European states and their former colonies we have witnessed a process by which representative institutions and constitutional law have specified procedures for the formation of the sovereign, a process that Foucault refers to as the 'democratization of sovereignty'. Such a phrase is connected to the oxymoron, the 'sovereign subject', which suggests that there might be occasions on which certain kinds of sovereign decision can be delegated to various personages and groups within the populations of these states. We shall pick up on this point in a moment.

The field of power also includes the powers of life, of the living, and of the processes of life, which have been previously assigned the title 'biopolitics'. We cannot turn to contemporary issues of biomedicine, bioethics and bioscience, without intellectual equipment that allows us to examine how the shaping of conduct and the exercise of choice concerns matters that deal with the organic and visceral materiality of bodies and the vitality, morbidity and mortality of the 'species body' of the population. Such choices are biopolitical in that they concern powers of the fostering of life and letting die. An example of this is the removal of life support systems for an individual in a coma or one defined as 'brain dead', as in the Schiavo case we have mentioned. Another example is the termination of pregnancy consequent upon genetic and other forms of screening or risk assessment.[4] These choices are often made by individuals – for example, relatives, carers, prospective parents, sometimes but less often by medical and health specialists – informed by expertise through which we attempt to govern conduct. The first point to note is that, in each of these examples, there is not only governmental regulation of choice but biopolitical concerns with the fostering of life and with letting die.

But we can push the analysis even further. The word 'choice' is perhaps too redolent of both the market place and its shopping mall consumer culture. The choices involved, in these examples, are to introduce and accent a rather different word, *decisions*. They are decisions on 'bare life', to employ Giorgio Agamben's evocative phrase (1998). Drawing upon Aristotle, he finds two concepts of life at work in Western political thought: that of *bios*, the morally and politically qualified life of the community; and the *zoē*, bare life, or life stripped naked, symbolized by the naked human individual (Agamben 1998: 1–5). For Agamben (1998: 83), drawing upon Walter Benjamin's account of the universal proscription against murder ([1921] 1978: 298–9), it is sovereign power that is at work in the making of such decisions on the life that can be terminated without the commission of homicide. These decisions are thus made as choices shaped by various kinds of expertise (or, if you like, governmental rationality), embedded within practices that concern the enhancement of life. There is thus sovereignty, governmentality and biopolitics. And while they might 'enter a zone of irreducible indistinction' (Agamben 1998: 9), they are not reinscribed within one another in the sense that one dimension of power has privilege over the other.

These decisions are sovereign decisions and not merely governmental or even 'biopolitical' choices because they involve not merely a matter of letting die but a form of killing without the commission of homicide. Or at least they involve a point at which it is difficult to know whether we are letting die or exercising a right of death. This is what I meant when I suggested that sovereignty itself could be 'dispersed' like other power relations onto individuals, parents, families and health experts. I call this a *delegation of sovereignty*, which parallels the delegation of sovereign powers onto legislatures, state governments, and so on. In the biomedical field, sovereign decisions of the continuation of life or its termination have, at least to some extent and in some cases, now been delegated onto individuals, parents and families. This delegation is caught within a network of forms of expertise of counsellors, bioethicists, institutional ethics committees, medical and legal professional bodies, as much as it is within the remit of legislatures, courts, judges and politicians.

Another example of an equally heterogeneous set of powers is found in the treatment of those groups variously called asylum seekers, illegal immigrants and refugees. While we can map fundamental transformations in the national and international government of refugees (Lippert 1998, 2004), these governmental regimes are incomplete without decisions on who is to be included and who is excluded from the juridical–political order. Some are thought worthy of inclusion as 'denizens' within a state. Others are placed in the paradoxical situation of being included through their exclusion. In Australia, for example, those awaiting 'processing' are placed outside the political order within the perimeters of 'detention centres'. These sovereign decisions on the value of populations are a condition for a government of such populations, which regulates their movements across national borders, assigns them particular statuses and treats them accordingly. There is also an unexpected biopolitical dimension to the treatment of refugees when we consider that their status depends upon forms of knowledge, policy and legislation associated with notions of human rights. Such rights are ascribed to individuals, under the Universal Declaration of Human Rights, at the moment of their birth, as Agamben notes (1998: 127). 'All human beings are born free and equal in dignity and rights', reads its first article. Indeed, the refugee might stand as an example of bare life in the contemporary world (see Agamben 1998: 131–3) who has rights only by virtue of his or her living existence. These rights, it should be noted, are to be upheld and promoted by the member states of the UN, as is made clear in the preamble.[5]

We should note that the effect of Agamben so decomposes the distinction between sovereignty and biopolitics as to problematically erase the shifts and transformations proposed by Foucault's work on biopolitics and state biologisms of the nineteenth century and to prevent an analysis of the character of contemporary shifts (see Part Three of this book for further critical consideration of Agamben's approach). However, there are contexts in which it is well not to draw the boundaries between these contemporary formations of power too tightly or one is likely to miss what he calls the 'zones of indistinction'. These are the regions in which these heterogeneous powers act in such concert that it is difficult to know whether we are in the presence of biopolitical or sovereign powers.

While an analytics decomposes the current regimes of power into their constituent elements, we should recognize that there are also key thresholds in which sovereignty, governmentality and biopolitics cease to exist as distinguishable categories. The powers of life and death enter into a network of indistinction with each other and with government. Biopolitical powers for the medical care of life might also entail sovereign decisions about the termination of life. Providing counselling for those deciding whether to terminate a pregnancy after genetic testing is not simply about 'conducting conduct', or the shaping of choice through contractually negotiated expertise, but about the sovereign decision on the termination or continuation of 'bare life'.

As the current government of refugees demonstrates, or the history of indigenous peoples within lands of colonization, there is hardly a form of the liberal government of the state that does not rest upon domination, coercion, violence or the threat and symbolics of violence. It is impossible to examine the constitutional legitimacy of the founding of states such as the United States, Canada, New Zealand and Australia, for example, without confronting the violent appropriation of land and extirpation of its inhabitants that this entailed. All this occurred with the blessing and active participation of the founding thinkers of modern constitutionalism such as John Locke, as James Tully (1995: 70–8) has shown, despite the apparent contradiction with the accepted principles of sovereignty and consent. A more recent example is the history of 'welfare reform' in the United States in the 1990s, particularly after the passing of the federal Personal Responsibility and Work Opportunity Reconciliation Act of 1996. This is partially a history of the forcible clearing off the welfare rolls those who would not conform to the requirements that they look and find paid employment or enter a training programme (Mead 1997; Peck 1998; Schram 2000).

This point about the multiform character of ensembles of rule can be quite easily made in relation to the 'ethos of welfare'. Of what does this ethos consist? From Foucault (1981, 2001c), it is about an effort to maximize the security of the population and the independence of its members. This entails balancing the labour of forming a community of responsible, virtuous and autonomous citizens with a pastoral care of their health, their needs and their capacities and means to live. The ethos of welfare is a potent admixture of rights *and* obligations, freedom *and* coercion, liberty *and* life. It is formed through practices of freedom by which citizens are formed and form themselves, on one side. Yet these are located within a web of sovereign powers by which subjects are bound to do certain things. These include the use of deductive and coercive powers of taxation, of systems of punishment, detention, expulsion and disqualification, and of compulsion in drug rehabilitation, child support, immunization, workfare programmes and so on for the achievement of various goals of national government.

More fundamentally, these sovereign powers consist in decisions as to what constitutes a normal frame of life, and hence what constitutes public order and security, and when such a situation obtains (Schmitt [1922] 1985b: 9). Today, as we saw in the previous chapter, there are various ways of governing domestic society that attempt to provide a means of deciding this normal frame. Among communitarians, such as Etzioni (1996), this normal frame is decided upon by the shared moral values of the communities. Among sociologists, such as Giddens (1998) and Beck (2000a), this normal frame is defined by the processes that lead to a new kind of institutionally negotiated individualization and cosmopolitanism. Among new paternalists, such as Lawrence Mead and his associates (1986, 1997), it is decided by the views of the citizenry made known by their representatives in the Congress. For neoconservative Christians, the normal frame is established by the faith of believers and their organizations. There is an agreement between all these groups that, however we decide the content of this normal, everyday frame of life, at least certain populations can be invited, expected, and indeed obligated, to follow it.

Fifty years ago, T. H. Marshall smuggled in sovereign notions of rights to justify the pastoral character of the welfare state in his classic essay, 'Citizenship and social class' ([1949] 1963). Today, 'welfare reform', and its instruments of workfare, emphasizes the converse of rights, obligations, when it demands the transformation of the individual as condition of the exercise of a pastoral, whether secular or religious, care. Both cross the threshold between the political–juridical order of sovereignty and the moral and pastoral government of conduct. For Marshall, pastoral care is a function of social rights; for compassionate conservatives, new paternalists, communitarians and Third Way social democrats, sovereign instruments bind those receiving pastoral care to paternally defined collective obligations.

Summing up this part of the argument, government, understood as the conduct of conduct, is one zone or field of contemporary power relations. To understand those relations we need to take into account heterogeneous powers such as those of sovereignty and biopolitics. The exercise of power in contemporary liberal democracies entails matters of life and death as much as ones of the direction of conduct; of obligation as much as rights; of decisions on the fostering or abandonment of life, or the right to kill without committing homicide, as well as of the shaping of freedom and the exercise of choice. Nevertheless, having distinguished this heterogeneous field of power, there are key thresholds that are crossed in which these distinctions begin to collapse. Sovereign violence, its symbols and its threat, is woven into the most mundane forms of government. The unemployed, for example, are to transform themselves into active jobseekers or participate in workfare programmes under the sanction of the removal of the sustenance of life. In contemporary genetic politics and ethics, too, we enter thresholds where it becomes unclear whether we are in the presence of the powers to foster life or the right to take it. The biopolitical, the sovereign, the governmental, begin to enter into zones of indistinction.

We would all, of course, prefer soft power to the 'hard power' of violence, coercion and obligation. However, it is clear that it is difficult to disentangle the soft power of governing through freedom from those 'hard' powers that secure the conditions of a form of life called freedom.

Liberal democracies

My second counter-premise concerns the nature of liberal democracies. It follows from the first. If regimes of power are constituted through multiform, heterogeneous trajectories and zones of power relations, then it is necessary to remain sceptical of the way in which contemporary liberal forms of rule are understood. It is my contention here that a liberal understanding of the government of the state systematically underestimates the manner in which liberal polities are engaged in sovereign decisions and a biopolitics of the population that concern, in their different and sometimes indistinct ways, fundamental matters of life and death.

There are three aspects of the liberal understanding of the state that are germane to the argument here. All three are present in the work of the most vigorous and able defenders of liberalism, such as Stephen Holmes (1993, 1995). These postulates are that of limited government, of individual liberty, and the anti-authoritarian character of liberalism. The first means that liberal government is one in which there are constitutional constraints on the sovereign powers exercised by the state. In liberal democracies, this can be presented as constraints on majority rule, popular sovereignty, or the will of the people. The second means that the principle of this limitation of government is found in the individual freedoms that exist in private life and in a sphere of civil society separate from the state. The third employs this system of limitations and rights to distinguish liberalism from authoritarian forms of government.

All three postulates are clearly a part of a liberal conception of government. They are, in other words, part of liberal ways of thinking about the means and objectives of the use of sovereign powers. They are all, however, easily shown to be a product of that specific standpoint. In other words, they are a part of the programmatic rationality of liberal constitutionalism. They do not consider the effects of such rationality in the practical domain to which it is linked.

That standpoint first presupposes the existence of an already existing sovereign power exercised over a distinct territorial domain. By famously defining the sovereign as 'he who decides the state of exception', Schmitt ([1922] 1985b: 5) was able to show, for example, that these sovereign powers are both inside and outside the rule of law which is established by constitutional democracies. The constitutional and juridical framework rests on something external to itself which both establishes it and which it claims to regulate, but which it cannot found. As Holmes agrees (1993: 57), 'liberal principles of majority rule and equality before the law can operate effectively only within the confines of legitimate territorial borders, yet these principles are totally incapable of creating or justifying such borders'. Liberal constitutionalism is a way of thinking about the use, restriction, democratization and regulation of sovereign power within a definite territory, which nevertheless it must simply presuppose. All discussion of mandates provided by representative institutions are discussions of how a determination is made on who is to use these sovereign powers and for what purposes. It is not a discussion of the existence of sovereign powers.[6]

More broadly, the development of liberal constitutionalism in the nineteenth and early twentieth centuries is accompanied by either the establishment or the extension of permanent police and armed forces, centralized ministries of state, government departments and large public service bureaucracies, mass compulsory schooling, national poor relief and social insurance systems, public health services and systems, and national taxation systems. The notion of government as an institutionally restricted sphere is thus compatible with what an earlier generation of historians called, in relation to England and controversies over Benthamite influences, the 'nineteenth-century revolution in government' (MacDonagh 1958; Parris 1960). As Holmes (1995) shows, this doctrine is at least as much an enabling one as a constraining one.

Much of the debate between liberalism and anti-liberalism, however, rests on whether the institutions of the liberal state (parliament, the executive, the legislative, the judiciary, government bureaux) conform to the ideal of how they should operate. Thus Schmitt's ([1926] 1985a) famous critique of parliament as an indecisive talking shop between opposed interest groups rests on its fundamental departure from the ideal as an arena of rational deliberation in which the people's representatives arrive at decisions on behalf of the general welfare. Stephen Holmes's rebuttal of Schmitt (1993: 57–8) is that parliaments can and do make and implement binding decisions that are backed by instruments of law and force and that, moreover, liberal thinkers have long considered the issues of the use of force, of the question of exception, of the control of asocial passions, and so on. The debate strikes me as interesting, however, less for the ultimate resolution of the issue of liberalism versus anti-liberalism and more for the way the attack and the defence of liberalism start to make visible the actual practices and operations of liberal kinds of rule. Both 'anti-liberals' such as Schmitt and 'liberals' such as Holmes move the analysis of liberalism away from its status as a moral philosophy that drives the institutional design of institutions of state and more toward its practical and technical operation.[7] They begin to highlight aspects of the paradox of liberalism as an ideal of limited government.

From a post-Foucauldian perspective, of course, this is only one, and quite small, aspect of the paradox of liberalism as limited government. Here, liberal government presents itself as operating through semi-autonomous non-state domains and specialist knowledges of them: civil society, culture, economy and population. Because of the idea that government must work through social, cultural, economic and vital processes external to the state to achieve the betterment of the life of the population, however, the potential for the government, whether through state or non-state agencies, of aspects of individual and collective life is boundless. Liberal government *is* total, not because it is equivalent to authoritarian rule riding roughshod over all civil liberties, or because it is completely successful in the realization of its aims. Rather it is total because its programme of self-limitation is linked to the facilitation and augmentation of the powers of civil society and the use of these powers, in conjunction with the sovereign, disciplinary and biopolitical powers of the state itself, to establish a comprehensive normalization of social, economic and cultural existence.[8]

A good example of an attempt to provide this kind of rationale for comprehensive government of life is found in the rationality of economic globalization. I have suggested elsewhere that the discourse of globalization is a manifestation of the transformation of the liberal problematic of security from the security of economic processes external to government to a kind of security of governmental mechanisms themselves (Dean 1999: 194). Here I want simply to note how the postulation of processes external to the formal apparatus of the state, indeed, external to the territory of the national state itself, can provide a standing reason for the reformation of all aspects of individual and institutional conduct to make them more efficient and competitive (Hindess 1998). Significantly, such a discourse should be understood as one of the national government of society, formulated through particular policies and using the resources of national states to achieve these goals. Moreover, such reformation of individual and institutional conduct can be done in the name of promoting freedom but by employing coercive means. Enforcing work obligations for the unemployed, single parents or people with disabilities, for example, can thus be linked to a discourse on the global necessity of economic freedom.

The contemporary politics of obligation of those in receipt of social assistance reminds us that liberalism attempts to govern as much through 'domination' – a word that covers a myriad of conditions – as it does through freedom. Liberal forms of governing are exceedingly 'ambivalent' about the idea of a self-determining subject. As far as the poor who might claim assistance were concerned, the formation of liberal government of the state in the nineteenth century in England was more fundamentally concerned with responsibility – certainly a capacity closely related to 'obligation' – than it was with freedom (Dean 1991). If it was about freedom at all, then, this form of liberalism was seeking to establish a positive conception of freedom in Isaiah Berlin's sense ([1958] 1997). An account of the formation of liberal government requires us to make reference to Reverend Thomas Malthus's injunction to create the conditions by which labourers would exercise what he called 'moral restraint', that is restraint from reproduction (Dean 1991: 77–81). If they did not, such conditions would dictate that they would starve to death and watch their children starve to death. The Malthusian diagram of 'domination' is one that seeks an enforcement of the ontological violence of nature by a decision of the state *not* to act, or to act in a particular way. This equality of all before the violence of nature, as much as Adam Smith's system of natural liberty, is the foundation of liberal conceptions of government and of law.

Consider even those who believed that the provision of subsistence was a necessary end of government and legislation, such as Jeremy Bentham and Edwin Chadwick (Dean 1991: 156–210). They envisaged a framing of administrative devices and centralized state bureaucracy that would ensure the maintenance of the forms of life appropriate to the class of labourers and those constituted as their natural dependents, that is, their wives, their children, and the mothers of those children. This administrative logic dictated a detailed regulation of the lives of those reliant on poor relief which would rival anything found in the German police scientists, if not exceed it. The late eighteenth- and early nineteenth-century liberal critique of police facilitates the attempt at the detailed regulation of the lives of the labouring classes, the poor and the indigent, under centralized state bureaucratic superintendence. And, infused throughout the administrative device of 'less eligibility' that was to ensure that the life of the pauper was to appear less advantageous than that of the labourer, was the Malthusian violence written into the bioeconomic realities of population and subsistence.

To sum up, liberalism presents itself as a form of limited government offering restraints on sovereign power. In contrast, liberal government offers the most fundamental and enduring extension of the powers of the government of the state so far witnessed. Moreover, this limitation is undertaken in the name of individual rights and liberty. Yet liberal forms of government of the state instrumentalize and shape various forms of freedom and choice. This is irrespective of whether liberals believe that freedom is an attribute of individuals exchanging on the market (Adam Smith), or that it is the product of specific social, institutional and cultural conditions, variously conceived.[9] Moreover, it is just as routine to attempt to form and to work through other kinds of capacities of certain types of individuals. The procreative prudence and economic responsibility of the Malthusian poor is one example. The obligation of the 'welfare mom' on workfare in the contemporary USA is another. Sometimes these and other capacities are viewed as a condition of freedom. On other occasions, working through these other attributes (obligation, for example), or transforming them (immaturity, idleness, and so forth) by *illiberal* means, are fundamental features of liberalism – a theme explored in full in the following chapter.

The attempt to govern through freedom is a contingent feature, not a necessary corollary, of liberal claims to be a limited form of government that respects individual liberty. Moreover, liberal government has no monopoly on notions of freedom. Given the excavations of Quentin Skinner in *Liberty before Liberalism* (1998), we know that the seventeenth-century 'neo-Roman' theory of free states in which the civil freedom of individuals is only possible in a self-governing political association is one example of another conception. The Ancient Greek notion of *sōphrosynē*, a state in which one could attain freedom in relation to the practice of pleasures, and not be a slave to them, is another (Foucault 1985: 78). And given that regimes that from a liberal point of view are called 'authoritarian' often justify themselves in terms of what Berlin long ago called a positive conception of liberty, the justification of domination in the name of freedom cannot be viewed as a distinguishing feature of liberalism.

I shall now make some remarks that use these two insights in an examination of the contemporary transformations of government. That is, I shall examine those transformations in relation to the postulate of multiple, heterogeneous and indistinct powers, and the view that contemporary forms of governing in liberal democracies have no necessary relation to individual freedom or the shaping of it.

Transformations of contemporary government

I have argued above that we cannot understand liberalism in its own terms, that is, as a system of safeguards against authoritarian rule. Nor can we understand contemporary formations of rule purely in terms of government defined as those zones of powers concerned with the 'conduct of conduct'. Both of these postulates run counter to certain tendencies of the literature on governmentality, and to many of the themes of the literatures concerning governance and globalization summarized in the previous chapter. Together, they reinstate the importance of biopolitics and sovereignty, and of situating shifts of government and rule within them. One of the effects of doing so is to render premature the obituaries for the ideal of a territorial state and the idea of governing society. I want now to suggest a 'thought experiment' for doing this (see Table 4.1).

Table 4.1 Contemporary governing in liberal democracies

Governing through freedom	⟷	Powers of life and death
Shaping of choice	⟷	Sovereign decision
Techniques of contract	⟷	Deployment of violence
Management of risk	⟷	Securitization of threats
Multiple communities	⟷	Society as realm of defence and source of obligation
Global economy and reform	⟷	Imposition of authority
New forms of citizenship	⟷	Obligation and techniques of subjection
Dissolution of territorial state	⟷	Protection of borders and assertion of sovereignty

Let me start with the transformations of rule that emphasize the subsumption of other formations of power under governance or government in Foucault's sense. If we do this, contemporary liberal government of the state might be described in the following way.

First, it is above all a form of governing through freedom rather than one that relies almost exclusively on domination or coercion. Freedom does not have to be an ineffable metaphysical principle: freedom can be both artefact and technical means for the realization of governmental objectives. As artefact it can be constructed: by establishing a market in health services, for example, or, in US foreign policy, by setting up a representative regime in Iraq that teaches the population the value of freedom and stands as an example for nearby countries. As technical means, it associates governance with attraction and empowerment and with the enabling, steering and facilitation of the networks and communities rather than with hierarchy and authoritative command (Rosenau 2000: 182).

Secondly, contemporary rationalities and programmes of government seek to elicit and shape choices often through the use of expertise and services provided by a range of different types of providers – for profit, non-profits, and public – often acting in 'partnership'. Those who are governed are thus often treated as 'consumers', 'customers', 'rational choice actors', and so on. Various social welfare, health and education clients are asked to make choices in a market in services so that services might be more individualized, tailored to particular needs, made more efficient by being customer-focused, and geared to combat welfare dependency and social exclusion.

Thirdly, the central instruments of these forms of government are the technique of the contract, the construction of 'quasi-markets', the use of formal rationalities of accounting and auditing, the utilization and formation of various communities, and the different forms of the expertise of risk. Older divisions between public and private sectors break down, market-based norms of competition and efficiency govern state as much as non-state institutions. Risk is no longer something managed by the state but devolves 'downward' onto plural agencies such as individuals, families, households, communities, businesses, insurance companies, and so on. Moreover, because risk is seen to escape the container of national societies it devolves 'upward' onto the attempts to manage by transnational corporations, multilateral agreements (for instance the Kyoto Protocol), intergovernmental organizations such as the World Bank and the International Monetary Fund, and international non-government organizations such as Greenpeace and World Wide Fund for Nature.

Fourthly, a central problem for contemporary liberalism is the reform of individual and institutional conduct so that it becomes more competitive and efficient. This problem is encapsulated in the rationality of globalization which envisages a global economy of transnational corporations and capital and financial flows and networks that vitiates – or severely limits – attempts by national states to govern what used to be characterized as their national economy for the benefit of the populations of such states.

Fifthly, the outcome of these new forms of governmentality in advanced liberal democracies is the production of new post-social and post-national forms of citizenship and identity. 'Below' the nation-state, we have economic citizenship, active citizenship, prudentialism, and the complex array of communal identities and identifications; 'above' the nation-state, the cosmopolitan self who identifies as a citizen of the world and is supported by an international human rights regime which is the foundation of a new cosmopolitan law.

Finally, the ideals, imagery and vocabulary through which we have previously conceived the task of governing society have suffered a series of mutations. The ideal of an omnicompetent state is in disrepute, and the imaginary of a single and unified society is in crisis. We have a language of spaces, mobilities and flows, a crossing of borders, of networks, regions, and communities that exist above and below the old nation-state.

This characterization might be understood as providing an excellent thick description of the programmes and rationalities of governing in contemporary liberal democracies. However, it fundamentally concurs with the three aspects of the liberal conception of the government of the state we have identified. One, it regards government as working through (the admittedly constructed) freedom and choices of life-planning individuals now operating in a globalized world and having cosmopolitan potential. Two, it characterizes contemporary liberalism as concerned to limit the extent of formal political authority on both domestic and foreign policy matters. On the domestic front, this limitation is by the implementation of market-styled techniques which transform state organizations and create partnerships with corporate and community bodies; on the foreign, it is limited by the multilayered governance of a new transnational civil society composed of international non-government and government organizations and transnational corporations (Habermas 2001). Three, it focuses on the transformation of liberal-democratic citizenship into new, active, economic forms, on the one hand, and a universal human rights regime, on the other, which continues to distinguish liberal democracy from authoritarian forms of rule.

The strength of the governmentality analysis has been its attendance to the actual rationalities and techniques through which the contemporary liberal government of the state is accomplished. If we stay at this level of thick description, however, such analysis confirms rather than criticizes much contemporary liberal social science. In the latter, current forms of governance displace systems of hierarchy and command with facilitative steering mechanisms and linkages and flows between horizontal networks (for instance, Castells 2000b; Rosenau 2000). Such an analysis is liable to downplay the role of the national state in favour of every other type of governmental and non-governmental agency and social movement, especially the actors of the global economy and civil society. Indeed, governing occurs through the global economy more than any other site and is about constructing networks, linkages and partnerships between different types of agencies for both financial gain and collective provision. In such a view, the world has become fundamentally depoliticized. It is one in which politics is an empty ritual seeking to gratify our appetites for mediatized spectacles (Castells 2000b: 80).

A rather different diagram of possible forms of contemporary liberal government emerges when contemporary transformations of the government of the state are located on multiple zones of power. Here shifts occur in relation to the powers of life and death characteristic of biopolitics and sovereignty as much as in the zone concerned with the conduct of conduct, that is, the zone of governmental power.

The freedom–domination relationship needs to be repositioned in relation to sovereign and biopolitical powers of life and death. In regard to sovereignty, there is a contemporary proliferation of the techniques of arrest, incarceration, punishment, expulsion, disqualification and, more broadly, coercion central to the treatment of populations of asylum seekers, of criminal and prison populations, even of idle youth and social welfare recipients. Of course, on some occasions some of these populations might be asked to exercise freedom and choice, but this should not distract attention from the renewed use of sovereign powers in programmes of mandatory detention and sentencing, zero-tolerance policing, tough love and new paternalist approaches to welfare.[10] Similarly, biopolitical issues of the fostering or disallowing of life, however modulated through individual freedom, cannot be reduced to it.

Thus the question of the shaping of choice by means of various forms of expertise leads to a sovereign decision on the forms of life that can be killed without committing homicide and those that can be allowed to live, and indeed be fostered by various biopowers. The clearest example here is the way in which contemporary biomedical practices employ various forms of expertise (risk assessment, prenatal screening, counselling, criteria on the futility of further treatment, notions of brain death, bioethics) to constitute family members, prospective parents, carers, doctors, and so forth, as loci of decisions concerning the termination of life or the attempt to preserve and foster it. In the language of Agamben, these are sovereign decisions on what constitutes life that can be killed without committing homicide.

The institutional means for the shaping of conduct thus also carry with them the threat of sovereign violence, the symbolics of violence and violence itself. Thus the establishment of institutions and markets to provide for the long-term unemployed or the single parent is accompanied by a fundamental threat to the life and dignity of the individual. Behind the agreements which the unemployed or the single parent must contract into in return for subsistence is the threat of an ultimate sanction, a withdrawal of assistance and thus a withdrawal of the means of life. Perhaps even more effective than the actual sanction are the symbolics of threat that accompanies the designation of a life that is deemed 'unworthy', in the language of National Socialists, or 'undeserving', in the language of nineteenth-century moralizing philanthropy. The question of violence, of micro-violences, of the symbolics and threat of violence, of legal and legitimate violence, as much as the various forms of the 'conduct of conduct' and the governing through freedom, including and especially the contract, is a component of certain types of contemporary liberal rule.

The key intelligibility of contemporary rule is given in more than in its economic self-image. The problem of new forms of productive, efficient and entrepreneurial economic citizenship and rights here meets new forms of moral discipline, restraint and, above all, obligation. The problem of contemporary rule is not simply about economic competition and networks in a globalized (or regional) economy, but about disorder, dysfunction, social pathology and welfare dependency. The personal disorder of the welfare recipient, and the beneficial moral effects of the supervision of the boss, are as important as increasing the productivity of the population for contemporary welfare reform in the USA (Schram 2000: 36–7). Moreover, the development of the 'working poor' in low-paid, insecure, non-unionized jobs establishes a population subject to wide discretionary uses of the arbitrary powers of the boss. These powers might decree no talking at work, no drinking of water during work time, and use of only designated breaks to go to the toilet (Ehrenreich 2001). At the heart of certain contemporary transformations of government is not simply the economic concern, in which the production of a certain form of economic citizenship is necessary for economic security in a global economy. It is also a political one in which the diagnoses of disorder and pathology require the reimposition of authority and the reinscription of not only the poor but all groups and classes within a hierarchy.

At least in certain key domains, notably relating to those on social support, notions of citizenship are being reconfigured so that obligation has become more fundamental than rights, and enforcement has replaced entitlement. While this notion of obligation can be understood as the converse of rights, I want to suggest that obligation is today breaking loose of the juridical discourse of citizenship and coming to assume a relation to the value of life itself. Obligations are enforced by sanctions in which the removal of the means of life or its threat is at stake. Obligation is thus underlined, even in its contractual form, with the threat, symbolics or deployment of violence.

Further, in rationalities and practices of rule concerning national or homeland security in the face of external or internal threats, the ideal of a unified political entity – a state – that claims the right to a monopoly of violence appears intact. In regard to the treatment of those who seek the protection of such a state from outside its borders, the notions of citizenship, nation and territory carry a terrible effectivity. And for those who seek to combat pathology and disorder, the construction of a unified society, characterized by common obligations and values, remains of central importance.

In so far as our studies of rule in contemporary liberal democracies conform to the first description, they replicate certain aspects of the normative understanding of liberalism in which the key dilemma is how a limited sphere of government might facilitate and activate the capacities of its citizens in a cost-effective way. Governing through the exercise of freedom and choice within constructed markets and in public–private partnerships, by plural agencies such as individuals, families, neighbourhoods, assorted communities, regions and other associations, and under the marketized pastoralism of experts, forms one contemporary response to such a dilemma. In this respect the contemporary ethos of welfare concerns how to provide for the needs of the population in such a way as to form and maintain an active and independent citizenry in a manner that strengthens rather than undermines economic performance. The contemporary liberal rationalities of this kind of government of the state concern markets, capital flows, globalization, risk, enterprise, individualization, agency, and so on.

This is, however, I think only a partial description of contemporary politics and what is at stake in the liberal government of the state. It rests to some degree upon a misunderstanding of the history of the formation of an autonomous rationality of government. For even Adam Smith, in his *Lectures on Jurisprudence* ([1752–4] 1978: 5), proposes that the problem of order or, as he puts it, 'internall peace', is 'the first and chief end of every system of government'. Modern governmental rationalities in general, and liberal rationalities of government in particular, are thus concerned with the conditions of social and political order, with the security of nation, society and borders. In so doing, moreover, they necessarily presuppose a power that determines what constitutes public order and decides when it obtains or is disturbed. They presuppose sovereignty. This is missing in not only the assiduous attempts to chart the mechanisms of contemporary rule by those inspired by governmentality approaches but also by the dominant narratives presented by contemporary social science.

I want to suggest that much contemporary discussion of the liberal government of the state is concerned with the establishment and maintenance of order in the face of perceived disorder, threat and disintegration. Whether we examine the new paternalism, social policy ideas of mutual obligation, or even sociologists' discussions of individualization and responsibility, we find the question of the political means of securing social order on the agenda. The contemporary debate here is about the content of a normal frame of life within a political order and the means of securing it. It is about how order can be restored or maintained and social pathology and dependency combated. Contemporary liberal rationalities might identify the emergent normal frame of life with the enterprise, partnerships and networking required by the global imperatives of economic competition and efficiency. But they also concern themselves with how that frame of life will be secured both collectively and individually.

Furthering the study of governmentality means continuing with, but also going beyond, a focus on those power relations conceived as the direction of conduct and the shaping of choice. An analysis of these relations is always in danger of acceding – like certain contemporary social science – to the normative content of liberalism and neoliberalism themselves. It is only by the sustained effort to reposition this analysis within an analysis of sovereign and biopolitical powers that we begin to gain an intelligibility of governing in liberal democracies that is no longer fundamentally colonized by liberal norms.

Conclusion

In Part One of this book we examined the notion of governing societies and the displacement and indeed rejection of it in broad social and political science discussions of governance, globalization and individualization and began to mark points of scepticism toward such narratives. While the post–Foucauldian literature on governmentality, to which this author has contributed, rejects the realism of such narratives, it too shares their suspicion towards the continued salience of the project and vocabulary of governing societies. The present chapter investigates this literature further, précising many of its evident analytical and descriptive strengths while focusing on a couple of potential problems. The first was the entrapment by its privileged object of neo- or advanced liberal forms of rule. Here we saw that the rejection of explicit normative frameworks meant that the description of contemporary liberalism often seemed to imply an endorsement of liberal values or at least of their preventive restraint on the authoritarian potential of sovereignty and biopolitics. The second was the way in which governmentality shared with the governance literature a kind of generalization of 'governance' or governmental power onto the entirety of the field of power relations. I have sought to avoid both these pitfalls by showing how liberal concepts of governing through liberty and limited government should not be taken as a description of liberal forms of rule and how governing through freedom enters into relations with other zones of power relations, in particular sovereignty and biopolitics. These are powers that in their different ways operate through life and death. Such intellectual shifts add up to a quite different description of the poles of contemporary liberal rule which are summed up in Table 4.1. In the next chapter, I follow up on this analysis by pointing to the fundamental nexus of authoritarian practices and liberal styles of rule and show the conditions of possibility of an authoritarian liberalism.

Authoritarian liberalism

In the previous chapter, I argued that it is necessary to offer a description of contemporary forms of rule that takes into account the existence of multiple and heterogeneous forms of power including not only government or governance, but biopolitics and sovereignty. With this in mind, I want to explore further the liberal task of governing society. I shall offer a description of contemporary liberal rule in terms that move beyond the sociological narrative analysed in Chapter 3 and the risk of narrowing of the Foucauldian alternative outlined in the previous chapter. To do this I bring into focus the relationship between a liberal governing through society and the coexistence of practices that might be described as illiberal, despotic or, to use the term employed here, authoritarian.

One of the consequences of Michel Foucault's approach to government has been to undermine the opposition, found in much social and political science, between power and domination, on the one hand, and individual freedom and subjectivity on the other. The art of government can take all sorts of stances toward freedom. It can try to shape it or treat it as an artefact of certain governmental arrangements. It can seek to educe it among some and presuppose it among others. It can treat the governed as free persons or citizens, and rely on their capacities to govern themselves rather than try to govern them. It can use freedom as a technical means for achieving its ends.

Such a view of government is particularly apposite to the study of liberal rationalities of rule. Liberalism is usually presented as a principled political philosophy that distinguishes a domain of limited government from a sphere of individual liberty, found and exercised within civil society, which must be respected. However, once we recognize that liberal political rationality might seek to create, work through or utilize freedom, then a set of complementary analytical openings emerges. Alongside the long acknowledged measures that attempt to protect and guarantee individual

liberty such as constitutional rule, representative government, the separation of powers and the rule of law, the liberal arts of government specify
the content of individual freedom, give it a particular form and turn it to
various goals. They employ techniques ranging from the earlier disciplines
found in institutional settings to contemporary practices of individual
and mutual empowerment, participation, self-help, and community
development and care.

Concentrating on such rationalities and techniques does not mean that
we should neglect the more coercive, binding or obligatory dimensions of
liberal governmental programmes and practices, as several writers have
demonstrated.[1] Here, I want to explore whether and how this approach to
government can account for what I shall call authoritarian mentalities and
practices of rule within liberal-democratic states. I shall argue that governing liberally does not necessarily entail governing *through* freedom or
even governing in a manner that respects individual liberty. It might mean,
in ways quite compatible with a liberal rationality of government, over-
riding the exercise of specific freedoms in order to enforce obligations on
members of the population. To illustrate and outline the argument I shall
make in this chapter, consider the views of well-known American advocate
of 'welfare reform', Lawrence Mead (1986: 6):

> American political culture gives pride of place to the value of free-
> dom. But a 'free' society is possible only when the conditions for
> order have substantially been realised. People are not interested in
> 'freedom' from government if they are victimised by crime, cannot
> support themselves, or are in any fundamental way insecure. They
> will want more government rather than less. Nor are they likely to
> vote or otherwise participate politically unless they are employed or
> have their personal lives in order. A 'free' political culture is the
> characteristic, not of a society still close to the state of nature, as some
> American philosophers have imagined, but of one far removed from it
> by dense, reliable networks of mutual expectations.

At first glance, Mead might appear to be using a fairly classical, negative
conception of liberty – as Isaiah Berlin ([1958] 1997) would have it – far
removed from the writers on liberal government cited above, that is, a
sphere of private individual liberty not prescribed by the law and regulation
of government. However, by suggesting that a free political culture can
only exist where there are 'dense, reliable networks of mutual expectations'
about the values and conduct of other individuals, Mead invokes a conception of the relation of freedom and government not far from the one
inspired by Foucault. Mead calls this pattern of mutual expectations the
'common obligations of citizenship' (1986: 12). These obligations are not
derived from the properly limited political sphere but from society itself.
'These *social* obligations may not be governmental, but they are public in
that they fall within the collective expectation that structures an orderly
society' (Mead 1986: 12, original emphasis). Thus Mead, like Foucault,

recognizes forms of regulation that exist within society but which are central to the achievement of social and political order and security.

Foucault suggests that liberal thought starts not with the state 'but rather from society which is in a complex relation of exteriority and interiority with respect to the state' (1997a: 75). The liberal task of governing society is as much a governing *through* society as a governing *of* society. In this respect Mead's remains an instance of liberal thought. State programmes of welfare, he argues, should not simply supply benefits as a right to those who are in a condition of dependency upon the state. They must adopt an 'authoritative policy' to enforce the common obligations of citizenship, and thus to replicate the conditions of obligation that already exist in society. As twenty years of debates on 'welfare reform' and 'workfare' in the USA and elsewhere have illustrated, one example of this obligation is the enforcement of work, no matter how routine and mundane, and irrespective of one's other responsibilities, for example, caring for and rearing children (Peck 1998; Schram 1995, 2000; Cruikshank 1999).

I want to suggest that Mead's argument is an example of how liberal rationalities and authoritarian measures are far from incompatible. Governing liberally, or governing in a free 'political culture', is quite compatible with the demand for a form of government of the state that places the question of order – whether personal or social – as its primary objective, and the reiteration of authoritative direction as its primary means. It is absolutely clear that rule in liberal constitutional states has routinely entailed authoritarian measures. But it is much less clear what it is about liberal approaches to government that makes this possible.

Previous accounts have argued that what they call 'despotism' or the 'liberal government of unfreedom' are necessary features of either liberalism's forms of ethical governance (Valverde 1996) or of its understanding of its commitment to individual liberty (Hindess 2001). The liberal governmental use of authoritarian measures is a necessary component of the liberal attempt to govern free individuals. In a contrasting yet complementary way, I argue that authoritarian measures follow not simply from the liberal government of free persons, but also from the liberal understanding of the sphere of government itself, and the implications of that understanding. This is to say, that the liberal reliance on authoritarian techniques is a consequence of the understanding of government as a limited sphere that must operate through the forms of regulation that exist outside itself, i.e. through those forms of regulation that obtain within what has been conventionally called 'civil society'. The term 'civil society' can serve as a convenient shorthand for all that liberal government must take into account that is exterior to the formal governmental domain of the state. It might include spheres of society, national or international economy, population, community, culture, biological existence, personal and psychological existence, or any combination of these. It has recently been said to include the social interconnectedness, civic engagement and civic trust that comprise social capital (Putnam 1995). It is interesting that the term 'transnational civil society' now refers to the domain occupied by international non-government organizations and is regarded as a domain of political participation in 'global governance' (Habermas 2001; Held 2004a).

I immediately anticipate an objection to this view. Surely, liberal governing through civil society strengthens the liberal attempt to govern through freedom. After all, the paradigmatic processes of civil society, most notably those of the market, are conceived by liberalism, from Adam Smith to F.A. Hayek, as relying on the actions and choices of free individuals pursuing their own interests. Aren't we thus led to the conclusion that the liberal problematic requires (state) governmental action that either does not interfere with such freedoms or actively shapes, supports or reinforces them? The response I offer here is that this view captures only the facilitative aspect of the liberal conception of government, and does this in a partial way. As I show here, there is a counter-side of the liberal conception of government, which might be called its authoritarian dimension. To understand the entwined facilitative and authoritarian sides of liberal government, we need to examine more closely the claim that liberalism seeks to govern through, reform and utilize the existing agencies, mechanisms and regulations of civil society. In the next section, I shall propose and illustrate some operations of the state–civil society double within the liberal government of the state. By these operations, a liberal approach to government generates specific norms of individual and collective life and hence of forms of freedom that become the means and the objectives of liberal governmental programmes. In such fashion, liberal ways of governing civil society can specify the kinds of freedom and autonomy that are to become the objectives of governmental policies and practices and which, under certain circumstances, will require the use of instruments of coercive authority and legal sanction.

My general point is that the limited sphere of the political ('the state') and the different conceptions of what is exterior to it ('civil society') interlace to turn the injunction to govern through freedom into a set of binding obligations potentially or actually enforceable by coercive or sovereign instruments. One might say that my objects here are the 'authoritarian folds' within the liberal conception of a limited government respecting and operating where possible through individual liberty and seeking to govern a national or, now, transnational civil society. I argue that these authoritarian folds are enduring features of liberal approaches to government, readily illustrated by episodes from the genealogies of economy, police, poverty and welfare and subject to certain transformations today.

To grasp these state–civil society doubles found within liberal approaches to governing, I next revisit the 'primal scene' of the birth of liberalism in eighteenth-century Europe as a form of critique of then extant forms of government such as 'reason of state' and 'police'. This allows me then to reconsider the authoritarian dimensions of governing liberally. I argue that authoritarian aspects of liberalism can be approached from either a legal and political order that seeks to guarantee individual liberty or from a liberal 'police' through civil society. However, it is only by considering their interconnection that it is possible to understand the liberal government of the state and its authoritarian possibilities. The legal and political figure of the autonomous individual is intelligible only by reference to that aspect of liberal government that relies on knowledge of the processes, modes of regulation, values and expectations that are located outside the formal political domain. Today what I shall call 'liberal police' is exercised throughout much of the world in some relation to a pervasive governmental rationality and perception of economic necessity, that of globalization. The fact that government is to be limited by processes of globalization and to work through non-government organizations located in transnational civil society hardly makes a scrap of difference to the liberal paradigms of governing.

Genealogy of liberalism

As we have seen in the previous chapter, liberalism as a normative political philosophy entails a commitment to individual liberty and to limited and accountable government. On the basis of this commitment, it is possible to distinguish between liberal ways of governing and those that can be regarded as authoritarian.

The approach to liberalism found in the work of Foucault takes a somewhat different tack. Rather than viewing liberalism as an underlying normative philosophy, it examines liberalism as a kind of practice or a manner of doing things (Foucault 1997a: 74). Explicit normative philosophy is but one dimension of this, and not necessarily even the most important normative aspect of liberalism. For Foucault, liberalism as practice must be viewed above all as a form of critique that is concerned with the idea that 'one always governs too much'. The activity of the government of the state is not an end in itself, as it is in doctrines of 'reason of state', but something done on behalf of what lies outside the state. It is society, not the state, that helps determine 'why there has to be government, to what extent it can be done without, and in which cases it is needless or harmful for it to intervene' (Foucault 1997a: 75). It is in this respect that the market plays a privileged domain in testing the limits of government and the effects of its excesses. Different kinds of liberalism vary as much by what it is they criticize as by their different philosophical principles, economic theories or juridical systems. However, according to Foucauldian genealogy, this critique was first undertaken in relation to the doctrine of 'reason of state' and the associated theory and practice of police. This critique thus makes intelligible some core and continuing aspects of liberalism, including the way in which it distinguishes itself from non-liberal or authoritarian exercises of rule.

The relation of liberalism to 'reason of state' and German cameralist police science (*Polizeiwissenschaft*) is indeed complex. Gordon (1991) provides a subtle account of the continuities between liberalism and its critical adversaries, among which is the preoccupation with security. To simplify, we could say that liberalism emerges as a critique of a theory and practice of rule that regards 'good police, security and public order' as conditions to be achieved by a *comprehensive* set of regulations based on a *transparent* and *detailed* knowledge of the population to be governed and the activities in which that population is engaged.

On this view, liberal forms of rule provide a critique of the pretensions to omniscience and omnicompetence of the agencies of police in order to advance the idea of a limited government that operates through the theoretical and scientific knowledge of immanent social and other processes external to the institutions of formal political authority. By implication, authoritarian rule ignores such processes, and the freedoms on which their security depends, and thereby risks what, in another theoretical context, might be called the 'total administration of life'. The liberal attempt to govern through freedom and concern with over-government thus acts as a safeguard against such eventualities.

Even given the acknowledged continuities, this reading overplays the distinction between police and liberal rule. If we use the term police in its most general sense as a concern for the good order of a community (Knemeyer 1980), liberalism proposes what is, in effect, a new form of police. This new form is a no less comprehensive police than the old one. However, it employs techniques and agencies located within civil society rather than merely issuing regulations and thus must rely on knowledge of economic, social and other processes outside the formal sphere of the state rather than a transparent knowledge of the minutiae of activities, things, humans. The first implication of this is that the different spheres and agencies of civil society, and the knowledge of them, are as much a component of liberal government as parliaments, public bureaucracies, judiciaries and the like. Liberal approaches to government thus cannot be divorced from the various forms of knowledge of civil society, including economics, biomedicine and the sciences of life, the 'psy' disciplines and the social sciences, and the practices and forms of intervention they codify and invest with specific goals. The second, perhaps more important implication is that the liberal fear of governing too much is not so much a fear that the population is being governed too much but that the state is doing too much of the governing (Dean and Hindess 1998b: 3–7).[2] Just as late medieval police relied on a variety of governing agencies other than the territorial state, so liberal police will seek to cooperate with, contract out, or enter into partnership with the agencies, groups and bodies of civil society.

Liberal police is thus anchored in civil society and attempts to guarantee the security of its processes. But how is this to be achieved? One way is for government to adopt what might be called a facilitating role. This means 'not to impede the course of things, but to ensure the play of natural and necessary modes of regulation, to make regulations which permit natural regulation to operate: *manipuler, susiter, faciliter, laissez-faire*' (Foucault, quoted in Gordon 1991: 17). Liberal government thus tends to present itself as enabling rather than prescriptive, guiding rather than directive. It 'steers' rather than 'rows' (Osborne and Gaebler 1993).

Liberalism thus works through the processes of civil society, paradigmatically through the quasi-natural and necessary processes of the economy. Yet there is another way liberalism connects formal state agencies and programmes to civil society and which emerged in early liberal states in Europe over the course of the nineteenth century. Jacques Donzelot (1979a: 53–8; Minson 1985: 180–218) long ago drew attention to the consequences of what he called 'the liberal definition of the state' in nineteenth-century France. On the one hand, the family would no longer be given a directly political role as it was in *L'Ancien Régime* with its infamous *lettres de cachet des familles* by which heads of households were direct agents of police and could enforce non-juridical confinement of their members. On the other, interventions into the family would now occur through philanthropic and other non-state bodies. The problem of 'too much governing' was thus not so much that the population were governed too much but that the state was liable to do too much of the governing. Indeed, the proliferation of non-state philanthropic, health and educational interventions into the liberal family in the nineteenth century suggests that the liberal problem of the state encompasses a sense in which there is *not enough* governing. A liberal police of families, according to Donzelot, will need to act not directly through the operations of the agencies of the administrative territorial state, such as before the Revolution, but through and in conjunction with a plurality of professionals, agencies and sites found within civil society. This is the lineage for contemporary theories of governance and slogans such as 'more governance, less government' and 'steering, not rowing'.

This steering function of government tells us about the broad rationality of liberalism but it does not tell us very much about the 'search for a liberal technology of government' itself (Foucault 1997a: 76). To put this in prosaic terms, we must find out what happens, and with what means, when one tries to govern liberally. Here, Mead's statements again prove perspicacious. He argues that government can only secure democracy by reproducing the values and expectations found in civil society within its own programmes and interventions. It is only by doing this that what Mead calls 'social policy' – which might be read here as a synonym for liberal police – will contribute to social order as it should. If it acts in a manner contrary to them, as the 'anti-authoritarian, benefit-oriented habits of federal politics' in the USA tend to, he argues, it will contribute decisively to a situation in which many citizens 'evidently are less able to take care of themselves and respect the rights of others than in earlier decades' (Mead 1986: 16, 8). Liberal government then must model its own interventions on the forms of regulation, expectations and values that are already in operation in civil society. While Mead himself argues for a statist form of delivery with regular homilies to the necessity of governmental control of workfare programmes (1997: 8), other versions of liberal government would suggest that the state must enter into alliance with the network of agencies of civil society (Putnam 1995; Giddens 1998).

This replicating or modelling of governmental regulation on the regulations that already obtain in civil society takes two forms. The first form is the modelling of state administration on the *processes* of civil society, including and perhaps especially that of the market. Here government is modelled on what is conceived to be the regulations of the market, best illustrated in the widespread 'neoliberal' adoption of models of public sector organization held to be derived from the market, or an image of an ideally functioning market, for example the construction of quasi-markets; the introduction of price-competitive tendering, devolved budgeting and funding per unit of throughput; the contracting-out to private companies or community bodies of what were formerly public services; the placing of senior public servants on performance-based contracts; the introduction of performance management systems into universities and health systems; the corporatization and privatization of public authorities and utilities, and so on. Such techniques may be regarded as fundamental features of the governmental constructivism of various forms of neoliberalism which differ from earlier liberalism in that they deliberately attempt to construct what are thought to be features of markets where such markets had not previously been in operation (Dean 1999: 153–65).

The second form of this replication is closer to what Mead has in mind. Here it is not the market-like forms of organization that are to be replicated but the patterns of values and expectations and hence the forms of conduct that are held to obtain in civil society, if civil society were to operate in its natural or ideal state not subject to the arbitrary imprecations of legislation and intervention. While many of these cultural values and forms of conduct can be viewed as being derived from the market, as Hayek argued (1979), there are many others that are derived from other aspects of civil society. Hayek himself suggested (1979: 162–3) that civil society was comprised of the different spontaneous social orders of the market, morals, law and language, each of which teaches us rules of conduct. Mead's notion of the 'common obligations of citizenship' can thus be read as an attempt to loosely codify such rules of conduct (respect for the law and for one another's personal rights, responsibility towards one's children) and to make them the basis for governmental interventions. While market constructivism is usually, and perhaps problematically (Polanyi 1957), thought to be restricted to neoliberal forms of rule, this attempt to model governmental intervention on values or principles that are held to be derived from civil society and its spheres is nothing new. The principal aim of the formation of a centralized system of state administration of poor relief in England was to make sure that the design of relief upheld and enforced the value that able-bodied men and their dependants (children, wives, mothers of their children) should survive through their wage-labour (Dean 1991). In this regard, contemporary 'welfare reform' (Peck 1998; Schram 2000), with its workfare practices for single mothers and the unemployed, and classical poor relief, with its deterrent workhouses for able-bodied men and those construed as their dependants, are different instances of this modelling of liberal government on the values and expectations held to exist, at least ideally, within civil society.

This view of liberal police has direct implications for our problem of the authoritarian dimension of liberal governing. If we focus on the legal and political discourse that accompanies liberal constitutional states, we are in danger of getting only one side of the story, and missing the sense in which liberalism connects governmental interventions of the state with the agencies, regulations, expectations, values and obligations embedded in the processes of society. Given that liberal government derives a particular and no less comprehensive form of regulation from the knowledge of civil society and the operation of its agencies, the distinction between liberalism and authoritarian police begins to look less clear-cut. Liberalism differs from earlier systems of police in it that it models its own interventions on the regulations and values it uncovers through a knowledge of civil society and consciously attempts to mobilize the processes and agencies of civil society.

Now I would like to suggest a clearer way of thinking about this liberal police (see Table 5.1). This liberal police works by two distinct but related operations: an 'unfolding' of the (formally) political sphere into civil society and an 'enfolding' of the regulations of civil society into the political.[3] The first marks the path of connection to what lies outside the state. This is illustrated today by the linkages, networks, partnerships and 'joining-up' of state organizations with the commercial, local and voluntary bodies found in civil society. It is found in the analysis of public administration and governance theorists (Kooiman 1993; Minogue *et al.* 1998), the prescriptions of advocates of Third Way politics (Giddens 1998) and the augmentation of social capital (Putnam 1995). It is also found in the role of faith-based organizations in the compassionate conservatism of President G.W. Bush. This is the *unfolding of the formally political sphere upon non-political agencies*. Its motto is 'more governance, less government'.

The second operation follows a line of 'implication' by which the features of civil society are folded back into the operations of the state – the *enfolding of civil society into the political sphere*. This is readily illustrated by the market constructivism of neoliberalism, which we have already addressed. It is also illustrated by the way in which values, expectations and conducts of civil society, real or ideal, form the means and objectives of governmental programmes. This is illustrated by Mead's 'authoritative policy', which overrides the inclinations of its subjects, to reinforce and revive the 'dense, reliable networks of mutual expectations' already found within civil society. Here, it may be necessary to enforce what the Australian

Table 5.1 Liberal government of society

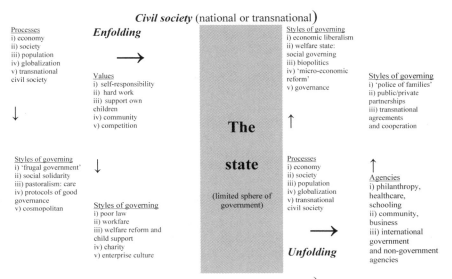

Civil society (national or transnational)

Enfolding

Processes
i) economy
ii) society
iii) population
iv) globalization
v) transnational
civil society

Styles of governing
i) economic liberalism
ii) welfare state:
social governing
iii) biopolitics
iv) 'micro-economic
reform'
v) governance

Values
i) self-responsibility
ii) hard work
iii) support own
children
iv) community
v) competition

Styles of governing
i) 'police of families'
ii) public/private
partnerships
iii) transnational
agreements
and cooperation

The

state

(limited sphere of
government)

Styles of governing
i) 'frugal government'
ii) social solidarity
iii) pastoralism: care
iv) protocols of good
governance
v) cosmopolitan

Processes
i) economy
ii) society
iii) population
iv) globalization
v) transnational
civil society

Agencies
i) philanthropy,
healthcare,
schooling
ii) community,
business
iii) international
government
and non-government
agencies

Styles of governing
i) poor law
ii) workfare
iii) welfare reform and
child support
iv) charity
v) enterprise culture

Unfolding

Civil society (national or transnational)

government has called the 'mutual obligations' of certain classes of citizens (principally welfare beneficiaries) by increased surveillance, compulsory workfare schemes (in Australia, 'work-for-the-dole') and sanctions for non-compliance (Australian Department of Family and Community Services 2000). The appeal to the values of civil society can give rise to arguments for approaches to the reform of public services and public provision that breach earlier modes of separation of Church and State, such as George W. Bush's advocacy of 'compassionate conservatism' (Olasky 2000; Kettle 2001). It can also lead to conflict between the values of the agencies of civil society and norms of public accountability, such as in the hiring practices of publicly funded religious voluntary agencies (Tingle and Gotting 1999).

My argument, then, is that to fully comprehend liberalism and its authoritarian dimension we need to attend not only to the effects of a political and legal order that tries to govern, wherever possible, through freedom, but to the liberal understanding of government itself. In regarding the state as secondary and as derivative of a 'civil society' outside its legitimate scope, liberal government is able to derive the substantive content of freedom and a society based on it, and transform that content into a set of norms enforceable, if necessary, by sovereign means. I want thus briefly to review liberalism as a specific political and legal order that seeks to respect and work through the liberty of the governed before moving on to the civil society side of the liberal police.

Liberalism as a legal and political order

Previous expositions of the authoritarian dimension of liberalism (Valverde 1996; Hindess 2001) have examined the way in which liberal forms of governing necessarily entail forms of categorization of subjects that provide it with subject or dependent populations who simply cannot, or cannot yet, be governed through freedom. They have also shown how at the heart of the juridical and political notions of autonomy lies an ethical despotism prior to any division between those capable of bearing the freedoms and responsibilities of mature subjectivity and those who are not. In so far as they focus on the problem of liberal conceptions of individuality, such approaches largely explain the authoritarian dimension of liberalism in terms of a legal and political order that claims to govern through and protect individual liberty. However, they also invoke concerns arising from the knowledge of civil society. Thus Barry Hindess (2001: 104–6) argues that the classical specification of which subjects may or may not attain liberal norms of autonomy relies on the notion of 'improvement' drawn from an evolutionist understanding of human populations. Mariana Valverde (1996: 362) identifies the notion of 'habit' as resting on a psychological conception of the human subject, and the overcoming of its addictions, inclinations and passions, as forming a key technique of this improvement.

A contemporary illustration of the use of therapeutic discourses and conceptions of improvement concerns those who are viewed as welfare dependent or, at any rate, at high risk of what is referred to as 'welfare dependency'. This term condenses and in a sense confuses moral and psychological characteristics with the simple administrative condition of requiring poor relief (Fraser and Gordon 1994; Schram 1995, 2000; Peck 1998). This risk does not apply to all those who require social welfare benefits. Certain applicants for social welfare, such as the temporarily unemployed who are regarded as 'job ready', require at most some assistance with placing them in a job and providing benefits whilst they find a job (Dean 1998a). For these people, who are regarded as members of the improved population temporarily inconvenienced by the lack of a job, assistance can be provided by relying on their liberty and by only limited resort to authoritarian means. For example, this population might be viewed as already having the capacity to exercise responsible market choices. This is so much the case in contemporary Australian social welfare that the 'jobseeker' can be treated as a customer making choices in a market of employment assistance services. The attitude towards such populations is similar to the approach to social citizenship found in T.H. Marshall's celebrated paper ([1949] 1963) in that these individuals are regarded as ones who can exercise citizenship given access to the appropriate assistance, whether of benefits or services of one kind or the other. There are clear differences, too, between Marshall's social citizenship and the 'neoliberal' economic citizen as customer, the most significant being the shift from provision through public services to provision through governmentally contrived markets in such services.

On the other hand, however, there are certain classes of individuals seeking social welfare assistance who are deemed at high risk of welfare dependency because they have not formed the requisite habits of punctuality, motivation and industry, and the techniques of self-presentation that would enable them to readily rejoin the labour market (Dean 1995, 1998a; Theodore and Peck 1999). For these populations, an altogether different regime might be indicated. Increased surveillance through the use of mentoring ('case-managers', 'advisers'), increased publicity about their obligations in respect of finding a job and the sanctions available to welfare agencies should they fail to meet these obligations, and none too subtle coercive measures such as workfare ('welfare-to-work' or 'work-for-the-dole') programmes are deemed necessary to render the individual autonomous, that is, as manifesting the sturdy independence and good character of those who prefer paid employment to welfare benefits as a source of their livelihood. A recent expression of such a view is found in the advocates of the 'new paternalism' (Mead 1997). The key to the new paternalist approach is the recognition, then, that coercion might be a condition of acting in the best interests of a certain, minority, class of individuals. In Mead's (1997: 23) succinct expression of this principle, 'those who would be free must first be bound'. As the example of those individuals at risk of welfare dependency demonstrates, the liberal governing through freedom, or in a manner consistent with individual liberty, does not necessarily mean that individuals should be governed as if they were already capable of such autonomy.

The case of those regarded as welfare dependent in contemporary liberal democracies demonstrates how liberal governing through freedom can be effected by using authoritarian methods. The division between those who can be profitably assisted in the exercise of their own freedom and those who must be coerced to fulfil certain obligations in order to accede to a condition generally agreed to be freedom may be a necessary feature of all liberalisms. The use of authoritarian liberal rationalities and techniques of government has also had a long history in colonial governmentality. A key illustration is afforded by the arguments presented by John Stuart Mill, drawn upon by both Valverde and Hindess. In 'Considerations on representative government', Mill ([1861] 1974: 409) argues for the necessity of a 'good despot', provided under the benign dominion of a 'more civilised people', for those nations incapable of 'spontaneous improvement' themselves. His comments on the necessity of routine and repetitive labour, including 'personal slavery', as hastening the transition to freedom (Mill [1861] 1974: 174–5), offer a clear analogy with the recent advocacy of workfare for the welfare dependant.

To summarize, one might wish to distinguish between the following (fluid) categories of liberal subjects of government grouped according to their capacities for autonomy:

- those who have attained capacities for autonomy, including the practice of exercising 'ethical despotism' upon themselves where necessary – Group A;
- those who need assistance to maintain capacities for autonomy as in the case of the social citizen under T.H. Marshall's welfare state and the 'job-ready' of contemporary workfare – Group B;
- those who are potentially capable of exercising liberal autonomy but who are yet to be trained in the habits and capacities to do so – Group C;
- those who, having reached maturity of age, are for one reason or another not yet or no longer able to exercise their own autonomy or act in their own best interests – Group D.

The latter group includes the chronically welfare dependent, those with certain mental and physical illnesses, significant sections of the elderly in liberal democracies, the vast majority of those who are living in the developing countries, as well as those whose capacities for self-government have been undermined by drugs, alcohol, tobacco and other addictive substances. What is indicated for them is a mode of government that acts in the best interests of those who cannot act in their own best interests, even were they to know them. This is the essential content of Mill's 'good despot' and today's 'new paternalist'.

There is of course a liberal government of those who disrupt or simply get in the way of the establishment and maintenance of a liberal legal and political order inside the state or in the international domain – Group E. I provide two extended examples. The first are those individuals and populations who stood in the way of the appropriation of land by Europeans and the establishment of a constitutional order in the Americas and Australasia. James Tully's (1995: 70–9) discussion of John Locke's constitutional arguments for the land appropriation of the indigenous populations of North America represents a case in point. For Locke, Europeans can wage war on these populations as reparation for any injury received from them during European settlement without recourse to constituted political authority because they remained in a state of nature. Further, land can be considered vacant and hence available for appropriation where use of the land does not conform to European norms of settled agricultural cultivation and improvement of the soil. This notion of an uncultivated state of nature advanced by Locke can be viewed as a component of European international law or the *jus publicum Europaeum* which Schmitt observes in action between the sixteenth and nineteenth centuries. Here the Earth is divided into civilized European soil which is divided into 'state territories with firm borders' and 'the "free" soil' of non-European princes and peoples open for European land appropriations' (Schmitt [1950] 2003: 148).

The second example are the agents of 'rogue' or 'criminal' states or of 'international terrorist networks' who commit such atrocities either on their own or on other countries' populations that constitute 'crimes against humanity'. Here liberal-democratic states engage in a version of the 'just war' against the agents, regimes and personnel that are held to be responsible for attempted genocide, violent suppression of ethnic minorities, suicide bombings causing mass death, and so on. In certain versions of this just war military intervention is justified by gross international human rights violations including genocide (for example, the NATO action in Kosovo in 1999). In others, doctrines of pre-emptive strike against states with 'weapons of mass destruction' are invoked (the US-led coalition against Iraq in 2003). In still others, it is to dismantle terrorist networks in the War on Terror, such as al-Qaeda, responsible for attacks such as those of 9/11. While these virtuous states, acting alone or in concert, might seek to limit the 'collateral' effects of such operations upon non-combatant populations, injury and death of civilians cannot be entirely eliminated either as a result of direct military intervention, economic sanctions or the fostering of civil war. In this regard, such populations simply unfortunately get in the way of the establishment of an international legal and political order. The conduct of such wars also manages to produce new forms of public enemy such as the 'enemy combatants' apparently denied the rights of prisoners under the Geneva Conventions in US detention camps such as Guantánamo Bay and subject to such measures as 'extraordinary rendition' by which they can be captured and flown to camps in third party states with greater acceptability of torture (see Chapters 7 and 8). Such military interventions represent a reversal of the principles of the *jus publicum Europaeum* which detheologized war and provided rules of engagement between sovereign states considered as equals and as 'just enemies' (*justus hostis*) and which held until early in the twentieth century (Ulmen 1996). Today, the ideas of criminal states and regimes and international terrorist networks provide a new moral and often quasi-theological basis for remedial military action by liberal-democratic states and the concomitant limitation of the juridical and civil rights of prisoners of war.

Presented as a list of different types of subject, organized according to their potential or actual capacities for liberal autonomy, the analysis of liberalism nevertheless remains at a purely formal and descriptive level. It reproduces the view that the autonomous individual is the rule to which the exclusions form practical exceptions. I now want to suggest that the reverse is in fact the case: that the liberal norm of the autonomous individual is a figure carved out of the substantive forms of life that are only known through these exceptions, for example insufficient education, poor character, welfare dependency, statelessness, underdeveloped human capital, absence of spirit of improvement, lack of social capital, absence of citizenship of civilized state, inadequate methods of labour and cultivation, and so on.[4]

Indeed, the partisans of Iraq, al-Qaeda terrorists and the members of Taliban militia in Afghanistan are arguably extremely autonomous people.

However, their autonomy is not of a kind consistent with the establishment of a liberal legal and political order in Afghanistan, Iraq and further throughout the Middle East. They are, to use Secretary of State Condoleezza Rice's delicious phrase, not on the right side of 'freedom's divide'.[5] Moreover, this construction of the norm of freedom through the diagnosis and treatment of its exceptions is only possible on the basis of rationalities of government drawing upon the human sciences and associated practices of normalization (cf. Foucault 1977: 193). To understand how these mass of exceptions are known and governed, and therefore how what the liberal political and legal order takes as its most universal norms are generated, we need now to bracket off the thesis of limited government. This entails moving from the juridical and political order of liberalism to the 'civil society' side of what we earlier characterized as liberal police and to the human sciences that claim true knowledge of it.

Liberal police

It would be possible to cite examples such as China's one child policy and Nazi Germany's notion of racial hygiene to illustrate how the human sciences can be implicated in the operation of forms of authoritarian governmentality (Dean 1999: 141–8). However, it is not necessary to focus on the catastrophic uses of biology, genetics and population control in non-liberal states to discover the generation of norms by human scientific knowledge strong enough to be enforced by sovereign powers. We need instead, perhaps, look no further than that region of knowledge that is paradigmatic of the processes of civil society, that concerning the market, and the disciplines of political economy and economics.

The unobstructed capacity of the majority of national populations to participate within the labour market is a key instrument of liberal police. Obstruction to that participation, conversely, is a disruption of that police and of social order. A paradigmatic example is provided by Adam Smith's detailed discussion in *The Wealth of Nations* ([1776] 1976: 152–7) of the law of settlements, by which parishes were responsible only for the relief of labourers who had been born or granted a certificate of settlement in their parish and entitled to remove labourers and their families without such settlement. Surveying their development over two centuries, Smith argues that such a law occasions the greatest disorder of 'any in the police of England' since it obstructs the 'free circulation of labour' and leads to grossly unequal wages in adjacent areas ([1776] 1976: 152, 156–7). Smith's account presents the attempts to enforce this law as 'an evident violation of natural liberty and justice' which has the effect of distorting the market in labour. In this extended analysis, Smith thus treats the 'system of natural liberty' of the market as an instrument of police.

For liberals like Smith or Hayek (1979), the effect of ill-conceived laws is not simply the distortion of the market but the distortion of the kinds of conduct associated with the market. In other words, the market is interesting not as a kind of natural entity but as a technique within civil society for the government of the conduct of individuals, institutions, and so on. According to this view, in the market we are subject to a system of signals about the prices of goods and labour that result from the decisions of other actors. The market thus regulates the conduct of individuals by making them calculate the costs and benefits of their actions. The market – together with morals, language and law – is among the most developed of what Hayek (1979: 163) called 'spontaneous social orders' by which the evolution of civilization teaches us 'the discipline of freedom' (Dean 1999: 155–9). Governmental or legal obstruction to the operation of the market distorts the way in which individuals learn to conduct themselves. In the market, we are no longer 'self-referential', as Mead would say, i.e. our actions are no longer simply tied to our own values, habits, and beliefs.[6] They are bound by the prices of goods and of labour. Rather than view the market as a naturally existing social order, as Hayek does, it can be understood as a way of naming a set of discursive–technical means for the regulation of conduct located within the domain of civil society.

Entering the market makes individuals no longer self-referential in a second and, in some respects, much more basic sense. It places them in authority relations within the workplace. If these relations are entered into, they establish virtues of punctuality, sobriety, regularity, industry, discretion and independence. In some versions, the kind of labour entered into is emphasized. In his earlier *Lectures on Jurisprudence* ([1752–4] 1978: 332–3), Smith suggested that those places that have the most security are not necessarily those where the greatest number of police regulations exist.[7] Rather, they are ones in which the 'common people' are independent and employed in manufactures rather than as servants and retainers as they are in feudal government or in France. Far from fostering the 'probity, liberality and amiable qualities' among the lower classes, such arrangements foster dependency and subservience. Manufacturing labour can be thus recommended to foster good police. By contrast, Mead's view is closer to Mill's that any kind of work is better than none at all. For him, the enforcement of work in social policy is necessary in the 'long struggle to restore the self-reliance assumed in Western politics' and in 'restoring some coherence in the lives of the poor' (quoted in Schram 2000: 36). Work needs to be enforced as the foundation of having one's personal life in order which, in turn, is a condition of social and political order.

With Smith, we see an early example of how a knowledge of processes in civil society helps begin to specify a set of norms and language to designate the forms of life and virtues that are desirable among the citizenry. But this knowledge of economic processes does not merely allow a specification of these norms. It is a condition of the emergence of an entire instrumentation and phantasmagoria of power, and it is perhaps here that contemporary advocates of workfare and 'mutual obligation' find their predecessors. Alongside and in the interstices of Smith's felicitous liberal economy, we find Jeremy Bentham's pauper management scheme, the centralized national administration of poor relief in England and Wales after 1834, and the nineteenth-century workhouse (Dean 1991: 173–92). The principle of 'less eligibility', formulated by Bentham, was – in the words of the *1834 Poor Law Report* – to ensure that the situation of the pauper 'on the whole shall not be made really or apparently so eligible as the situation of the independent labourer of the lowest class' (Checkland and Checkland 1974: 335). The administrative principle thus draws the line between the sturdy independence and prudential existence of those who subsist through the exchange of their labour and those who enter into a state of dependency upon relief, social assistance or charity for that subsistence. In Bentham's dream of a centralized administration of pauperism, the fact of falling into the latter category alone makes it possible for paupers to be subject to a regime of confinement, forced labour including child labour, strict disciplinary routines and comprehensive inspection, therapeutic and reproductive experimentation, systems of punishment based on petty infractions, and so forth. The obverse of the generation of new norms of what we might call economic citizenship, which are central to the installation of a market regime, is a liberal technology of government that seeks to form and transform the population by routine labour, supervision, sanction, punishment and deterrence. Both the Poor Law and workfare are instruments of liberal police, Bentham and Mead versions of its governmental imagination.

We can thus describe the configuration of what might be loosely described as classical liberal rule, instanced in this case by early nineteenth-century Britain, in the terms broached earlier. This instance of liberal government demonstrates an unfolding of the political upon civil society in Smith's market economy and the enfolding of the knowledge, values and norms imagined to exist within an unfettered operation of civil society onto the instruments of government themselves. Thus poor relief is to be organized to reinforce the natural–social state of depending on labour rather than relief for subsistence. Liberal modalities of government work as a double: the government *and* its other(s), which is not to say the forms of their folding cannot become extremely complicated. Broadly, we might say that this 'classical' economic liberalism was transformed along these two folds. First, the initial fold of government upon the market and market actors is complicated by the use of other organizations and agents within civil society, such as philanthropic bodies, doctors and educators, and police and public health reformers, as instruments for the achievement of the various kinds of ends, for example the protection of children or the prevention of crime. Second, the enfolding of the values and norms of civil society and the knowledge of civil society often produced within it (for instance by statistical societies) came to set limits to and act as a condition of the operation of the market economy. Along both folds, liberal rule thus acted as a condition of the emergence and expansion of the field of social government that, in conjunction with the emergence of mass representative institutions, gave rise from the beginning of the twentieth century to a social politics and to programmes of the welfare state (Dean 1999: 129–30). In this social kind of liberal governing, as in the early liberalism it at least partially displaces, there remains the fundamental division of the government and its other, state and society. In fact, this social liberalism establishes a further condition of acceptability of the role of government itself. The knowledge of civil society, during this entire process, provides a key mechanism for the specification of the social, as well as political and legal, rights of the governed as citizens. It also divides populations in such as way as to allow the flourishing of a range of disciplinary, paternalist, tutelary, sovereign and punitive measures for the potentially improvable (Group C), the chronically unimprovable (Group D), the iniquitous, the criminal, their accomplices and their unfortunate neighbours (Group E). The specification of the autonomous subject of liberalism is only possible given knowledge of populations, personalities and forms of life, within and outside families, normal and pathological, found within civil society.

Rule in contemporary liberal democracies can also, very broadly, be approached through these operations. First, it continues the enfolding of the norms and values of civil society onto the political, as we see with the new paternalist and workfare measures we have dealt with throughout this chapter. It also continues the enfolding of the processes and modes of regulation of civil society into the limited sphere of government itself. This can be illustrated by contemporary notions of the global economy.

Secondly, it continues the folding of the political onto civil society. This can be illustrated in the notions of 'joined up' and public–private partnership approaches to government and the effects this has in particular areas, such as community policing and crime control. It can also operate through new civil society agencies such as transnational or international non-government agencies (INGOs) and intergovernmental bodies (IGOs). I shall illustrate these two operations in the rest of the chapter.

Concomitant with the retraction of the redistributive and social justice objectives, issues of crime control, policing and punishment regimes occupy increasing importance within liberal government (O'Malley 1999; Stenson 2000; Stenson and Edwards 2001). In these areas, like so many others, the solution to problems of maintenance or even establishment of order at a local level takes the form of advocacy of partnership approaches to government in which established police forces work with local communities, businesses, citizens' groups, other statutory authorities and even private security firms. In Britain, for example, local partnerships compete with one another for grant aid from a central government concerned with targeting those communities most in need of regeneration. Among the effects of such partnerships and funding arrangements are the displacement of crime to other areas, erosion of trust between different groups, and so on, as Stenson and Edwards have shown (2001). However, the major concern here is that the advocacy of such partnership as a part of progressive politics does not necessarily lead to the implementation of gentler approaches to youth crime on housing estates and street prostitution, such as community outreach and educative and therapeutic interventions. Instead, these coalitions often favour 'punitive sovereignty' approaches that seek to cleanse neighbourhoods of criminalized street gangs, pimps and prostitutes, or which use 'target hardening' approaches that increase security against things like burglary. It is within such contexts that zero-tolerance policing techniques, promoted through media-driven political communities, can appear as a solution to local community problems. A second effect of these approaches, also germane to our concerns here, is that while police forces themselves are subject to mechanisms of review and accountability and subject to legislative regulation, many of these other partners (for example, private security firms) are not.

Another example of the dual character of governing through a knowledge of economy and civil society is the contemporary understanding of globalization and the global economy and its impacts. I cite this as a key illustration of the enfolding of the processes of civil society, now projected onto a global scale, into the mechanisms of government themselves. In the contemporary social sciences we find a massive literature on this topic (for example, Held and McGrew 2000). Yet, comparatively little work has sought to understand globalization as a framework of national governmental policy rather than a determinate social structural process involving the greater interconnection of parts of a global capitalist economy (Larner and Walters 2004). If, however, we bracket off the truth claim entailed in the later conception, it is possible to view globalization as an 'interpretive grid' or 'conceptual apparatus' (Larner 1998: 601) that shapes ways of thinking about, problematizing and reforming the institutions and populations of nation-states.

Viewed from this perspective, the notion of 'the economy' as a self-regulating system and part of a system of national economies engaging in mutually advantageous international trade has been largely displaced in recent years by the less benign governmental imaginary of a global economic system that distributes countries and regions into winners and losers in a new 'zero-sum' competitive game (Hirst and Thompson 1999: 6). The task of national government, according to this view, is no longer to engage in the prudential management of a self-regulating national economy so as to fund benefits to the national population out of the increment of economic growth – benefits such as social welfare, education and national defence. Rather, given the zero-sum game between parts of the global economy, the promotion of economic efficiency and competitiveness becomes the paramount goal in what amounts to a new liberal problematic of security (Hindess 1998). All other activities of government, such as those of the welfare state, higher education or migration, must first be assessed in terms of the availability of resources, and secondly as to whether they contribute to or inhibit economic efficiency (Hindess 1998: 223). Thus the main objective of domestic policies is to reform those kinds of individual and institutional conduct that are considered likely to affect economic performance compared to that of the members of other national and even regional populations. A corollary of this view is that this is often best achieved by contriving and constructing market systems of allocation in domains where they had not previously been in operation.

This governmental perception of economic globalization provides the rationale for a range of remarkably similar remedies to be prescribed for the ills of the institutions and the populations in established liberal democracies and for those outside them in 'developing' countries. While these policies are commonly embraced by the national governments of liberal democracies and their international associations, they are also promoted among countries in Asia, Latin America and the former Soviet bloc by the World Bank, the IMF and other agencies.

Just as classical economic liberalism gave rise to both Smith's benign vision of the 'free circulation of labour' and Bentham's less than benign 'pauper panopticons', so contemporary discussion of global economic transformation represents something of a paradox. Considered as a rationality of the government of the (national) state, the discourse of economic globalization can simultaneously hold 'there is little (or, at least, less) we can do to exercise national sovereignty' *and* 'it is imperative to engage in comprehensive reforms of the public sector, welfare, higher education, finance and the labour market'. Under explicit authorization of a discourse that claims a significant diminution of sovereign powers of states, we have a view that national governments must do or become all sorts of things and that it is necessary to resort to more direct and even coercive measures upon certain sectors of their own and other populations. Viewed as rationality of the government of the state, there is no contradiction between a contemporary conception of borderless economic liberalization and the emergence of a kind of authoritarian liberalism that invokes Schmitt's ([1932] 1998) authoritarian liberal formula of 'strong state and sound economy'. This formula can be linked to political programmes that render the return to juridical and administrative compulsion in various languages: the moral claims of community, the obligation of individual citizens, social inclusion and social order, and so on. 'New paternalist' conservatives (Mead 1997), Third Way social democrats (Giddens 1998; Latham 1998; on whom, Lund 1999), and communitarians (Etzioni 1995, 1996), all concur on the need for governmental mechanisms to enforce obligation on the part of the poor, welfare recipients, single parents, non-custodial parents, homeless youth, recovering addicts, and so forth. In practice, this means governing substantial minorities (social welfare recipients, illegal immigrants, delinquent parents) in a way that emphasizes increased surveillance, detailed administration and sanction. In certain South-East Asian countries, such as Malaysia under Dr Mahatir, this formula has been allied to the positive commitment to traditional social values that regard the majority of the population as culturally unprepared to govern themselves in a liberal-democratic fashion. There is thus at a minimum some kind of convergence in the processes of economic and political reform undertaken by certain liberal democracies and at least some postcolonial states.

The rationality of globalization clearly indicates the way in which a knowledge of the economic sphere considered to be at least formally outside the institutions of political authority can authorize a comprehensive government and reform of personal and social life and institutional patterns of organization. Liberal government of the global economy can act to install as comprehensive a police as anything imagined by the German police scientists in the eighteenth century and to advance as 'total' a specification of appropriate kinds of life as that of state socialism and fascism in the twentieth. The liberal distinction between a police state prone to an authoritarian encroachment of civil society and limited liberal government governing through free individuals thus once again proves unstable. In earlier police, a comprehensive government of life was based on a thorough knowledge of individuals and populations and manifested as the attempted complete regulation of those behaviours that promoted or impeded human happiness and the strength of the state. In contemporary liberal government, the comprehensive government of life is based on the knowledge of the processes of a global economy, and additionally the processes discovered by other human sciences such as psychology, demography and biology which we have not touched upon here. In place of a detailed specification of behaviours, we find the claim to be governing though the freedom of individuals and groups. But this freedom is based on the norm of an autonomous subject that is specified in a detailed fashion, not through the contents of specific police regulations but through the exceptions, pathologies and dependencies that are discovered, diagnosed and remedied by the human sciences in conjunction with governmental practices and the sovereign powers of states. Where both eighteenth-century police states and twentieth-century totalitarian regimes undertake a comprehensive reformation of social life by asserting versions of the autonomy of reasons of state, contemporary liberal government seeks to accomplish a similar task by asserting the diminution of state sovereignty in the face of forces within a global civil society beyond its control. The paradox is that the discourse on the diminution of sovereignty calls forth the use of often directly coercive measures enforced by the very same sovereign powers in the treatment of certain populations.

Conclusion

In this chapter, I have sought to show how the opposition between liberal and authoritarian governmentality is highly unstable. It is unstable because the liberal project of governing through freedom entails divisions between and within both populations and individual subjects, in such a way as to require authoritarian or despotic government in a wide variety of instances.

This is a feature of liberal government that has long been noted from a variety of intellectual stances, including postcolonial and feminist, as well as governmentality, literatures. What has remained less obvious is how the liberal conception of government as arising from knowledges of civil society feeds the authoritarian dimension of liberal government. The substantive content of the self-governing individual and its others that are at the heart of liberal divisions of populations can only be understood by examining this, second, dimension of a comprehensive liberal police. This can been exemplified in relation to classical economic liberalism, the long recent history of 'welfare reform' or colonial government, or contemporary discussions of global economic and political transformations.

My argument, then, can be restated in this way: the liberal government of the state encompasses both the constitutionally defined legal–political order of limited government and a liberal police established by a knowledge of spheres, processes and agencies outside this domain, for example, civil society, economy, population, and so on. In order to understand the authoritarian potential of liberal government we need to comprehend both aspects of the liberal order. For the abstract and universal freedoms protected by legal powers are given normative content by the specialist knowledges that frame the forms of life found within formally non-political domains of civil society, as well as the pathologies, dependencies, and exceptions to these forms of life.

I want to suggest further that as well as the ordinary despotism and authoritarianism we find in liberalism, for example that which is applied to those who have not, or perhaps cannot, achieve extant versions of liberal notions of self-government, there are certain contemporary formulae of the liberal government of the state that might be best described as 'authoritarian liberalism' with its dual principles of strong state and free or sound economy. Today, such formulae are not merely hybrid assemblages of liberalism and conservatism but necessary effects of contemporary liberal understandings of global economic changes. The 'dirty secret' of many contemporary liberal governmental discourses of globalization, moral obligation, the new paternalism, social exclusion – and many of those political discourses that seek to mobilize them across the political spectrum – is that a story of the diminution or end of national state sovereignty is aligned with the deployment of sovereign and coercive powers, as well as forms of culture-governance, over the lives of a substantial majority of the world's inhabitants.

An investigation of this fundamental notion of sovereignty is therefore required.

PART THREE

Departures

Sovereignty and violence

At the core of the problem of 'governing societies' is another one, that of
sovereignty, and of sovereign powers. And at the core of the problem
of sovereignty is the question of violence. The emergence of the sovereign
state system was a condition for both national and international projects of
governing societies. While there is no political and social relationship that
can be viewed as eternal, the idea of sovereignty as a fundamental and
extant operation of power is essential to understanding the kinds of
societies in which we live and their directions. To deny this is both
apolitical and utopian whether one adopts a neoliberal perspective of the
march of globalization or a vision of cosmopolitan social democracy. To
deny a form of power with constitutive links to violence and to territory is
to deny oneself the analytical capacity to grasp how a self-avowedly liberal
and pacific social and economic international order is constructed and
defended. To demonstrate this I want to start with a consideration of the
concept of sovereignty and its constitutive dualities around violence and
supremacy.

The concept of sovereignty in recent thought

The position that sovereignty is fundamental to contemporary liberal
democracies is of course anathema to much current thinking. It runs
counter to the emergence of theories of governance and globalization
which stress the fact that social and political organization has become less
hierarchical, taken a network form, and erased the old borders of the
nation-state. In most social and political narratives, sovereign power is
being undermined, decentred, flattened, deterritorialized, pluralized, and
conceptually displaced (see Table 3.1). It appears as a second-order

phenomenon, even an archaism or survival of absolutist or monarchical power, as something undergoing transformations as a result of far deeper and more fundamental processes. At best such an approach implies that we should examine how sovereignty is being reconfigured. At worst, it suggests there are a lot more interesting phenomena to analyse.

The latter option appears as a recurrent move in Foucault's work despite whatever complexity we might find there. At different points the characterization of sovereignty permits the analysis of modern systems of punishment (Foucault 1977: 48ff.), the definition of biopolitics (Foucault 1979a, 2003), the delineation of an analytics of power (Foucault 2003: 34), and the emergence of government (Foucault 1991a). Sovereignty is displaced and subordinated by those elements that Foucault contends are more defining of our contemporary era – whether it is discipline, biopower or governmentality. Of course there are other possible uses of Foucault's frameworks and his indications on the assemblages of power relations which we pursue in this book. Similar, but less sophisticated, moves are made in Hardt and Negri's *Empire* (2000). While these authors spend considerable time tracing the 'first articulations of a new imperial form of sovereignty' they then proclaim the need to descend into the hidden abode of 'immaterial' production to understand the political subjectivities that might contest and overthrow Empire (Hardt and Negri 2000: 205). Sovereignty is something that is historically, logically, analytically and theoretically displaced.

In a sense, Foucault, as much as Hardt and Negri, reproduces the structure of both liberal and Marxist critiques of sovereignty. For these critiques, the economy forms the real location of social and political order. For Marxism, the mode of production is merely justified and concealed by 'formal' political and legal relations (or superstructure). For liberalism, the market is the dynamic component of civil society to be facilitated by appropriate legal and political forms. For Foucault, sovereignty and its concepts need to be penetrated to discover the more fundamental relations of power – those of discipline, of biopower and of government. For example, at one point he argues that if the theory of sovereignty persists today, it is because 'this theory [of sovereignty], and the organization of a juridical code centred upon it, made it possible to superimpose on the mechanism of discipline, a system of right that concealed its mechanisms and erased the element of domination and techniques of domination involved in discipline' (Foucault 2003: 37). For Hardt and Negri, much closer to Marxism than Foucault, it is because production is logically prior and determining of the political order that we must penetrate sovereignty and descend to its hidden domain. Indeed, for them there is a sense in which sovereignty has been transformed into something else. After noting the fundamental incompatibility of sovereignty and capitalist production, they argue that sovereignty is forced to come down from its position of transcendence within modernity (that is, its self-definition as supreme) and enter into 'the plane of immanence', ultimately to be transformed into governmentality (Dean 2003b). There thus appear to be two incompatible positions in Hardt and Negri: that sovereignty has been transformed into a new kind of sovereignty ('imperial sovereignty') and that it has become something else ('governmentality' or the kind of power relations characteristic of what Gilles Deleuze [1995] called a 'society of control'), that is, it has lost the specific characteristics of sovereignty. Indeed, these incompatible positions suggest the tensions of different gestures made in poststructuralist theories of sovereignty.

When the displacement of sovereignty is applied to international law, we return to the fundamental tenet of much of cosmopolitan critical theory: that national sovereignty as an untrammelled exercise of force has been displaced by a cosmopolitan law based on individual human rights and even democratic values. Ulrich Beck (2000a: 81–2) contends that human rights have precedence over national sovereignty in the 'second age of modernity'. Similarly, David Held (2004a: 137) argues that the regime of what he calls 'liberal international sovereignty' means that 'sovereignty can no longer be understood in terms of the categories of untrammelled effective power' and state legitimacy must be understood 'through the language of democracy and human rights'.

According to such a view international law and human rights have already taken precedence over national sovereignty and all that remains is to reform existing institutions of the United Nations, particularly the Security Council, utilize the organizations of transnational civil society, and enable a cosmopolitan post-national citizenship (Habermas 2001). Military intervention will take the form of a defence of human rights undertaken when it satisfies a 'just cause threshold'. Further, the notion of governance allows such thought to neatly sidestep the old problem of One World Government and talk instead of 'global governance'. The reference to the international organizations in transnational or global civil society reminds us how much this diagnosis is still rooted in a liberal view of governing society even if now 'society' has broken the container of the state and become global. Indeed, David Held (2004a: 132) has recognized this liberal provenance when he notes that in many respects, 'the changes [in international law] represent the extension of the classic liberal concern to define the proper form, scope and limits of the face of the processes, opportunities and flux of civil life'.

This cosmopolitan, post-sovereigntist, world order is presented as the only alternative to American unilateralism and the neoconservative ascendancy in Washington. Yet in many respects the Washington hegemonic view is no less universalist and also proclaims the cosmopolitan character of the values of freedom, democracy and peace. What is at stake in the debate between American unilateralism and European multilateralism is principally the ultimate source of authority for such things as military action. Rather than deferring to the deliberations of the United Nations, the United States claims the right to decide what constitutes a just cause for military action. However, the United States, like Europeans, views its enemies through a similarly cosmopolitan lens: they are not its particular enemies as a nation but those who would commit crimes against humanity.

However, this contest between European cosmopolitanism and American conservatism misses the point of the intrinsic connection between the contemporary liberal critique of sovereignty and the authorization of the use of deadly force. Even that most Kantian and philosophical among contemporary commentators on international affairs, Jürgen Habermas, recommended a police action in the name of human rights and justified the NATO bombing of Yugoslavia in 1999 as a possible anticipation of the leap 'from the classical conception of international law for sovereign states toward the cosmopolitan law of a world civil society' (2000). At the very least such a stance would seem to suggest that that even cosmopolitans are willing to suspend current international law in an emergency in order to advocate the use of military violence if their morality dictates it (Giesen 2004). Habermas paradoxically endorses the use of sovereign force by states in anticipation of a law that is higher than state sovereignty. What such advocacy does suggest is that whether war is authorized through the United Nations or undertaken by the United States and its allies, it is no longer made for the advancement or defence of national sovereignty and national interest, that is, as an act of national policy, which is viewed as a crime, but as an act of international policy outlawing criminal acts and human rights violations. There is less a transformation of the use of sovereign violence in the international sphere than a transformation of its justification.

It is thus necessary to place the use of sovereign violence at the heart of an examination of contemporary power relations whether in domestic or international domains. While this conclusion might appear to contravene Foucault's old injunction to cut off the King's head in political theory, an understanding of sovereignty should begin with his concept 'the right to take life and let live' or 'right of death' (1979a: 136), or, to put it more gently, the right to use 'legitimate violence' in Max Weber's expression. My hypothesis here is that we need to understand the dual character of sovereignty in both its relation to violence and its claim for supremacy within a given domain.

The first duality concerns sovereignty as the sufficient monopoly of violence in a specific territorial domain. In this respect sovereignty makes governing societies possible. It is a condition for the effective internal government or governance of that which lies within their boundaries and of stable and enduring agreements between states. State sovereignty, in this sense, opens the spaces under which social, legal and political institutions can be built and markets can be constructed and operate, and in which various governmental, biopolitical and even geopolitical powers and strategies can be deployed. A world divided into functioning state-societies is an aim and tool of many projects of the effective international governing of societies. In this respect, the project of sovereignty is a civilizing one on both domestic and international fronts in that it restricts the arbitrary use of violence for political ends. It can do this, however, only because sovereignty is defined by a constitutive relationship to violence whether in domestic or international spheres. In the former, the state has to have enough of a monopoly of violence to defeat or contain internal enemies. Internationally, it needs something that can maintain its own territorial integrity: its means of defence either alone or in concert with its allies and/ or a system that guarantees that integrity.

If one stresses the first side, state sovereignty can be recommended on the grounds that it is a condition of order and thus of a pacified, civilized and prosperous society. It is beyond morality and a condition of moral projects. Sovereignty can become a project extended to all regions and territories of the world, especially those currently without law and order. It is thus relatively insulated from critique. If one stresses the second, the constitutive violence of state sovereignty can appear as something abhorrent and to be morally regulated. Here we can locate the demands that national sovereignty be subordinated to human rights and prescriptions of the moral conditions under which aggressive war can be justified. Yet the discourse of sovereignty is formed between its realist endorsement and its attempt at moral transformation, between its existence as a condition of moral action including democracy and the demand that it be subordinated to moral principles.

There is a second duality that we also need to grasp here. This is between sovereignty as state sovereignty and sovereign power as a component of different power relations. As we noted in Chapter 4, sovereign forms of power are present within other social, cultural and governmental practices and are essential to their forms of operation. The power to decide life and death can be delegated to, for example, police officers or air marshals confronted with life-threatening criminals or the prevention of terrorism, and regulated, such as in the legal and ethical controls on abortion and euthanasia. Legitimate violence can be claimed or even arrogated by other organizations such as sporting associations. Perhaps the latter case can be thought of, in terms that would be familiar to both Bodin ([1576] 1992: 11–12) and Hobbes (1651), as *derogatory* of sovereignty, that is, a partial retraction, limitation or detraction from sovereign power. Thus, in a discussion of how we know that laws issued by various authorities under their seals are the will of the sovereign and thus should be obeyed, Hobbes writes: 'For the constant permission of these things is a manifest signe enough, and evident declaration of the Commanders will; provided there be nothing contain'd in the Law, Edict or Decree, derogatory from his supreme power' ([1651] 1996: 14, xiii). While sovereignty might be a supreme power within a domain, it can be derogated within specific arenas.

There is state sovereignty, on the one hand, and the sovereign forms of power found in everyday practices. It is clear that the two concepts are far from unrelated. The relationship between the internal pacification of a territory, the development of representative parliamentary democracy, and the development of modern sporting contests has been subtly analysed by Elias and Dunning (1986). It would seem that there is a loose historical correlation between the development of a body capable of claiming a monopoly of legitimate violence and the development of highly rationalized and rule-governed violence in sports such as boxing, rugby, football, and so on. The state monopoly of violence would seem to be bracketed – or more properly 'derogated' – at the sidelines of the field or the ropes of the boxing ring unless the effects of sporting violence lead to demands for its legal regulation or proscription.

If the sovereign claim to violence can be derogated, it can also be delegated. Indeed, it can only work by being delegated. The state monopoly of violence can only be claimed through the institutions to which it delegates the right of death. Standing armies, and later navies and air forces, were formed as instruments for the exercise of sovereign violence against external attack and threats and internal civil war. The constabulary force of police officers, on the other hand, develops as a means of keeping domestic order through the more or less carefully calibrated exercise of sovereign violence (Dean 2006a).

Despite the enjoyment of violence as a component of leisure pursuits, mainly as spectators, the assertion of the existence of power relations connected with violence offends civilized sensibilities. This is undoubtedly why sports such as boxing have declined in recent years and authorities have sought to outlaw those activities such as the duel which entail a right to kill or a possibility of killing. This now extends to sports that involve the killing of animals such as fox-hunting and cockfighting. This distaste for a power and an action rooted in the right to kill is most abstractly evidenced in liberal forms of rule concerned with the limitation of sovereignty in both domestic and international settings and with the kind of social and political theories discussed throughout this book. This distaste of course does not stop authorities from engaging in foreign military intervention to dislodge a tyrant – defined as one who rules in a permanent, as opposed to a temporary, 'state of exception' (Beasley-Murray 2005) – despite the fact that such adventures can and do lead to the deaths of tens and even hundreds of thousands of civilians. Nor does this distaste prevent legislators from passing bills on the use of lethal force to protect domestic populations against terrorism. In our time the exercise of the 'legitimate' right of death is less as a form of punishment, despite the exception of many of the states of the United States, and more as the prevention of the 'illegitimate' power to kill. The question of 'legitimacy' is always one to be put into brackets given that the problem of who decides, and how, remains an open and contested matter.

Any discussion of sovereignty today is thus caught between these two sets of problems. One centres on the constitutive violence of territorial sovereignty and the goods it delivers, beginning with social peace, and the potential evils it entails, beginning with the dangers of a police state and international aggression. The other focuses on the question of a supreme power which, perhaps oddly, can also be divided and only works through its delegation and derogation. In the remainder of this chapter I shall focus on the questions of supremacy and violence in outlining some general themes of sovereignty.

Sovereignty as supreme power

A focus on the right of death should not pre-empt a discussion of the more conventional understanding of sovereignty as the 'absolute and perpetual power of a commonwealth', after Bodin ([1576] 1992: 1), or, even more basically, the quality or condition of 'being supreme or pre-eminent in some particular domain', as a recent glossary entry puts it (Hindess 2005: 339). The latter might mean the sovereignty of reason over the passions or the sovereignty of the individual over his or her life. Some, such as Georges Bataille (1991), have addressed sovereignty as having little to do with the sovereignty of states. For our purposes, we need to grasp the dual nature of sovereignty. It is a supreme power within governing societies, that is, a supreme power over a territory that bounds society and the population within the territory. Yet it is also something that can be uncoupled from sovereignty and states. We shall address the issue of the sovereignty of states in this section and the potential delegation, derogation and arrogation of the sovereign right of death in the next section. The paradoxical theme of the divisibility of a self-proclaimed indivisible power is fundamental to our understanding of its status in contemporary societies.

Recall the discussion of the historical conditions of governing societies in Chapter 1. There we saw that these conditions entailed the project of a political unity capable of putting an end to religious conflicts, and subsuming the plethora of medieval authorities under the centralized jurisdiction, legislation and administration of a territorial sovereign. We should not imagine that this was a task readily accomplished. There was an enormous labour of formation of such a political unity. This labour includes the treaties, covenants and conventions that made up the system of European interstate law of which the Peace of Westphalia is a key example and perhaps even the symbol. It also includes numerous doctrines that concerned state security and strength, an art of government expressed as reason of state and civil prudence, maxims derived from the revival of pagan thinking such as Stoicism and Aristotleanism, and the development of the science and practice of maintaining domestic order, police.

Moreover, as Ian Hunter (1998) has pointed out, the establishment of political order was also the central concern for contemporaneous political science, such as that of Henning Arnisaeus at the beginning of the seventeenth century. Sovereignty itself could form an end of government. Arnisaeus argued against those who would shield lethal religious communities and their spiritual disciplines behind the protection of states. He claimed that political order should be the ultimate end of politics, that there should be a distinction between political and moral–theological concerns, and that 'the preservation of political order can only be achieved by the domination of contending estates and powers, which necessitates the deployment of a power superior to all others' (Hunter 1998: 252). The prince should therefore, Arnisaeus concludes, withdraw from the legal enforcement of religious belief and observance, eject the Church from the state apparatus, and move to acquire such things as absolute legislative power, a monopoly of armed forces and weapons, powers of taxation and appointment of magistrates. It is only by the production of a secular sovereignty that civil peace could be established and maintained. To cite such views is to locate religious tolerance less in the liberal private domain than a state policy for securing sovereignty.

Sovereignty, however, is about more than order. It is also about disorder, and in particular about the disorder wrought by time and change. One does not have to posit a thoroughly apolitical sphere of civil society, globalism or the mode of production to recognize that the goal of producing order within a particular territory is subject to a wide range of contingencies. This challenge is suggested by the other aspect of Bodin's definition. Sovereignty is, or at least tries to become or represent itself as, *perpetual*, that is, immortal. There is an enormous symbolic investment put into the establishment of the idea that state sovereignty is perpetual (Neocleous 2003: 16–18). In medieval political theology, according to the famous account of Ernst Kantorowicz (1957: 7), the problem of the immortality of sovereign power confronted with the mortality of the monarch was linked to the doctrine of the king's two bodies. The classical formulation of this doctrine posits a 'body natural' which is mortal and subject to human infirmities, age and other defects, and a 'body politic' which is devoid of such finitude and limits. With the 'democratization of sovereignty' this feature of sovereignty no longer resides in the king's immortality but in the impersonal state as the 'body politic' and, later, the 'social body' and the nation, and in the symbols and rituals associated with national identity (Corrigan and Sayer 1985; Neocleous 2003: 21–8). Sovereign is divisible and indivisible, mortal and immortal, mutable and immutable.

Schmitt ([1922] 1985b: 36) pointed to the relationship between the dominant theological and metaphysical ideas of an age and its fundamental legal and political concepts. One can see in the notion of absolutist sovereignty a power with parallels to the idea of an omnipotent God. Otto Gierke ([1913] 1957: 41) had already suggested that the idea of sovereignty acts as 'a kind of magic wand' in which the doctrine of a power that is superior to any other is transformed into the idea, proposed equally by defenders of monarchical or popular sovereignty, of the absolute omnipotence of the state. All this underlines the notion of sovereignty as an aspiration, a more or less accomplished fact, reliant not only on the effectiveness of state policies, and the capacities of its military and police forces, but the ability of ceremony, ritual and symbol to awe, to inspire and enrapture its subjects and to project durability and permanence.

One reason that sovereignty remains an aspiration is that it is not simply a matter of putting an end to civil war and establishing the rule of law underlined by sufficient force to maintain it. The development of the modern state sovereignty occurred within the 'great transformation' of feudal society and property relations and the emergence of modern capitalist societies (Polanyi 1957). Foucault (2001a: 202) even speaks of 'the shattering of the structures of feudalism' as a condition for the posing of the problem of government in the sixteenth century. This small phrase includes the new forms of property and land-appropriation that Marx called the 'expropriation of the peasantry'. This process is a condition for the emergence of new kinds of property and a new class of wage-labourers. The liberal exercise of this sovereignty, including a liberal art of government, addressed a context in which it was necessary to construct the conditions under which the mass of the population would be rendered into a condition of wage-labour and cultivate a specific set of attributes such as independence from charity and poor relief, regularity, punctuality, and responsibility for self, family and for one's children (Dean 1991).

In short, sovereignty as supreme power within a territory was and is something that had to be achieved, maintained, defended, proclaimed, symbolized and ritualized. Sovereignty entails rendering the divisible indivisible, the mutable immutable, the mortal immortal. One should not imagine that this is a task, once accomplished, that can be forgotten or put to one side or that, having been established with the absolutist monarchies in Europe, can be taken as a kind of given. Sovereignty is not merely a 'survival' or 'archaism' from the absolutist monarchies, or a task identified solely with law and the legal order, however important these may be, but an always open question, a matter of historical, political, linguistic and symbolic construction and contestation. Above all, the existence of something that approximates a sovereign agent within a geographical space is open to empirical investigation and not, as many influential forms of social and political thought would have it, dissolved by theoretical gesture.

Thus many of the theories studied here can be viewed as making quite radical empirical claims about sovereignty. Liberal cosmopolitans claim that the territorial state is, or at least should be, no longer supreme in international affairs. Economic globalizers claim that it is no longer supreme in domestic economic matters. The key point here is that if sovereignty means the ongoing achievement of supremacy within a particular domain, then the question of whether or not something or someone is sovereign is not to be foreclosed by theoretical narrative but remains and ought to be approached as an open one.

One argument by liberal cosmopolitans is that given that nation-states are prohibited by the articles of the United Nations Charter to engage in aggressive wars with other nation-states, they no longer freely have the right to pursue their sovereign interests by means of military action or

threat.[1] Such a view needs to confront the recurrent US military interventions, typically in concert with other states, into other nation–states for
various ends. The liberal cosmopolitan might respond that the USA – or
any other state – makes such interventions, however imperfect they may
be, in terms of the principles of international law rather than sovereign self-
interest. Thus US–led military actions have been justified in terms of
human rights abuses (the NATO bombing in Yugoslavia in 1999 to stop
the genocide of Kosovars), the violation of territorial integrity (the first
Persian Gulf War) and increased international instability caused by the
stockpiling of weapons of mass destruction (second Gulf War). However,
given that only one of these actions received UN authorization it would
seem that the United States is sovereign in so far as it can pass judgment not
only on when international law and order have been breached and act
accordingly but on how one interprets and uses key concepts such as
territorial integrity, international stability and human rights.

The idea of a new liberal international order or sovereignty rests on the
doctrine of *jus cogens* (literally higher law) by which international law
overrides domestic law (Danilenko 1991). The first problem with
regarding the existence of such a doctrine as evidence of the erosion of
nation–state sovereignty is that there exists no form of compulsion to
enforce ratification of such law. Thus the United States has not at the time
of writing ratified the Kyoto Protocol on limiting carbon emissions to
combat global warming (nor have some other states, taking their cues from
the USA, such as Australia). The USA has not ratified the International
Criminal Court which has been established to prosecute individuals for war
crimes and genocide. More fundamentally, the United States has signed but
not ratified the very convention, the 1969 Vienna Convention on the Law
of Treaties, that is held to have first embodied *jus cogens* and which requires
states to refrain from undermining the treaties they sign, even if they
subsequently do not ratify them (Hindess 2005: 331).

The second problem with the doctrine of *jus cogens* is that a condition for
the effectiveness of such a doctrine would be the existence of a supreme
legislative body to enact such law and a supreme judiciary to interpret and
apply it. In the absence of such institutions, or agreement as to which
institutions have priority (for instance, those established under the United
Nations Charter or the United States Constitution [Koskenniemi 2004]),
the interpretation and enactment of such laws will always be open to
competition. In such a case, sovereignty would mean the prerogative to
determine the meaning of such words as 'human rights' and 'democracy',
which, as we have seen, the United States has regularly exercised. From
this perspective, it is not surprising to find that we are much closer to a
world order that is currently governed according to the dictates of a sole
hegemon than a liberal cosmopolitan order subject to international law.

This is not to say that sovereignty in the international domain has
remained fundamentally the same. Under the UN Charter, there is an
explicit prohibition of wars of aggression against member states, as we have

noted. This first of all means that the existing historical order of sovereign states is taken as a given. Largely, the settlement reached at the conclusion of World War II remains in force with some adjustments for decolonization during the Cold War and for the breakup of the Soviet bloc after 1989. It also means that this order will have a protector: thus one or several sovereign states with sufficient means will undertake to preserve this order. It follows, thirdly, that wars of national purposes have been replaced by legitimate wars for international purposes. The right of sovereigns to conduct wars for self-interest is replaced by the sovereign rights of one state, acting alone or in concert with other states, to decide when there is sufficient reason to conduct international wars. In the absence of a trans-national military force, the legal doctrine of *jus cogens*, like the political notions of a cosmopolitan governance and democracy, presupposes the existence of a sovereign power or powers capable of military action and right to wage war.

There are other cases in which the issue of the existence or otherwise of forms of state sovereignty is important in contemporary rationalities of governing. One is the case of those societies without an effective state described by the British diplomat, Robert Cooper, as 'zones of chaos'. He describes, for instance, Afghanistan in September 2001 in the following terms:

> Sometimes a zone of chaos can turn into a major direct threat to state security elsewhere. It is true that the circumstances of Afghanistan were unique. What was left of the state was dominated by an extreme Islamist regime that contracted out different state functions to different bodies: finance to drug barons, health and welfare to the United Nations and various NGOs, and defence to Osama Bin Laden. In return for shelter and facilities to train terrorists he provided men and arms to prosecute the civil war against Ahmed Massod.
>
> (Cooper 2003: 68)

The obvious conclusion here is that, without particular political conditions within a country or territory, so-called 'zones of chaos' become security problems to rich parts of the world, the most dramatic example of which were the events of 9/11. It is interesting that after the US military interventions in Afghanistan and Iraq, and in the context of their occupation after the defeat of state forces, the idea of 'state-building' is once again on the agenda, whether from a conservative public policy perspective (Fukuyama 2004) or from the perspective of a self-consciously liberal historical approach to American Empire (Ferguson 2004). If sovereignty is the supreme power within a domain, rather than the inviolability of whatever regime happens to be in place, then a key condition for international security and for domestic governance is the existence of an agency that has enough of the monopoly of force to deter any challengers. Such an agency can then be supported to accomplish basic state functions. This might include instituting and operating according to the rule of law, providing basic public welfare and education, and protecting and enforcing different kinds of property rights.

Sovereignty in this sense can also be viewed as a resource of government and something that can be traded off against other benefits. Since World War II, for example, a European project has emerged which was wary of the devastation the unfettered pursuit of national sovereignty had brought in the first half of the twentieth century and has been willing, to a certain extent, and with advances and retreats, to trade aspects of national sovereignty for a pacific European sphere. Hence there has been a European approach to international government which represents both a 'pooling of sovereignties' and a deliberate attempt to embed national sovereignties within a system consisting of multiple layers of agreements, rules, norms, laws and regulations. One argument here might be, however, that it is the resilience of the national state structures, and their capacity for international cooperation in policing and border patrol, for example, that have allowed for this rendering interdependent of sovereignties (Held and Hirst 2002). This latter point comes across very strongly when one considers the different kinds of cooperative 'geostrategies' that are constitutive of the borders and frontiers of the EU under the Schengen agreement (Walters 2004).

A final point can be made with respect to sovereignty as supreme power within a territory. Foucault argued (2003: 35–7) that one reason for the persistence of the 'juridical theory of sovereignty' was the process of the 'democratization of sovereignty' and the development of representative parliamentary institutions since the French Revolution 'as an alternative to absolutist or monarchical administration'. This democratization of sovereignty has, in turn, two sides. The first is the national side. For several centuries, Foucault shows, the discourse on the nation appears first as a kind of historical memory of invasion, victory and domination and, in the context of a discourse on war, a binary war of races or of nations. As such, it was used against monarchical sovereignty in the service of those who claimed a right of war against the state which, far from being the settled trade-off of obedience and protection promised by Hobbes's image of the great human body, was merely a temporary lapse of this memory, a temporary cessation to a war between two adversaries. The historical discourse of nation was invoked in popular and bourgeois struggles against the English monarchy at the time of the Civil War and by the aristocracy in France against the establishment of the administrative monarchy under Louis XIV. Yet it is part of a binary image of society, instanced by historical memory of the Norman Conquest and the national dualism of France. In such a discourse, the nation was used against the juridical theory of sovereignty to show that:

> War has not been averted. War obviously presided over the birth of States; right, peace and law were born in the mud and blood of battles ... Law is not pacification, for beneath law, war continues to rage in

all the mechanisms of power ... There is no such thing as a neutral subject. We are all inevitably someone's adversary.

(Foucault 2003: 50–1)

When the same themes are taken up by the bourgeoisie, such as in Sieyès's tract, *What is the Third Estate?* ([1789] 1963), it is to proclaim the possibility of an end to this permanent civil war in the form of a nation that is now capable of seizing and running the state on behalf of all. The democratization of sovereignty is thus the process by which sovereignty is transferred from the body of the monarch to the body of the people. Governing is no longer about the sovereign subjugation of subjects but about the government of and by citizens. According to this liberal nationalism, the nation-state establishes a true civil peace by putting war outside the social body in a space of exception. War is replaced by a struggle or rivalry over the universality of the state. 'We will have civil struggle, and the military struggle or bloody struggle will become no more than an exceptional moment, a crisis of an episode within it' (Foucault 2003: 225). When we talk about sovereignty as supreme power it will no longer be the power of the sovereign over the people to establish a state of subjugation but the sovereignty of the people or the nation itself.

The birth of the nation-state means that war is taken outside the body of the nation and beyond the border of the territory of the state and the normality of life of the people. But the life of the people is inscribed in the state and the state will come to take care of that life, and seek to foster and shape it. For Foucault the nation-state will be the crucial condition for the modern discourses of state racisms and biologism.

On the other hand we can see another set of consequences of the democratic nation-state which we should also not dismiss lightly. One effect of this process of electing representatives who would exercise sovereignty is that they can, at least in an ideal sense, be held accountable. It is only within the internal arrangements of the territorially enclosed democratic state that doctrines of 'responsible government' and the practices of representative democracy have been effective. Sovereignty is both a condition and a target of democratic political struggle. It is a condition in the sense that only in a relatively pacified territory that 'contains' a civil society would it be possible to envisage two parties that might take turns in operating the institutions of supreme power without open civil strife arising. It is a target in that the exercise of sovereignty is at stake in such competition. Moreover such a system, once established, can be held accountable classically by its own citizenry and today by the standards of international organizations and the views of the incipient international community of societies.

We keep coming back, in different ways, to the duality of sovereignty and we find a new kind of duality in the critique of the nation-state today. The great virtue of the idea of a multilayered governance in which individuals identify with community, region, city and 'the world', rather than

the nation, is an end to all those dreadful consequences of national identification and national sovereignty, including the genocides of those
beyond the nation or the demand that the nation be expanded into the
space of the biologically inferior others. At this level it is hard to be
anything but cosmopolitan. However, the great problem with multilayered
governance, which includes unelected non-governmental organizations
and corporations in its notions of transnational civil society, such as that
envisaged by most advocates of cosmopolitanism, is that in the absence of
a supreme set of institutions it is very difficult to imagine anything or
anybody being held responsible.

Sovereignty as a form of power that seeks to present itself and act as the
supreme and perpetual power of the state is of course never as supreme or
as perpetual as it would like both its subjects and its enemies to believe.
While it is difficult for us to imagine a world without the great republic of
the United States, even this state has a date of birth and a history which
portends its mortality and is likely to meet competitors to its current
dominance of the international sphere in the present century. However,
just because we can show that sovereignty is never as complete as it would
have us believe and that the form of the state is contingent upon economic
conditions and technological changes, this does not mean that we should
rush to dispense with the concept and the analysis of the project of
sovereignty and its maintenance in the twenty-first century. The dissolu-
tion of national sovereignty is just as problematic as the immortality of the
state. Globalizers applaud 'governance without government' without
recognizing that the first term usually presumes the second.

Most twenty-first-century critical political theorists of sovereignty
would be uncomfortable with this straightforward definition of sovereignty
as supreme within a domain. Many of them emphasize its founding in a
right of death to which we now turn.

Sovereignty and violence

From Max Weber to Giorgio Agamben, twentieth-century social theory
and cultural critique reminded us of the constitutive link between sovereignty and violence, a link that is crucial to understanding the relation
between politics and death. This link is found in Max Weber's definition of
a state as 'a human community that (successfully) claims the *monopoly of the
legitimate use of physical force* within a given territory' ([1918] 1972: 78,
original italics). Although he believed that sovereignty was an archaic
mechanism of power used to build and justify absolutism, Foucault most
strongly links sovereignty and violence in his conception of sovereign
power as 'the right to decide life and death' (2003: 34–5; 1979a: 135). In
his lectures, he is even more explicit when he talks about how the right of
life and death is always tipped in favour of death so that '[s]overeign
power's effect on life is exercised only when the sovereign can kill. The

very essence of the right of life and death is actually the right to kill ...'
(2003: 240). For Agamben, drawing on a fragment from Pindar, 'the
sovereign *nomos* is the principle that, joining law and violence, threatens
them with indistinction' (1998: 31). The names of those who linked
sovereignty and violence include Benjamin, Bataille and Anthony Giddens
(1985), and many others in various social and critical traditions. Recently
political theory has begun to consider the relationship between the political
thought of conservatism, Marxism and fascism and the cultural understanding of death (Neocleous 2005). While Foucault (1988b: 160) spoke
about a *thanatopolitics*, a favoured term in recent cultural studies debate
which links death to sovereignty is *necropolitics* (Mbembe 2003).

Strangely, one who does not make a direct definitional link between
sovereignty and violence is Schmitt. Note the word 'decide' in Foucault's
definition. The word 'decide' is undoubtedly not accented in the way it is
in Schmitt's definition ([1922] 1985b: 5): 'Sovereign is he who decides on
the exception'. Given his reputation as one who emphasized the extreme
elements of politics, Schmitt ([1922] 1985b: 13) explicitly disavows
Weber's view when he states categorically that the 'essence' of state
sovereignty is to be located 'not as the monopoly to coerce or rule, but as
the monopoly to decide'.

Schmitt also adds an important methodological insight to our discussion
of legal and political concepts when he suggests that '[a]ll significant
concepts of the modern theory of the state are secularized theological
concepts' ([1922] 1985b: 36). The key methodological precept Schmitt
makes here is that 'the sociology of juristic concepts' rests on the idea that
'the metaphysical image that a definite epoch forges of the world has the
same structure as what the world immediately understands to be appropriate as a form of its political organization' ([1922] 1985b: 46). He then
makes the point through tracing the movement from transcendent notions
of the sovereign and supreme lawmaker in the seventeenth and eighteenth
centuries to the more immanent notions of democracy, of organic theories
of the state and the identification of state with the legal order in Hans
Kelsen (Schmitt [1922] 1985b: 49–50). One might want to say that the
theory of representative democracy posits a kind of compromise between
transcendence (the representative) and immanence (the people).

From this perspective, a world in which the image of the political order
is one of multilayered governance consisting of flat relations between
heterogeneous entities without borders is just as metaphysical as its predecessors and corresponds neither to the image of God, machine or
organism but perhaps to the world as a kind of a global information and
communication network, inhabited by knowledge workers – or, better
still, the world as a kind of computer software package, Globalization 3.0,
in Thomas Friedman's image (2005: 10–11). To the extent that such a
metaphysics can even overwrite and reprogramme the primitive software
of war and violence, it is a 'virtual war' conducted by pilotless Drone
aircraft feeding digital images from Iraq into several communicating

command centres and being operated by a low-ranking officer at an air-force base in Las Vegas (Friedman 2005: 38–9). The metaphysical picture of the world today is one that seeks to exclude the problem of sovereign violence and of death from political relations, or to purify the political through ideas of governance. The repulsion we feel about violence in the form of war and insurgency, or state executions, makes it hard to grasp and think about the problem of the relationship between sovereignty, violence and death.

How then should we approach the question of sovereignty and its relation to violence? How should we approach a politics of death? First, I think we need to reject a model that criticizes the very concept of sovereignty because it is appalled by such a link. The idea of a supreme power which monopolizes legitimate violence is as much about limiting and restraining 'necropolitics' as it is about engaging in it. Secondly, we need to keep in mind that sovereignty and sovereign powers are historical constructions both in concept and in practice. The concept and practice of sovereignty today is not of course identical to that advocated during the European religious wars of the sixteenth and seventeenth centuries but it does retain some important continuities. We must thus reject universalist and bipolar notions of sovereignty found in various theories or an approach that suppresses the link between politics and death by treating it as an archaism. Thirdly, we need to keep open the space of the relations between sovereignty, law and the state, or state and nation, so that they might be characterized by shifting rather than fixed relations. One of the effects of both contemporary critical thought and globalization narratives is to freeze such concepts by identifying a certain form of sovereignty with law, or by eliding the state with the nation, or by imagining sovereignty and state are inseparable. Finally, we should acknowledge that the territorial form of sovereignty was a precondition for a project of governing society both by pacifying the space occupied by civil society and defining the constitutional limits of the sovereign encroachment upon that space. The project of governing society emerges, from this perspective, as a component of the project of territorial sovereignty. With these points in mind, we shall return to the critical theory of sovereignty.

For Foucault (1979b: 135), sovereign power is, in a formal sense, 'derived no doubt from the ancient *patria potestas* that granted the father of the Roman family the right to "dispose" of the life of his children and his slaves . . .'. Agamben agrees that the right of life and death is a right of the father to unconditional power over his sons in Roman law (1998: 87–9). He nonetheless argues that the power of life and death over the son is to be distinguished from the right to kill others such as adulterous wives and daughters and, even more so, slaves. The latter right remains within the *domus*, that is, it is a component of his domestic jurisdiction as head of household, while the power of life and death, the *vitae necisque potestas*, '. . . attaches itself to every free male citizen from birth and thus seems to define the very model of political power in general' (Agamben 1998: 88).

The link between sovereignty and a patriarchal heritage is also recognized by Weber (1978: 56) when he argues that, despite the state's monopoly of legitimate violence, 'the right of a father to discipline his children is recognized – a survival of the former independent authority of the head of household, which in the right to use force has sometimes extended to a power of life and death over children and slaves'. Whether the lineage of sovereignty can be found in such a power of life and death is beyond the scope of the present study. We would want to note that this power of the householder father (*paterfamilias*) is itself already conditional in Aristotle on the proper civic education of women and children '... if the virtues of either of them are supposed to make any difference to the virtues of the state. And they must make a difference: for the children grow up as citizens, and half the free persons in a state are women' (Aristotle in Dubber 2005: 7).

For Foucault, the early modern versions of sovereignty also have a conditional character. Because sovereignty exercises a right of life only by killing or refraining from killing, it is really 'the right to *take* life and *let* live' (Foucault 1979b: 136, 2003: 241). He argues that, in the seventeenth- and eighteenth-century juridical theories of Hobbes and Pufendorf, this is a right conditional upon the defence of the sovereign against domestic and external enemies. Such an understanding of sovereignty cannot tell us when the security of the sovereign is threatened, and thus does not tell us on what occasions that right might be activated. In this regard, Schmitt's accentuation of the role of decision in sovereign power adds a key element. For the latter (Schmitt [1922] 1985b: 9), 'sovereignty (and thus the state itself) resides in deciding this controversy, that is, in determining definitively what constitutes public order and security, in determining when they are disturbed'. We shall return to this 'sovereign nominalism' in the next chapter.

In addition to these, both Georges Bataille and Walter Benjamin must be mentioned. Indeed, Foucault's definitions seem to echo Bataille's theme of sovereignty as linked to the denial of the sentiments that death controls. 'Life beyond utility is the domain of sovereignty' states Bataille (1991: 198). The implication of this is that sovereign existence is the capacity to live in the present moment beyond the concern for the need to sustain life. The moral corollary is that 'sovereignty requires the strength to violate the prohibition against killing' (Bataille 1991: 221). Yet Bataille claims his definition of sovereignty has little to do with the sovereignty of states. The possibility of uncoupling concepts of sovereignty and state suggests an interpretative use of the concept considered by neither Schmitt nor Weber, and oddly probably neither Foucault nor Agamben.

Benjamin's 1921 essay on the 'Critique of violence' also offers a significant contribution to the constitutive link between sovereignty and violence. In this essay, Benjamin shows the irreducible relation between law and violence. He distinguishes between violence as a means to achieve the aim of establishing law and violence as an inseparable component of the law that is established, echoing Sieyès's distinction between constituting power and constituted power (Benjamin [1921] 1978: 295). He thus distinguishes between law-making violence and law-preserving violence, the oscillation between which defines the rise and fall of various kinds of state power and the way in which such power is punctuated by revolutions. Benjamin emphasizes the permanent relation between law and violence, and, in a vein that betrays his continuing dialogue with Schmitt, offers a critique of parliaments as cultivating compromises that ignore the latent presence of violence in legal institutions, including contract ([1921] 1978: 298).

Benjamin ([1921] 1978: 293) further claims that 'every conceivable solution to human problems ... remains impossible if violence is totally excluded in principle'. This view would seem an important challenge to all those who would claim a 'governance beyond government' which operates through non-hierarchical networks. To move beyond legal violence, he therefore looks for a different kind of violence unrelated to the justification of the means or preservation of the ends of law. He first seeks this in the violence of the Greek gods. Their mythical violence, however, replicates the structure of law-making violence, and can be contrasted with what he calls 'divine violence', which is truly law destroying. Mythical violence works through guilt and retribution for those who challenge fate. It can be viewed in constitutional law and treaties that leave one party, like Anatole France's bridge-dwelling poor, more exposed to the equality of legal violence. Divine violence strikes with lethal force without blood in a way that is 'unalloyed' with law. Benjamin ([1921] 1978: 297) argues that, while the mythical violence involved in the making of the juridical order is 'bloody power over mere life for its own sake', only divine violence can truly purify life, not simply by expiating the guilt of mere life, but by purifying the guilty of law itself. Only in the final sentence of the essay does Benjamin ([1921] 1978: 300) link violence to sovereignty: 'Divine violence, which is the sign and seal but never the means of sacred execution, may be called sovereign violence.'

In these passages Benjamin seeks to establish the link between law and violence and yet gestures to a 'pure', 'divine' or revolutionary violence outside the sphere of law. Benjamin here proposes something like an emancipatory violence, a 'line of flight' completely external to the dialectic of constituent and constituted power which are moments of a juridical order (Neal 2005b). Here violence, as Agamben notes, exists in anomie, an anomic zone, a zone without norms (2005: 59). Unlike Schmitt who would bring violence back into a relation with law in his discussions of the state of exception, Benjamin seeks the possibility of a human violence outside law and any specific actual or future legal order.

Benjamin's passages on the pure or divine violence today must remind us of the actions of suicide bombers and the agents of jihadist necropolitics. Here purity is gained from guilt and from the law, or at least from what is understood as the corrupting law of Western liberal imperialism. However, the wanton destruction of human life is far from bloodless in that it shatters bodies and lives and reduces them to pieces of inert flesh dripping with blood. Moreover, it receives justification from another kind of law, divine law, which promises immortality and happiness in the next world. Mbembe (2003: 39) is correct to point to the connection between Palestinian martyrdom in the name of a freedom to come and the discipline of life and the hardships and excesses experienced under occupation. However, such a relationship does not exist in the case of the jihadist martyrs of London, Madrid and Bali, and the 9/11 conspirators. Jihadism has distinct resemblance to the features of fascism: necrophilia, that is, extolling the virtue of death; the immortality attained through death in the service of a political struggle; the willingness to turn the politics of killing upon its own weak or corrupted population; and, finally, a virulent anti-Semitism which views Jews through vampire blood myths (on Nazism, see Neocleous 2005: 72–112).

Certainly those who would arrogate to themselves the Deity's judgement on good and evil and declare holy war give pause to those who might idealize violence as political resistance. The suicide bombers remind us that what is viewed as an emancipatory potential of a divine violence by its perpetrators is experienced by its innocent victims as death, maiming, dismemberment and loss. Not divine, but demonic; not emancipatory but destructive.

There are other ways in which these insights can be taken. The idea of a bloodless violence appears in Elias's notion of a highly rationalized and instrumental violence which would have none of the features abhorrent to a civilized sensibility such as public brutality and spectacle, randomness and pleasure-giving (Elias and Dunning 1986: 226). In the case of the Pentagon's recent 'revolution in military affairs', and related notions of virtual/virtuous war, we find the aspiration of a kind of bloodless violence, at least for the forces of the US and its allies. As James Der Derian puts it (2002: 8, original emphasis): 'At the heart as well as the muscle of this transformation [of kinds of war] is the *technical capability* and *ethical imperative* to threaten and, if necessary, to actualize violence from a distance – but again with minimal casualties when possible'.[2]

Benjamin's deliberations also lead him to a reflection on the meaning of the sanctity of human life and the proscription of murder in the constitution of sovereign power and violence. Again this begins to bring the question of sovereignty apart from that of the state and sets us on a path of considering violence within more mundane institutional practices. The commandment against killing, he argues (Benjamin [1921] 1978: 298–9), does not exist as a 'criterion of judgement' but as a guideline which individuals and communities have to wrestle with and 'in exceptional cases, to take on themselves the responsibility of ignoring'. He regards the sacredness of life as a relatively recent dogma, 'the last mistaken attempt by a weakened Western tradition to seek the saint it has lost in cosmological impenetrability'. Benjamin thus extends the analysis of sovereignty and violence to our ideas of life and its sanctity, and the exceptions we make to

the commandment 'thou shalt not kill'. For those who accept this commandment, Schmitt's decision on the exception is thus presupposed in any
assertion of a right to kill.

Agamben (1998: 71), as a close reader of Benjamin, takes up this theme
of the sacred man, *homo sacer*, in whom mere existence or 'bare life' is
sanctified, and who may be killed but without this being condemned as
homicide. For Agamben, *homo sacer* is subject to recurrent examples
throughout history. These include its paradigmatic manifestation in
National Socialism. He analyses or mentions the Holocaust, the Nazi
extermination of the Jews, the death camps (*lager*), the Nazi euthanasia
Program for the Incurably Ill, and the use of the *Versuchspersonen* or human
guinea pigs by the Nazi doctors. Outside National Socialism, he focuses on
the history of the concentration camp and contemporary refugee camps,
experiments parallel to the Nazi one in US prisons on prisoners sentenced
to death, and notions of 'brain death'. In later writing (Agamben 2005), he
takes up the treatment of captured combatants by the USA in the War on
Terror.

The treatment of the Jews and other victims (gypsies, homosexuals,
mentally ill) of the Nazi Holocaust as *homo sacer* captures the full bloody
machinery of sovereign power when fused together with the state management and control of the life of the population – with biopolitics. This
form of sovereign power divides populations with respect to life; some
groups are consequently declared 'life unworthy of living'. They are thus
placed completely outside the existence of the political community
(defined in terms of the fatherland, and the purity of the race) and stripped
of the possibility of any positive value. Because they are placed outside the
proscription against murder, they are deprived of human right (for example
protection in law) and divine right (the sanctity of life) and their execu-
tioners are relieved of all moral and criminal responsibility for their murder
(Agamben 1998: 8; Bauman 2005: 161).

In many ways, Agamben's analysis of Nazism is continuous with the one
proposed by Foucault in the final lecture of the 1975–6 series (2003: 239–
64). Here the notion of race first acts as a way of dividing populations
between those whose lives are worthy of living and those whose lives are
not and, secondly, makes the quality of the life of the former dependent on
the killing of the latter (Foucault 2003: 254–5). Nazism takes this logic,
born of colonization and imperial war, to another level. Foucault describes
it as an 'absolutely racist State, absolutely murderous State, absolutely
suicidal State'. The superimposition of these gave rise not only to the
genocide of the Jews and others but also the orders for the destruction of
the life support for the German people in April 1945 (Foucault 2003: 256).
In the introduction to the *History of Sexuality* he summarizes the way two
very distinct 'regimes of power' were constitutive of Nazism:

> Nazism was doubtless the most cunning and the most naïve (and the
> former because of the latter) combination of the fantasies of blood and

paroxysm of a disciplinary power. A eugenic ordering of society, with all that implied by way of extension and intensification of micro-powers, in the guise of an unrestricted state control, was accompanied by the oneiric exaltation of a superior blood; the latter implied both the systematic genocide of others and the risk of exposing oneself to a total sacrifice.

(Foucault 1979a: 150)

Such a description might be viewed as a special case of the general framework we elaborated in Chapter 4. Here the biopolitical management of life acting in the name of racial hygiene, disciplinary practices in the family, procreation, education and everyday life, and a sovereign power rooted in the symbolics of blood, soil and fatherland, are combined, recoded and reinscribed in a very definite way. This underlines the point about the heterogeneity of power relations, they way they combine in various regimes, and the manner in which they recompose each other in different recombinations.

The question remains whether we can ever feel protected from the bloody potentialities of sovereignty and the ever new forms of biopolitics (whether in contemporary genetics and the technologies it makes possible, or in biomedicine and the ethical dilemmas its presents). For Foucault, or at least for some of his followers, as we saw in Chapter 4, the liberal arts of government often appear to offer us a safe haven from the most bloody excesses of these powers of life and death in contemporary liberal democracies. For these societies, such an argument would run, place limits on such powers first in the name of the exercise of economic freedom now projected onto a global scale, and secondly through the assertion of human rights and the rule of law.

Agamben's provocation is quite the opposite. The evidence: that the figure of *homo sacer* enters into the political domain of contemporary liberal-democratic societies in, for example, the reappearance of detention camps for refugees, and the confinement of 'unlawful enemy combatants' in such prisons as those found at Guantánamo Bay (Cuba) and Abu Ghraib (Iraq) in the early years of the new century. This kind of provocative approach can be summarized as follows.

Agamben regards sovereignty as a kind of originary political figure which has its roots in ancient Greek and Roman conceptions of political community. This rests upon a structure of inclusion and exclusion: an inclusion of *bios*, or the moral and political life of a community and the exclusion of *zoē*, or bare life. The two concepts of life are present in Aristotle's assertion that 'the good life then is the chief aim of society but men come together for the sake of life merely' (1957: 201). Sovereignty is a kind of limit or threshold concept which both transforms bare life into the good life and leaves bare life outside the political order in a relation of 'exception', a concept betraying some relation to Schmitt. The problem of contemporary politics is not that political power has finally taken hold of

life at the end of the eighteenth century, following Foucault, but that *zoē*
and *bios* have become indistinct. Questions of bare life, coded as birth, that
is, 'nativity', and its etymological derivative, 'nation', and of human rights,
have flooded the juridical and political order and are linked to the crisis of
the old hidden order, or *nomos*, of politics. Such a crisis is manifest in the
figure of the refugee, on the one hand, and the camp on the other. The
camp as the place of the inclusion of the excluded bare life in the legal–
political order becomes the biopolitical *nomos* of modernity.

The camp in this sense exemplifies our current world order and the
manifestation of the crisis induced in it by globalization. In this respect
Agamben's perspective on the inability of the nation-state to inscribe life
within itself as citizenship is not far removed from the narratives of the
decline of the nation-state and the critique of society as 'container' in
writers such as Ulrich Beck. However, rather than leading to the latter's
cosmo-democracy, the crisis of the nation-state leads to a recharged
sovereignty. The problem for the contemporary nation-state is that 'it
enters a period of permanent crisis and the state decides to undertake the
management of the biological life of the nation directly as its own task'
(Agamben 2000: 42). The appearance of the camp is 'the sign of the
system's inability to function without transforming itself into a lethal
machine'. Because of this crisis, the state of exception, which used to be
invoked only on specific occasions to maintain the security of the sovereign state or to protect democracy, has itself become generalized as 'the
dominant paradigm of government' (Agamben 2005: 2).

According to Agamben, the old political distinctions between war and
peace, civil and foreign war, and war and police action cease to have any
meaning. After the first Gulf War, Agamben argues, 'sovereignty has finally
been introduced into the figure of police' (2000: 104). Domestic law is in
disarray due to its incapacity to inscribe life within the nation-state.
International law is in equal disarray as it too enters into a global state of
exception in which war is no longer legally conducted war between
sovereign states but a police operation outside international law which
criminalizes and then seeks to eliminate the enemy (Agamben 2000: 105–
6). 'Such an operation', asserts Agamben (2000: 106), 'is not obliged to
respect any juridical rule and can thus make no distinctions between the
civilian population and soldiers, as well as between the people and their
criminal sovereign, thereby returning to the most archaic conditions of
belligerence'.

Liberal or social-democratic cosmopolitans like Beck (2000a) and
Habermas (2000) would first support a conception of a new form of just
war undertaken to combat genocide and gross human rights violations
and secondly seek to reinscribe this new just war within a regime of
cosmopolitan law. Agamben takes the opposite tack. He sees the current
criminalization of the enemy, and war as police in service of rights, as a part
of the problem rather than its solution. Instead of trying to force the state of
exception presented by the current world order back within a legal frame-

work, and to assert the primacy of legal norms and human rights over sovereignty, he argues we must try to keep them apart, and to free the hold of law on life in an effort 'ceaselessly to try to interrupt the working of the machine that is leading the West toward global civil war' (Agamben 2005: 87). While Beck and Habermas accommodate critique to a new form of just war which emerges with the crisis of an international order built on state sovereignty, Agamben takes the much more radical option of seeking to abandon law altogether.

In this respect, Agamben seems to present just as totalizing a view of the present as the narratives of globalization and cosmopolitan governance he would otherwise appear well placed to contest. Moreover, his continuous historical narratives of the relation between science and politics are equally all-encompassing. For example, his view suggests that the practices of contemporary biomedicine have a direct heritage in the eugenics of the early twentieth century and are hence linked to the practices of racial hygiene of the Nazis. For those such as Nikolas Rose (2001), such an approach would be of very little help in respect of the analysis of complex issues concerning 'etho-politics', or a politics in which life itself and its quality is at stake, which is at least partially conducted from below, that is, by those who seek to control fertility and pregnancy and to enhance and prolong their lives by using biomedical technologies, pharmaceuticals, surgery and medical know-how. Far from a state-controlled management of populations, Rose suggests, this new etho-politics entails a self-shaping and self-judgement by individuals in a relational dialogue with experts in a kind of fuzzy zone between coercion and consent in which choice is guided and shaped. It is thus reasonable to conclude that Agamben misses out on much of what is characteristic of contemporary or advanced liberal forms of governing.

Similarly, in relation to contemporary geopolitics, Agamben analyses power relations in their rawest manifestations and tends to generalize from there. He focuses on the re-emergence of the 'camp' in the contemporary world in the detention of refugees (1998), the way in which military interventions become police actions in the name of a just cause (2000), the treatment of 'enemy combatants' in US prisons at Guantánamo Bay, and the curtailment of rights and democratic freedoms to provide security against the threat of international terrorism in the Patriot Acts and Presidential Military Orders (2005). Just as his biopolitical outlook allows very little for the complexity of the current politics of life, including the aspirations of individuals and families to better their own lives, so too his geopolitical outlook refuses the public debates in which practices of detention, counter-terrorism and security are contested, and the process by which detention is subject to legal procedures, juridical and administrative review and norms of human rights. He similarly fails to analyse the multiple uses and forms of military action, including the possibility that peace-keeping and certain deployments of police could exist in close proximity to concerns about establishing the rule of law and acting in accord with the international human rights regime (Dean 2006a). He also ignores the larger issue of a new sphere of action and humanitarian intervention which has emerged with the organizations of what some have called transnational civil society.

Nevertheless, I submit, there is another way in which we can read Agamben. If, rather than a total explication and critique of the present, we read Agamben as offering an analysis of certain zones of power, such as sovereignty, and its configuration in domains of constitutional law, philology and philosophy, then I suspect there is much more we can do with his work. Agamben then becomes someone who offers an argument more to do with the irreducibility of sovereignty than the necessary over-determination of all bio- and geo-political orders by the most violent and bloody dimension of it. In our present context, Agamben can thus be approached as offering a powerful, if flawed, counter-narrative to the ones of globalization, governance and cosmopolitanism we have met throughout this book. Foucault once suggested that the potentiality of the recombination of different zones of power made 'our societies' really 'demonic' (Dean 2001). Agamben can be read as an extension of the question of the demonic potential of such arrangements.

Conclusion

The discussion of sovereignty in critical theory leads us onto fiendishly difficult intellectual terrain and to conclusions that contradict and offend our civilized sensibilities. The preceding discussion proposes, however, that it is grounded in a right of death which can be suspended, retracted and derogated within certain domains and delegated onto other agents. This right of death enables the states that have emerged over the last three centuries both to secure a peaceful domestic order and to negotiate the possibility of international peace and order. However, as radicals such as Agamben and Foucault remind us, this sovereign right is also deeply problematic, particularly when combined with modern technologies, knowledge and forms of power such as biopower, to divide populations with respect to life, and to place some outside the frame of legal and moral right.

In the work of such thinkers as Agamben and Foucault, sovereignty is a complex and irreducible mechanism of inclusion and exclusion which is constitutive of the political, which operates in law but exceeds it, and whose ontology is thus bound to that of violence as much as law. In this regard, Agamben has provided us with an important elucidation of the concept of sovereignty *pace* narratives of its decline or displacement consequent upon globalization. And against the imagery of networks and flows, he gives us the notion of the concentration camp as the paradigm of the present crisis of the nation-state.

Foucault locates the emergence of a biopower or power over life in the eighteenth century, which is in many respects the opposite of sovereignty.

Agamben, by contrast, discovers a politics of life within ancient ideas of sovereignty itself. I wish to defend neither of these bipolar narratives in which sovereignty is displaced by biopower (Foucault) or 'bare life' becomes indistinguishable from the good life (Agamben). Sovereignty must be torn apart from such narratives and analysed in its diverse historical forms. However, I do wish to draw the conclusion that within contemporary regimes of power, sovereignty enters into zones of contact with the 'productive' powers of contemporary societies, such as disciplinary power and biopolitics. Indeed, if we follow Agamben, it sometimes enters into 'zones of indistinction' with such powers. What is important from an analytical point of view is that sovereignty and other powers change as they enter into new figurations of power, they reshape and recompose each other and combine and recombine in new and different forms. One of the fundamental tensions of liberal ways of governing society noted throughout this book is the way the liberal attempt to shape freedom, choice and aspiration through the deployment of expertise, law, ethical regulation and administrative procedure meets and recomposes but does not dissolve the sovereign decision on matters of life and death. In fact, as I shall argue in Chapter 8, accounts of contemporary liberal governing need to understand the force of the sovereign power of decision which is embedded in particular regimes of power and practices.

To do this, however, it is necessary to reiterate the other argument of this chapter. That is: while sovereignty has been historically identified with the territorial state as a supreme power within a given domain, it is also able to be dispersed onto different agents in various situations and for different ends. Sovereign power, as the power to decide on life and death, is delegated to various agents, arrogated by others and derogated within certain domains, as we have seen. The call to decision arises at multiple and unpredictable sites, as too does the exception, to which we now turn.

State of exception

○————————————————————————————————

The most provocative view of contemporary governing under current
global conditions has been put forward by Giorgio Agamben (2005: 2–3),
who claims that:

> Faced with the unstoppable progression of what has been called a
> 'global civil war', the state of exception tends increasingly to appear as
> the dominant paradigm of government in contemporary politics. The
> transformation of a provisional and exceptional measure into a
> technique of government threatens radically to alter – in fact, has
> already palpably altered – the structure and meaning of the traditional
> distinction between constitutional forms. Indeed, from this perspec-
> tive, the state of exception appears as a threshold of indeterminacy
> between democracy and absolutism.

The question of the exception in contemporary governing appears to
pick up on two key issues which have emerged in the course of our earlier
discussions. The first is the question of authoritarian liberalism raised in
Chapter 5. Does the diagnosis offered by Agamben, encapsulated in the
final sentence, offer us any assistance in the formulation of that problem?
The second is the issue of the imbrication of sovereignty within practices,
procedures and rationalities that might be described as liberal, biopolitical
or governmental. Can we use the problematic of the exception to clarify
and further our understanding of this relationship?

I first return to Schmitt's discussion of sovereignty to understand the
now classical reference on the exception. Schmitt's work is characterized
by two tensions which parallel one another: the first is between his personalist and institutionalist conceptions of sovereignty; the second between
his idiosyncratic and sociological conceptions of the decision. I then discuss
Agamben's arguments on 'the state of exception' and follow his application

of the concept to the one example he considers paradigmatic of contemporary politics, Guantánamo Bay, or, more broadly, 'the camp'. This will enable us (in the following chapter) to consider the relations between the decision on the exception and administrative process, government, expertise, law, and even normal life, in the US detention facility located there. It will also allow us to review the position that the 'camp' is the exemplar of all social and political relations in the contemporary world and to give further consideration to how sovereignty is embedded in liberal ways of governing and how the sovereign decision on the exception operates across a range of styles of contemporary liberal rule – some of which might be better described as authoritarian.

Sovereign exception

In 1922 Schmitt thought he had cracked the precise notion of sovereignty when, basing himself on a reading of Jean Bodin's chapter 'Of the true marks of sovereignty' rather than his canonical definition, he asserted, 'Sovereign is he who decides the exception' ([1922] 1985b: 7). There is something stunning in the simplicity of this formulation and it no doubt gives us a conceptual leverage on the kind of issues raised in the previous chapter. While Bodin ([1576] 1992: 58–9) argued that the 'power of making and repealing law' and of receiving law from no one but God is the power that subsumes all of the rights and prerogatives of sovereignty, he did pay particular attention to the 'right of judging in the last instance [or final appeal] (*dernier resort, extrema provocatio*)' ([1576] 1992: 67), and it is here perhaps we can glimpse Schmitt's argument that to be supreme within a particular domain is to be the locus of a final decision. For Schmitt ([1922] 1985b: 13), the sovereign '. . . has the monopoly over this last decision. Therein resides the essence of the state's sovereignty, which must be juristically defined correctly, not as the monopoly to coerce or rule, but as monopoly to decide.' The reference and critique of Max Weber's definition of the state is clear. So too is the personalist identification of the sovereign with an individual – a particular *he*.

Schmitt's formulations give rise to a series of well-known paradoxes. The sovereign both constitutes law and is constituted in law. The sovereign is a part of the legal order and yet outside it. Most importantly, the formulation stitches together the sovereign naming of the exception and the sovereign acting on the decision. The sovereign decision includes naming the situation as one of 'extreme peril, a danger to the existence of the state', an 'extreme emergency', of which 'the precise details . . . cannot be anticipated . . . nor can one spell out what may take place in such a case . . .' (Schmitt [1922] 1985b: 6–7). For Bodin, he argues, the indivisibility of the prince's sovereignty beyond either the estates or the people is linked to these conditions of 'urgent necessity'. Under them 'the authority to suspend valid law . . . is so much the actual mark of sovereignty' (Schmitt

[1922] 1985b: 9). The sovereign decision combines a sovereign nominalism with the decisive authority to take action on the part of a particular person.

But this nominalism goes even further. To be sovereign might be to guarantee public order and security but it also consists 'in determining definitively what constitutes public order and security, and in determining when they are disturbed' (Schmitt [1922] 1985b: 9). Above all, the sovereign, in deciding the exception, 'definitely decides when the normal situation actually exists' (Schmitt [1922] 1985b: 13). The sovereign not only names and decides the exception but in doing so names and decides the normal.

Schmitt is clearly thinking as a legal theorist and these passages on sovereignty reveal him at his most personalist and decisionistic, that is, he is proposing a framework that emphasizes the decision as a kind of personal and ruptural event. At this stage in his thinking, Schmitt ([1922] 1985b: 18–22) distinguishes between two types of legal thinking: a normativist one, where sovereignty is viewed as a unity of given legal norms, and this decisionist one. In the preface to the 1934 edition of this same book (1985b: 3), however, Schmitt adds a third type of legal thinking, an institutional one, in which law and legal thinking arise from institutions and modes of organization. After World War II, in *The Nomos of the Earth* (Schmitt [1950] 2003), sovereignty will come to be grounded in the concrete spatial order of a community, its *nomos*, which has acts of land-appropriation or land-taking (*Landnahme*) and later appropriations of sea, air and industry, as its precondition. The *nomos* will link the taking of land (*Landnahme*) with the exception (*Ausnahme*) or taking of the outside, the '*ex-capere*' in Latin. (Agamben will pick up on on these common derivations of the German words.) Some have maintained that this insistence on the basic character of land-taking represents a symptomatic link with the Nazi concept of *Lebensraum* or 'living space' (Diken and Lausten 2005: 39). My own view is that it is more symptomatic of the inability of modern European political and social thought to imagine any other kind of *nomos* than one involving the settled community and cultivation of the soil, and thus the lack of recognition of the claims of nomadic and indigenous peoples to sovereignty and land ownership. While Schmitt recognizes the possible etymological link between *nomos* and nomad ([1950] 2003: 326, n.4), he regards the latter word as derived from the Greek *nome*, which meant 'grazing or wandering in search of pasture', and thus as preliminary to a land-appropriation.

The institutionalist thinking of the concept of *nomos* is not, however, so much an alternative as a contextualization of the sovereign decision. Thus, in Schmitt's discussion of what he regards as the first (and only) truly global *nomos*, that expressed in the early modern European international law, the *jus publicum Europaeum*, the global order is constituted as a relation between formally equal sovereign states which has as a corollary the 'de-theologization' and de-moralization of war between such states (see

Schmitt [1950] 2003: 156–7). In such an institutional framework, it is the sovereign, and no third party, who decides the juridical rights and moral legitimacy of its own cause. Within such an international institutional order, sovereigns decide to abolish the question of right from international (more precisely, inter-*state*) affairs including the notion of war from just causes (*bellum ex justa causa*), and leave it to one another to decide on the justness or rightness of their own causes.

There is a further tension between the idiosyncratic and sociological aspects of Schmitt's notion of the decision as a decision on the state of exception. In *Political Theology*, Schmitt argues ([1922] 1985b: 13) that the exception escapes all codification and derivation from and in terms of norms or procedures. It is that which 'cannot be subsumed' and 'defies general codification'. It is a specific juristic element, 'the decision in absolute purity'. He continues (Schmitt [1922] 1985b: 15) that in 'the exception the power of real life breaks through the crust of a mechanism that has become torpid by repetition'. He quotes Kierkegaard, who states that:

> The exception explains the general and itself ... If they [exceptions] cannot be explained, then the general also cannot be explained. The difficulty is usually not noticed because the general is not thought about with passion but with a comfortable superficiality. The exception on the other hand thinks the general with extreme passion.
> (Kierkegaard, quoted by Schmitt [1922] 1985b: 15)

The Danish philosopher might be read, of course, as simply offering a radical version of the plea for an idiographic rather than nomothetic social knowledge found in thinkers in the *Verstehen* or interpretative tradition. As his catchphrase 'he who decides the state of exception' suggests, however, Schmitt is concerned to locate the decision within a definite decision-maker.

Schmitt ([1922] 1985b: 9–10) nonetheless realizes that the decision has definite sociological forms: 'Public order and security manifest themselves very differently in reality, depending on whether a militaristic bureaucracy, a self-governing body controlled by the spirit of commercialism, or a radical party organization decides when there is order and security and when it is threatened and disturbed.' In later work (Schmitt 1993) he will follow Max Weber in linking the emergence of particular forms of decisive authority and their capacity to name central antagonisms to social, cultural and technological conditions. Schmitt's sovereign is far from the classical sovereign of Bodin. Under conditions of liberal, constitutional democracy the position of sovereign is much more contested and much more likely to be one that is arrogated by a particular actor in a given situation. On the basis of Schmitt's jurisprudence, there could thus be a political sociology of the conditions of the arrogation of the right of final decision.

Schmitt's presentation of sovereignty clarifies Foucault's discussion of modern domestic rationalities of government in an important respect.

Foucault (1991a: 95) juxtaposes the 'self-referring circularity' of sovereignty as found in Samuel von Pufendorf to the productive arts of
government derived from 'reason of state' thinkers and the German
cameralists who succeed in giving content to the achievement of public
order and security. Foucault is correct to identify these latter intellectual
formations as contributing to modern rationalities of government.
Schmitt's point, however, reminds us that such observations cannot write
sovereignty out of the picture and that sovereignty cannot be dismissed as a
barren and empty way of thinking about rule whose concern is nothing but
its own augmentation through producing obedient subjects and eliminat-
ing threats to itself. For Schmitt, the sovereign decides not only what the
ends of government are but how to understand such ends and the practical
content when applied to life. A discussion of the various rationalities of the
government of the state, including liberalism and biopolitics, cannot avoid
sovereignty as a structure of decisions that define the thresholds at which
order and security obtain and how they are to be applied to life. Modern
powers over life and individual and collective conduct (that is, biopower,
discipline and government/governance) cannot do without sovereignty
when it comes to the government of the state. Moreover, they cannot do
without sovereignty when it comes to questions of life and death.

Further, where Foucault tends to identify a government of life and the
living as a feature of distinctively modern *biopolitical* formations, Schmitt's
view of sovereignty already contains a notion of a power concerned with
life. He writes that '[e]very general norm demands a normal, everyday
frame of life to which it can be factually applied and which is subjected to
its regulations ... For a legal order to make sense, a normal order must
exist, and he is sovereign who definitely decides whether this normal
situation actually exists' (Schmitt [1922] 1985b: 16). As a corollary to the
definition of sovereignty in terms of the exception, sovereignty is a set of
decisions on what this normal everyday frame of life is and whether or not
this normal frame of life is effectively operating.

The implication of this view is that the sovereign structure of law refers
not simply to a juridical and political order or a power that is external to
law but to how life itself is captured or taken by law. Thus Schmitt shows
how law already refers to a normal standard of existence. 'The law has a
regulative character and is a "rule"', he writes, 'not because it commands
and proscribes, but because it must first of all create the sphere of its own
reference in real life and *make that reference regular*' (Schmitt [1922] 1985b:
26, original emphasis). The sovereign aspect of law as a decision on the
state of exception both frames real life and normalizes or regularizes its
relation to that life. The sovereign decision is not thus on the margins of
governance and its normal and normalizing workings. It penetrates and is a
condition of every effort to render life governable.

The tension between the personalist versus institutional view of sovereignty and the legal order is useful in that it emphasizes the sense in which
an institutional order can be delegated onto or arrogated by individual

persons as its agents. From the perspective of the European international legal order the sovereign is a moral person who has been delegated specific right within its own territorial domain and is bound by specific rules in its conduct toward other such moral persons. The tension between the idiosyncratic and sociological dimensions of the decision is also important to maintain because it reveals how the radically undetermined character of the decision can still be shaped within forms of expertise, paradigms of conduct, legal precedent, wise counsel, and so on. While what is exceptional cannot be known in advance, and the decision itself is unpredictable, we can analyse how the necessity of the call for decision is made within given forms of knowledge and expertise and in different practices and how the decision is devolved onto various agents.

There is much to be learnt from Schmitt. We would be giving him too much credit, however, if we allowed his sovereign nominalism to pass without raising some questions. Certainly his strongest claim is that the sovereign decides the exception and *thereby* decides the normal. If this is taken to mean that the sovereign decides the normal as it does the exception then this is surely making too large a claim. Any basic understanding of norms would want to distinguish between legal norms, technological norms, organic or vital norms and social and cultural norms (cf. Canguilhem 1991). Schmitt would seem to elide legal and social norms in a kind of sovereign overreach. Thus while it might be said that the sovereign can decide when a normal legal order exists, it does not readily follow that he thereby decides what constitutes a 'normal' social existence. The definition of the latter opens up the field of normalization in the knowledge and practices of the social and human sciences, approaches to education, the 'psy' knowledges, and so on (Foucault 1977). Moreover, across the different fields of social, technological, medical and biological knowledge, the concept of norm itself varies: from an agreed-upon standard (for the measurement of medicines), to those of healthy organic function (of heart rate, blood pressure and so on), to a prescribed conduct of life (e.g. one of work and self-responsibility). Norms can be in opposition to the abnormal or pathological (for example, sane versus insane) or in a continuum with it (for example, fluctuation of the value of currency in relation to other currency). Schmitt's version, by contrast, of the normal/exceptional couple remains locked into a dichotomous, either/or logic. He both ignores the specification of social norms by disciplinary practices and forms of expertise and freezes the normal into a single side of a dichotomy. If the governmentality perspective misses the sovereign decision imbricated within regimes of practices, Schmitt misses the normalizing practices that surround the exception.

The tension between Schmitt's personalist/decisionist and sociological/institutional elements thus has parallels in the attempt to tease out the role of the sovereign decision in contemporary liberalism and its regimes of practices in healthcare, policing, and so on. Against Schmitt's statism, I would suggest that there are many mundane, routine, institutional practices and procedures which do rely on sovereign decisions devolved to political and legal persons and which are, to use another term, 'derogatory' of state sovereignty. These decisions are made within *various* normalizing frames and the exceptions thus generated, but the agents of such decisions are not necessarily state agents and the normalizing frames are not ones decided by the sovereign. Among these decisions are the various delegations and institutionalizations of sovereign decisions on the life that can be killed without committing homicide, to return to Agamben. Indeed, I shall characterize authoritarian liberalism as a way of governing that delegates and arrogates the sovereign decision while simultaneously annihilating its exceptional status by trying to convert it into the norm – examples include the treatment of 'enemy combatants', the enactment of counter-terrorism policing, or current biomedical interventions. The political sociology of authoritarian liberalism seeks the intelligibility of the relationship between sovereign decision, norms, persons and institutional practices. In order to do this, however, we must call into question the assumptions that the sovereign decision is exercised by the executive arm of the state, and that the only source of the normal is that generated by the decision on the exception.

The next steps in my argument are first to consider Agamben's interpretation on the state of exception as a technique of government and his understanding of the camp as the 'biopolitical *nomos* of modernity'. I then follow Agamben's application of this notion of the 'camp' to the US detention camps at Guantánamo Bay.

Agamben and the exception

After surveying these passages from Schmitt's work in the Weimar Republic, Agamben presents himself, perhaps unjustifiably, as going somewhat further than Schmitt himself ([1932] 1998: 28):

> If the exception is the structure of sovereignty, then sovereignty is not an exclusively political concept, an exclusively juridical category, a power external to law (Schmitt), or the supreme rule of the juridical order (Hans Kelsen); it is the originary structure in which law refers to life and includes it in itself by suspending it.

The 'force of law', then, at least for Agamben, is that it holds life in its 'ban' by abandoning it. The relation of exception is one of the ban: in abandoning bare life, the law does not merely put it in a sphere of indifference, but rather leaves it 'exposed and threatened on the threshold in which life and law, outside and inside, become indistinguishable' (Agamben 1998: 28). To be banned is to be placed outside the juridical-political order that defines the normal frame of life of a political community. But in the act of being placed outside this order, who or what is banned is included in the power that places he, she, them or it there. This act gives content and validity to that normal frame.

To be abandoned means to be placed in a position where law has withdrawn and where one is exposed to death. *Homo sacer* is the originary figure of life taken in the sovereign ban which recalls the original exclusion of bare life (*zoē*) which founds the political community (Agamben 1998: 83). This figure may be manifest as the traditional object of the ban, the bandit, or as the exile. Like them, Agamben concludes (1998: 183–4), he 'is pure *zoē*, but his *zoē* is as such caught in the sovereign ban and must reckon with it at every moment, finding the best way to elude or deceive it. In this sense, no life, as exiles or bandits know well, is more "political" than his.'

As a locale in which the 'naked' or 'bare' life produced by the breakdown of the nation-state is taken or captured outside (*ex-capere*) the normal life of the political community and juridical order, *the camp* is the very spatial and material manifestation of this state of exception. It is the 'fundamental biopolitical paradigm of the West' (Agamben 1998: 185).

Yet the camp is even more than an exemplar of political or power relations in a civilization. Its topographic structure is for Agamben the structure of contemporary *nomos* or world order itself and the crisis introduced into it by the crisis of the nation-state. One might observe that most visions of world order are founded on geopolitical cartography – Huntington's (1996) mapping of the 'clash of civilizations' is a recent example; the antithesis of land and sea in classical European international law after Grotius would be another.[1] Others might be based on historical teleologies such as Fukuyama's 'end of history' (1992) or even globalization theses. Agamben's concept of *the camp* acts as a kind of riposte to both these tendencies: it is an intensive rather than extensive spatial concept and its assertion disrupts narratives of the ever-widening sphere of commercial and political freedom. The camp is a rhetorically loaded counter-concept against the claims of a movement to cosmopolitan citizenship and global civil society, on the one hand, and the paradigmatic status of the transnational corporation and the city (the 'cosmopolis') itself. Moreover, for Agamben, the camp will be found in very different locales including football stadiums, zones within international airports, and even housing estates: 'if the camp consists in the materialization of the state of exception and in the subsequent creation of a space in which bare life and juridical rule enter into a threshold of indistinction, then we must admit that we find ourselves virtually in the presence of a camp every time such a structure is created' (Agamben 1998: 174).

Against extensive visions of the geopolitical order, Agamben asserts that the camp is the 'new biopolitical *nomos* of the planet' (Agamben 1998: 176, 2000: 42–4). By this assertion Agamben makes a claim about world order conceived as the concrete spatial character of the global political community. In so doing, he takes issue with the institutionalist, post-World War II work of Schmitt. For the latter (Schmitt [1950] 2003: 47–8), the first corollary of the idea of *nomos* as a concrete spatial order is 'law as the unity of order and orientation'. As such, every *nomos* presupposes land-appropriation or land-taking and it is on land that human communities orient and order themselves. While we might reject the blindfold of the philosophical anthropology underlining this view, we can accept it as a component of modern European perspectives on space. Under the *jus publicum Europaeum*, for instance, the concrete spatial order of the Earth is conceived first of all as a division between the territories of state sovereigns, and, more fundamentally, in terms of the antithesis between the 'engraved and embedded' element of land and the characterless (as in 'scratchless') element of the sea – *terra firma* and *mare libre* (Schmitt [1950] 2003: 42–3). Such international law is further premised on the division between the sphere of European law and the free spaces for conquest and competition found in the New World.

The particular order of modern political existence is thus condensed within the sovereign European state and its orientations to the rest of the world – colony, free lands, free seas, territorial waters, protectorate, and so on – are based on its territorial status. *Nomos* is thus a fully spatialized concept. Now, Agamben argues that Schmitt has failed to connect this concept to his earlier work on sovereignty as a decision on the state of exception. He argues that *nomos* not only entails land-taking (*Landnahme*) but also a 'taking of the outside', an exception (*Ausnahme*) (Agamben 1998: 19). However profound this linking of exception and land-taking, Agamben is mistaken and concedes as much (1998: 36), when he notes that this relationship between *nomos* and its constitutive outside is already found in Schmitt's passages on the way early agreements between sovereigns drew global lines on the face of the Earth to determine where European law no longer held or which divided the Earth between the Catholic powers and later between Catholic and Protestant powers. The Spanish–Portuguese '*raya*' and the Anglo-French 'amity line' are key examples of what Schmitt calls 'global linear thinking' ([1950] 2003: 87–99).

In the most general sense, sovereignty, for Agamben, needs the exception in order to function. A sovereignty exercised over a territory inhabited by a nationally identified population requires the exception as 'the creation and definition of the very space in which the juridico-political order can have validity' (Agamben 1998: 19). The camp responds not to a need to control and discipline the excess masses, as in the 'great confine-ment' analysed by Foucault, but to the need of the sovereign state itself to assert the validity of its control over a territory.

But, it might be asked, why the camp? Why not some other kind of exception? After all, for all their systems of confinement, and their spec-tacles of punishment, the absolutist states of the classical period did not invent the camp. It was the liberal constitutional and imperial states of the late nineteenth and early twentieth centuries, among them Great Britain in South Africa and Spain in Cuba, that appear to accept that dubious honour of the invention of the concentration camp.

Agamben's response links the exception back to the question of life. Contrary to Schmitt, he argues that the *nomos* of early modern European law is thrown into crisis along neither of the dimensions of the legal order identified in the first corollary cited above, that is, in neither order nor orientation (or localization). Rather *nomos* is thrown into crisis along a third aspect of the modern state, neither state, nor territory, but birth. For the nation (with its etymological linkage to 'nativity') seeks to inscribe human life within itself in its concept of citizenship by virtue of birth. The existence of ethnic populations and their denationalization in Europe in the early twentieth centuries, including the Nuremberg Laws on Reich citizenship, and the more recent attempts at controlling the flows of refugees, stand as evidence of how the nation-state must turn itself into a lethal machine to inscribe life within itself. 'To an order without localization (that is, the state of exception during which law is suspended) corresponds now a localization without order (that is the camp as the permanent space of exception)' (Agamben 2000: 43). Under contemporary conditions, the exercise of sovereignty which seeks to inscribe life within the nation-state needs the camp to assert and to justify its sphere of legal validity.

Giorgio in Guantánamo

There is something compelling about Agamben's counter-intuitive diagnosis of modernity as having 'the camp' as its exemplary organizational form. For those living in liberal democracies, the camp as an institution has a way of creeping up on us. It emerged in recent years as a way of dealing with the 'problem' of those seeking refugee status. The camp has moved to headline status after the beginning of the War on Terror in late 2001 and has now entered into the iconography of the critique of American power. Among the chief of such icons are the orange overalls or jumpsuits worn by prisoners at Guantánamo Bay and the pictures that revealed the scandal of Abu Ghraib.[2] Some of the latter, such as ones of naked prisoners being threatened by barking dogs, could appear as the definitive illustration of Agamben's thesis of the confrontation of sovereign power and bare life.

After 9/11 the United States launched a war in Afghanistan against the Taliban regime whose government was accused of harbouring the al-Qaeda terrorist organization led by the men held responsible for the terrible events of that day. In January of 2002 many of those captured by US forces in Afghanistan were transported to detention camps for 'unlawful enemy combatants' sited at Guantánamo Bay. The latter had been a naval base on Cuba occupied by the USA since 1903 pursuant to a permanent lease with the Cuban government which gave the USA 'complete jurisdiction and control' over a forty-five square mile area while Cuba retained 'ultimate sovereignty' (Johns 2005: 616). In the early 1990s Guantánamo had been used as a facility for the interdiction, detention, processing and possible repatriation of some 36,000 Haitians and 20,000

Cubans seeking asylum in the United States. From 2002, it has been used to hold terrorism suspects, some of whom were captured in Afghanistan. The number of such detainees is relatively small. Several estimates put the number at a little over 500 in 2005. According to the United States Department of Defense, as of 7 November 2005, some 256 had been moved out, 180 on release and 76 transferred into the custody of other governments.[3]

Guantánamo Bay is only one of the facilities in which the USA currently holds what Amnesty International estimates are 70,000 detainees around the world. They are held in Bagram and Kandahar airbases in Afghanistan, Camp Bucca, Abu Ghraib, Camp Cropper and others in Iraq, and in the cells of foreign governments acting at US request. Some are subject to secret transfers or 'renditions' to third countries and some are held in undisclosed CIA locations. As Neal (2006a: 44) has put it, Guantánamo appears to act as 'an object for domestic and global public consumption'. This is so in the case of popular film (for example, Michael Winterbottom's *The Road to Guantánamo* in 2006) or in the case of ongoing media stories such as that of the Australian David Hicks, or the failure of US military policy under Secretary of Defense Donald Rumsfeld. It has come to stand for the practice of US exceptionalism, and even the exceptionalism of the George W. Bush presidency within the US, and it functions in Agamben's discussion as standing for contemporary exceptionalism more generally.

As we noted at the beginning of this chapter, Agamben (2005: 2) has continued his provocative line of analysis by arguing that, faced with the unstoppable progression of global civil war, the state of exception tends increasingly to appear as the dominant paradigm of government in contemporary politics. As a consequence the state of exception has moved from 'temporary and exceptional measures into a technique of government'. Although Agamben (2005: 3) references the contemporaneous use of the notion of a 'global civil war' in Schmitt and in Hannah Arendt, he does not bother us with a consideration of the concept. However, it would appear to invoke a diagnosis in which war has escaped its classical representation as a formally declared and conducted war as a duel between sovereign states – that is, the 'war in form' of the *jus publicum Europaeum* (Schmitt [1950] 2003: 141). This European interstate war sought to put an end to civil war, war within states, and to externalize and thus limit war by making it a form of action between states. A 'global civil war' can only be inferred from a situation in which international law has broken down. War is no longer conducted by states for national interests but, like a civil war, in the name of a just cause (*ex justa causa*), which, in principle, implies that there is no limit to war. War is no longer conducted for national purposes but for international ones.

The more immediate context is given by the post-9/11 Presidential Orders and the USA Patriot Act which leave the status of those captured in the War on Terror in a kind of legal 'limbo'. Agamben argues that the effects of the Presidential Military Order of 13 November 2001 on the

inmates of places like Guantánamo Bay are the following: 'Neither prisoners nor persons accused, but simply "detainees", they are the object of a
pure *de facto* rule, of a detention that is indefinite not only in the temporal
sense, but in its very nature as well, since it is entirely removed from the
law and from juridical oversight' (Agamben 2005: 3–4). Guantánamo then
would be a space outside law in which those detained are objects of a kind
of arbitrary rule rather than subjects of a legal process. For Agamben, the
stripping of the legal status is even more radical than the Nazi death camps:
'The only thing to which it could be possibly compared is the legal
situation of the Jews in the Nazi *Lager* who, along with citizenship, had lost
every legal identity but at least retained their identity as Jews', he proclaims
(Agamben 2005: 3).

For Agamben (2005: 3), 'what is new about President Bush's order is
that it radically erases any legal status of the individual, thus producing a
legally unnameable and unclassifiable being'. Those captured in Afghanistan are thus neither prisoners of war under the Geneva Conventions nor
even criminals under US law. Their detention is entirely outside the law.
The camp, as he told us in *Homo Sacer*, is a place of *de facto* rule where what
actually happens becomes law (Agamben 1998: 170–1). In the camps, he
says, citing Arendt, 'everything is possible'.

Agamben (2005: 6) goes on to cite a number of authors who are the
'heralds who announced what we have before our eyes – namely that "the
state of exception ... has become the rule"', that is, who are heirs to
Benjamin's claim in the eighth of his *Theses on the Philosophy of History*.
Among these texts is Clinton Rossiter's *Constitutional Dictatorship* ([1948]
2005), which Agamben cites (2005: 9) in evidence of the view that
democratic regimes have undergone a fundamental change during the
world wars of the twentieth century and the following period. Rossiter
states ([1948] 2005: 297, 313) that in the Atomic Age 'constitutional
emergency powers may well become the rule and not the exception' and
that measures such as 'executive dictatorship, the delegation of legislative
power, and lawmaking by administrative decree ... may eventually in all
countries, become lasting peacetime institutions'. This is how, according to
Agamben (2005: 28), we must view the actions of President Bush, who
refers to himself constantly as the 'Commander in Chief of the Army' in
order to claim sovereign powers to meet the emergency and is thus
'attempting to produce a situation in which the emergency becomes the
rule, and the very distinction between peace and war (and between foreign
and civil war) becomes impossible'.[4]

If the camp is the new *nomos* of the planet, then Guantánamo Bay is one
of its most recent and disturbing materializations, a place of normless
exceptionalism beyond the law, geographically and legally separate from
the national territories of the United States. But the assertion of a sovereign
exceptionalism is tied to the transformations of US domestic law and
foreign policy within which the executive has arrogated to itself emergency
powers to confront a condition of necessity afforded by the War on Terror.

The relationship between law and state of exception in Agamben is complex and in some ways contradictory. On the one hand, the force of the critique of the camp, and of Guantánamo Bay, gathers its momentum from the notion of a state of exception beyond the law. The state of exception is 'a place devoid of law, an anomic zone in which all legal determinations – and above all the very distinction between public and private – are deactivated' (Agamben 2005: 50). He can thus excoriate all those including Schmitt who tie the state of exception to the defence of the juridical order. On the other hand, it is only because it is juridical in form and effect and nourishes the law that it is a vital scene for the development and deployment of governmental techniques. The law, according to Agamben, thus employs the exception 'as the original means of referring to and encompassing life'; the state of exception must address 'the relation that binds, and, at the same time, abandons the living being to law' (Agamben 2005: 1).

A more limited critique of Agamben is that the association of the 'global civil war' with the breakdown of international law needs some qualification and reconsideration. One could point to the efforts of many international lawyers, through the adoption in 1977 of the second additional protocol to the Geneva Conventions and in other international law initiatives, to ensure that civil war remains within the reach of international norms. The more recent effort to instantiate a new right of humanitarian intervention as an exception to international legal prohibition on the use of force against another state, and the related argument that a state's legitimacy on the international plane is contingent upon its remaining responsive and attentive to the basic needs of its citizens, might be regarded as a further example of this inclination. This is to say that a recharacterization of war as no longer a prerogative of states directed toward each other need not be associated with the breakdown of international law. Rather this reframing might be regarded as making possible a new round of legal renewal and reform efforts.

It is telling that Agamben makes little reference to Schmitt's writings on international affairs and remains fixed on his early Weimar work and with excavating, however interesting, the subterranean debate between Benjamin and Schmitt on the state of exception. Indeed, where the question of *nomos* reappears in Agamben's work in *State of Exception* (2005) it is derived from this debate and from the pair *nomos*/anomie. If we were to draw upon these later writings what would we find that was relevant to this discussion of Guantánamo? If we have taken Giorgio to Guantánamo, we might ask Carl to join him there for a while in the knowledge that it is the latter who had direct experience as inmate of both Russian and later American camps after World War II.[5]

Schmitt, as we have seen, noted the effects of the breakdown of international public law and its law of war from the early twentieth century. This breakdown had its technological correlate in the development of airwar and the disorder and disorientation this introduced into traditional theatres of war. Airwar renders obsolete the notion of a battlefield relatively separate from civilian populations and defined by a front. More importantly, airwar dissolves the relation between the 'occupying' military personnel and the civilian population (Schmitt [1950] 2003: 320–1). The pilot drops his bombs and leaves, or today an operative might 'pilot' a drone aircraft from a distant command centre. Schmitt would note the replacement of the just enemy with new kinds of absolute enemy, and the displacement of the war in form, the war legally conducted between sovereign states, with a new kind of total war between all sorts of different actors. He would also note that war is no longer morally 'bracketed' and has become a new form of just war often undertaken to defend not only moral values but religious doctrine. There is a kind of parallel between the new 'discriminatory' kind of war which regards the enemy and its population as 'troublemakers, criminals and pests' and the lack of relation between occupier and a civilian population made possible by aerial bombardment.

Guantánamo Bay would appear then, in this framework, to be the result of a new kind of just war conducted against those who, by their action or association, place themselves beyond the reach of not only law but human morality and decency itself and who would conduct attacks on civilized peoples not in the form of war undertaken by sovereign states but by shadowy networks. The War on Terror is a war against a new perfidious non-state enemy who by its actions has been conducting an undeclared war, an aggressive war, against civilized humanity. There is a new moralization of war and thus a new 'discriminatory concept of war' (Schmitt [1950] 2003: 321). Those captured in such a situation do not bear the markings of the soldier of the standing army and cannot be treated as such. Moreover, because they have placed themselves outside the regulatory framework of states and war, and are willing to conduct operations by all kinds of unpredictable means, such as witnessed on 9/11, they can be treated outside the law of war. Further, this status, which is even beyond that of the criminal states that harbour such organizations, forms the legal foundation of the use of interrogation practices to gain information which will provide humanity protection against their malfeasance. Such tactics as the legal redefinition of torture, the outsourcing of interrogations to third parties not subject to US law and Western values and practices such as human rights, and the use of psychological and medical expertise to extract information, all find their justification in this new kind of enemy. The War on Terror thus emerges as a new and frightening kind of just war, a new kind of total war, a new war on annihilation which knows no legal limits because of its vilification of the enemy as an absolute enemy.

The value of placing Guantánamo Bay and its like within the historical framework of the transformation of war is that it allows us to link the treatment of the prisoners there back to the exception. The prisoner, as absolute enemy, is placed/places himself outside the pattern of behaviours and beliefs that could be expected of the just enemy who shared with his opponent an agreed set of rules of the conduct of war. War is not simply a contestation between two parties within an agreed framework of civility and hostility and a common value framework but a life and death struggle between those who would defend civilization and even humanity and those who would seek to annihilate both. The implication of this from the point of view of those engaged in a just war is not to completely annihilate the enemy or that 'anything goes' but that it might be necessary to suspend liberal values in the defence of them – the very condition analysed by Rossiter. This is the moral conundrum of those conducting a War on Terror. Secondly, because the absolute enemy does not play by the rules he represents not only a danger but a totally unpredictable danger, characterized by his shadowy and secretive networks. Who after all could foresee 9/11? And isn't the very fact of suicide bombing a transgression of accepted rules of war and evidence of a set of impossible-to-understand values? Much of what we know has occurred to the inmates of Guantánamo underlies this moral conundrum and experience of unpredictable and uncertain danger in this condition of just war.

As a by no means entirely sympathetic international lawyer has put it, 'readers have been struck by the expressive force of his [Schmitt's] critiques of American policies and attitudes' (Koskenniemi 2004: 493). While Agamben is willing to apply Schmitt's concept of *nomos* he makes no systematic address upon the thesis of the *Nomos of the Earth*, nor Schmitt's writing in the 1950s on the new *nomos*. In an essay of 1955 entitled 'The new *nomos* of the Earth' ([1950] 2003: 351–5), Schmitt signals three possible orders after the Cold War. The latter acts as a kind of interregnum between the old and new *nomos* and would defer the question of the new world order for some half a century (until the Presidency of George H. W. Bush in fact). The first would be that one party to the Cold War would be victorious and would act as the sole sovereign of the world. The second would be a new balance of land, sea and air administered by the United States taking over the role of Britain as the 'greater island that could administer and guarantee the balance of the rest of the world' ([1950] 2003: 355). The third would be a world of several independent regional blocs, or *Großräume*.

Something of each can be detected in the present. At times the USA acts like the sole sovereign and is hence unbowed before any international law. Guantánamo Bay, Abu Ghraib, and the practices of the 'rendition' of terror suspects to third states, as well as the 'torture memos', would appear to confirm this interpretation. The notion of balance would place the USA in a position of guarantor of order for the rest of the world. The debate between a cosmopolitan and pacific European view of world order and the realist American view has been read as the irresolvable tension between those who provide security for the current world order and those who most benefit by it (Kagan 2002). And finally, the period of the end of the Cold War has corresponded to the period when the USA nervously awaits and tries to forestall the emergence of a global competitor in the East, whether Japan in the 1980s and early 1990s or China in the early twenty-first century.

Now all of these alternatives are representations of a possible *nomos* and we have the difficulty, and the privilege, of living in uncertain times. At times, American policies and politics act in terms of the second *nomos*: consider President Clinton's engagement with his European NATO allies in Kosovo in 1999 in the name of human rights and the prevention of genocide. In more recent times, in the post-9/11 world, the USA has acted like the sole sovereign of the world, acting out a blueprint which was already written by the authors of the Project for the New American Century (2000).

Schmitt would of course think that – compared to the issues involved here – Agamben's characterization of the camp as the new *nomos* of the Earth is somewhat risible. Specific camps, such as Guantánamo Bay and Abu Ghraib, could be viewed as manifestations of the assertion of American sole sovereignty. Detention centres for the interdiction, processing and repatriation of illegal immigrants would be viewed less as the materialization of a state of exception and more as means for the defence of leaky territorial sovereignty. The strength of Agamben's notion of the camp, as we see, is to remind us of the ignominious history of the last century in which liberal constitutional and democratic states invented the concentration camps that found their terrible culmination in the Nazi death camps. From our perspective, the trope of the camp disrupts the smooth flow of globalization theory. However, it does nothing to address the difficult questions of world order and international law and the basis on which the latter might be framed. This does not mean that Schmitt offers us a superior solution to such questions despite the force of his critique. His universalization of the European spatial outlook, his dogmatic 'grounding' of the key concept of *nomos* in land-taking, his apparent nostalgia for the *jus publicum Europaeum*, and his totalistic rejection of what we might call humanitarian military intervention mean that we must look elsewhere for a more pragmatic, nuanced and secular view of contemporary international law to which international lawyers could contribute (Koskenniemi 2004: 507).

One might want to note that Agamben is not as radical as he would seem in his appreciation of Guantánamo as having the status of 'a state of exception' beyond national and international law. This is a view shared by many international lawyers and judges and seems to have reached to the ranks of journalism. Both Lord Steyn of the House of Lords (2004) and a judgment of the English Court of Appeal refer to Guantánamo as a legal black hole, a term also used in a *Newsweek* report (Barry *et al.* 2004). Other international lawyers refer to it as a 'legal no-man's land', a 'place beyond the law', an 'exceptional rights-free zone' (Johns 2005: 620). In her foreword to *Amnesty International's 2005 Report*, the Secretary-General restated this view in slightly different terms: 'The detention facility at Guantánamo Bay has become the gulag of our times, entrenching the practice of arbitrary and indefinite detention in violation of international law. Trials by military commissions have made a mockery of justice and due process' (Khan 2005).

There are two jurisprudential responses to such a situation (Johns 2005: 621–3). For many lawyers the response is to seek to subject this space of lawlessness to the law or to some legal body such as the courts of the United States or the United Kingdom, the Inter-American Commission on Human Rights and the United Nations' Working Group on Arbitrary Detention. For others it is to redefine the law in such a manner as to fit the circumstances and the necessities after 9/11.

For Agamben, neither of these responses are the answer for both lead back to law and the legal order. In his view it is necessary to finally sever the hold of law on life and 'ceaselessly to try to interrupt the working of the machine that is leading the West toward global civil war' (Agamben 2005: 87). The agents of such disruption and their means are nowhere specified.

Conclusion

The purposes of this chapter are primarily expository. Starting from Agamben's provocations about the state of exception as a technique of government, I have sought to explicate his position and its roots in Schmitt's theory of sovereignty. This proves a difficult task given the many paradoxes of this definition of sovereignty, and the tensions between a personalist and institutional account of sovereignty and idiosyncratic and sociological approaches to the decision on the exception. These tensions, however, are useful because they keep in focus the way sovereignty can be exercised through moral and legal persons, on the one hand, and yet be enmeshed in expertise, law and regulation, on the other. Critically, I focus on the overreach of Schmitt's sovereign nominalism when he claims that it is the sovereign that decides not only the exception but the norm. Such a critique serves to underline the claim that the sovereign decision needs to be analysed as a component of different regimes of practices, a point developed in the next chapter.

I explored Agamben's concept of the state of exception through his understanding of the camp as the *nomos* of modernity (of which Guantánamo Bay becomes the exemplar) and as a site of normless exceptionalism. I find that he poses contradictory relations of the state of exception to law. The state of exception, he claims, is both radically outside the law and yet legal in form and nourishing of the law. I argue that recent legal developments have undermined his argument that what we have is a 'global civil war' as a symptom of the breakdown of international law. Agamben's view of the camp certainly shares much with contemporary legal and popular criticism of Guantánamo as a black hole outside the law. Despite Agamben's use of Schmitt's legal theory, a much more interesting understanding of the nature of current military conflict is given by Schmitt's genealogy of war and peace with the collapse of the *jus publicum Europaeum* and the re-emergence of notions of just war, the absolute enemy, and so on.

I want now to evaluate Agamben's view of 'the camp as the new biopolitical *nomos* of the planet' by, first, examining the practices of Guantánamo Bay with the help of two recent critical commentaries from international law and international relations perspectives and then applying what we learn to a range of contemporary governing practices. Such an examination will enable us to make some broader points about styles of contemporary liberal rule and exceptionalism without lapsing into the sociologism of Agamben's camp followers.

Contemporary liberal exceptionalism

According to Agamben, the camp is a spatial structure of exclusion which simultaneously asserts the legal validity of territorial sovereignty. It first made its recent reappearance, if it ever went away, in liberal democracies in the form of 'detention centres' for refugees and illegal immigrants. However, its most notorious recent examples include the facilities housing 'unlawful combatants' in the War on Terrorism which included Abu Ghraib and Guantánamo Bay and others. There are no doubt many other camps found outside Western liberal-democratic nations (or beyond their effective jurisdiction) but the scandal associated with the ones mentioned concerns the fact that their existence is justified by the very values and practices that they appear to violate at every turn. This is particularly the case when we read the infamous US Government 'torture memos' which advised on lifting the legal threshold of actions that constitute torture and attempted to quarantine captives from the most elementary legal rights including the right to be publicly charged of a specific crime and have one's case heard by an independent tribunal (Greenberg and Dratel 2005). The scandal is intensified further by the practice of 'extraordinary rendition' whereby detainees are flown to third-party locations 'beyond the line', as Schmitt might have said, of respect for human rights and international law.

The practice of 'rendition' directly links the detention camps of the West with the torture practised by countries without any avowed respect for human rights. More broadly, the practice of torture by the United States of America can be viewed as acting as an exemplar to the rest of the world. As the Secretary General of Amnesty put it:

> The USA, as the unrivalled political, military and economic hyper-power, sets the tone for governmental behaviour worldwide. When

the most powerful country in the world thumbs its nose at the rule of law and human rights, it grants a licence to others to commit abuse with impunity and audacity. From Israel to Uzbekistan, Egypt to Nepal, governments have openly defied human rights and inter-national humanitarian law in the name of national security and 'counter-terrorism'.

(Khan 2005)

In regarding 'the camp' as an exception outside the law, Agamben joins hands with human rights activists and liberal lawyers in his critique of Guantànamo and similar institutions but, as we have seen, he breaks with them in that he does not share their faith in the project of bringing them back into the rule of law. There is no doubt that the appearance of such camps, and those in which refugees are detained, is a disturbing feature of contemporary liberal-democracies and a feature of their government. However, as I now show, it is important not to allow this insight to be overblown into claims that the camp is 'the new biopolitical *nomos* of the planet' (Agamben 2000: 44) or 'that the *logic* of the camp tends to be generalized throughout the entire society' (Diken and Lausten 2005: 5, original emphasis). The first assertion would appear to so enclose *nomos* within the camp as to occlude the possibility of a discussion of the political, legal, economic or social conditions of contemporary world orders and international law. The second stands as a good if colourful example of the way in which sociological discourses on contemporary modernity tend to reduce the present to a single logic, principle or thematic. Whatever the virtue of such positions as counter-narratives to mainstream social and political discourse, they are open to exactly the same accusations of hubris and empirical unsustainability. The figure of contemporary liberal gov-erning is neither the network nor the camp: although both tell us quite a bit about it.

Against – and to some extent with – such positions, we can say that there is much to learn from the experience of specific kinds of detention centres. Not only is there no single paradigm of the planet today or logic of society, there is probably no single form or paradigm of 'the camp'. However, the analytics of governmental practices and forms of power within particular camps can illuminate much. My purpose here is thus a limited one. It is to contribute to understanding of how practices of rule operate in con-temporary liberal democracies, especially ones entailing the operation of sovereignty, by examining and drawing upon two possible and very dif-ferent lines of argument and critique concerning Guantánamo Bay con-structed in response to Agamben (Johns 2005; Neal 2005a). I argue that what is interesting about Guantánamo is not that it provides the hidden key to the logic of power or even of society but that it provides us with clues about how sovereignty can be imbricated within distinctive governmental regimes in liberal democracies. As such, this discussion nourishes our understanding of what I have earlier called authoritarian liberalism.

Assemblage and decision

The first line extends the view put forward in Chapter 4 that power relations and practices of rule can be multiform, composed of hetero-geneous elements, and open to different forms of combination. Rather than the camp as simply an instrument of a publicly declared state of exception linked to the exercise and defence of sovereignty, we can approach particular camps as a combination of diverse practices and rationalities in which multiple zones of power interact to a point of 'indistinction'. Here I follow Andrew Neal (2006b: 189; 2005a) in iden-tifying what he calls the 'novel recombination' of sovereign, disciplinary and national elements in the practices and the rationalities associated with Guantánamo Bay. The camp in this sense has no essential form: it has a history of transformations and mutations and is a site invested with multiple purposes. It can be turned to different ends and invested with different political purposes. It can be a site of aspiration, investment and opportu-nity. It can be a labour camp with enforced work for the workshy and unemployed, a concentration camp for political prisoners, a detention centre for processing the claims of would-be refugees, and a death camp for the extermination of inferior races. For the guards, their supervisors and administration staff, the camp can also be a training facility, an institution of career advancement, a place of consumption, and a place to live.

One of the most disturbing things about the camp is *not* that it can have many forms (transit camps, collection camps, processing centres, labour camps, concentration camps, gulags and ghettoes) and subjugate different populations (POWs, refugees, political prisoners, forced labourers, those regarded as sub-races), and subject them to different treatment (forced labour, discipline, torture, mass murder). It is rather the way in which the camp has shown a relatively unpredictable capacity to switch from one function to another. Guantánamo Bay has moved from a processing centre for asylum seekers to a prison for unlawful enemy combatants in the War on Terror over a period of ten years.[1]

However, probably the most interesting thing about the camp today is its replication of all that is usually conceived as opposite to the exception (Johns 2005: 616). Guantánamo has its own schools, power systems, supply and transportation systems, its fast-food franchises, gyms and college. It is 'small-town America', according to its base commander. In it, excep-tionalism is located at the heart of 'mainstream' liberal normality.

Neal bases himself on the Report on the 'Tipton Three', a condensed summary of the evidence provided by three former British Guantánamo detainees (2006b: 194–5; Rasul *et al.* 2004). This report is also the basis of the recent film *The Road to Guantánamo*, released in 2006. First of all, Neal identifies elements of the legal procedure and forms of punishment more akin to the medieval criminal process of monarchical sovereign punishment described by Foucault in *Discipline and Punish* (1977). These include the secrecy of the criminal procedure to the accused, the opacity of the rules of truth governing the investigation and the symbolic affirmation of the sovereign. In such a process, Foucault puts it (1977: 42), suspicion is the 'mark of a certain degree of guilt as regards the suspect and a limited form of penalty as regards punishment'. The experience of those at Guantánamo appears to resemble such a process in that the detainees were not told of what they were accused within repeated and often repetitious interrogations by different organizations including the US Army, the FBI, CIA and MI5. The objective of such interrogations was to extract a confession irrespective of whether it would meet any legal standard of proof or serve any discernible juridical purposes (Neal 2006b: 196). Further, interpreting 9/11 as a symbolic crime against the sovereign, the investigatory practices of Guantánamo could be viewed as the sovereign taking revenge for an affront to its person and the exercise of its right to make war on its enemies (Foucault 1977: 48; Neal 2005a). However shrouded in mystery, Guantánamo Bay could also be viewed as a spectacle which manifests 'the dissymmetry between the subject who has dared to violate the law and the all-powerful sovereign who displays his strength' (Foucault 1977: 48–9).

Neal (2006b: 199–201) also finds elements closer to Foucault's well-known account of discipline. This is a place of 'enclosure' of course. It is also an extreme form of 'partitioning' and 'cellularization' in two-foot square fully observable mesh cages. There is the observation and even recording of every detail of behaviour and spoken word and even the control of movements within the cages. There appears to have been a hierarchical ranking system based on degree of cooperation. There are also micro-penalties of reward and deprivation around such items as blankets, towels, facecloths, toothbrushes, toothpaste and Styrofoam cups, all of which were considered 'comfort items'. Neal (2006b: 202) also emphasizes the politics of resistance in which apparently trivial actions such as scratching 'have a nice day' on the cup produces a fearsome response such as time in solitary confinement. There are limits to this disciplinary power, however, especially the lack of attempt at training and reform of the prisoners. In this respect, Neal (2006b: 26) concludes that what we witness at Guantánamo is the reverse process that Foucault detects in modern systems of punishment: rather than sovereign punishment being permeated by the network of productive new disciplinary power, 'a modern regime of disciplinary power has been permeated by a reawakened modality of sovereign vengeance and war'.

To imagine a particular regime of practices – such as the camp – as a combination or recombination of different strategies and techniques of power is not to imagine a stable and predictable set of outcomes. The different elements are shaped and reshape each other in unexpected ways. Moreover, this brief summary cannot do justice to the subtlety of what is clearly an analysis in development. However, one clear implication of this approach is that contemporary liberal exceptionalism is *not* an exception to extant and earlier forms of power but must be understood in terms of their functioning in a particular context.

Finally and most interestingly, at least in one version of his account, Neal (2005a), building on this insight, argues that the form of sovereign exceptionalism practised in places like Guantánamo is not a monarchical but, again following Foucault (2003), a *national* one. On this reading, the violation of 9/11 was not simply that of the taking of the lives of nearly three thousand people but a violation of national sovereignty itself. As G. W. Bush (2001) put it on television on that evening, what was abominable was not simply the ending of lives by despicable acts of terror but that 'America was targeted for attack'. As a result, a 'great people has been moved to defend a great nation'. What is at stake is not simply the body of the individuals murdered but the body of the nation under attack from evildoers. While it could be argued that America itself was never threatened by the attacks of 9/11 (unlike perhaps those of the Japanese on Pearl Harbor), its government certainly acted as if the imagined pristine body of the nation had been violated by these acts. In so far as the atrocities of 9/11 prompted the USA to act as if its sovereignty had been threatened and to convert the potentiality of sovereignty into the actuality of the two wars it has since conducted and the horrors of its camps, the 9/11 architects and conspirators have been eminently successful in exposing the excesses of *Pax Americana*.

Neal's argument is that the 'material functioning of contemporary exceptionalism' is a 'recombination of already-existing discourses and mechanisms of power'. To the sovereign, disciplinary and national discourses and mechanisms, I would like to add a further one: mediated electoral politics. While President Bush would proceed to a narrow victory in the 2004 election, we can adduce a better example.

That example concerns the refusal by the Australian government to allow the Norwegian freighter, the Tampa, to enter Australian ports with its cargo of boat people in August 2001 (described in the Introduction). The Australian Prime Minister, John Howard, said of his policy of intercepting boat people by the navy in his campaign speech: 'We have had a single irrevocable view on this, and that is we'll defend our borders and we'll decide who comes to this country' (Howard 2001). The solution to this crisis would be to look for an offshore camp beyond the jurisdiction of Australian immigration law and its consequent international obligations, which would be found on the bankrupt island nation-state of Nauru (Marr and Wilkinson 2004: 136–9). This was to be the Pacific Solution and among the models of such a camp would be Guantánamo itself, at least in its earlier incarnation as a refugee-intercepting and processing facility. The Australian example adds a further dimension to our discussion of sovereign exceptionalism. In the US case, the President is the sovereign head of state; in Australia, like the UK, the Prime Minister is merely the leader of the party or parties that form government and acts under commission from the sovereign, or the sovereign's representative in Australia's case. President Bush declared a national emergency on 13 September 2001, and later arrogated extraordinary executive powers under the Military Order of 13

November which were pursuant to this national emergency. The example of Prime Minister Howard is much more intriguing in the Tampa case. Here, he clearly decides the exception: refugees will be excepted from Australian territory by not being allowed to land on its soil; part of the Australian territory will be later excised from its migration zone by law (Marr and Wilkinson 2004: 202–3). So we have the similar suturing together of a kind of sovereign nominalism – to name an event as exceptional – and a sovereign decisionism – to take exceptional measures. However, Howard simply *speaks* the language of emergency – of border protection, of national sovereignty, of military and exceptional solutions – without actually declaring an emergency. How could he do this? How can an elected, formally non-sovereign official arrogate the right to name and decide an exception, without an officially declared state of emergency, while at the same time convincing enough voters to vote to return his government with a greater majority in parliament, particularly after lagging behind in the opinion polls only weeks before the election? And if there is any doubt that this issue was central to that election, consider that the poster and pamphlets for the Prime Minister's Liberal Party 'showed a resolute John Howard with his fists clenched, flanked by flags' (Marr and Wilkinson 2004: 365–6). The message read: '*WE* DECIDE WHO COMES TO THIS COUNTRY AND THE CIRCUMSTANCES IN WHICH THEY COME.' On the morning of the ballot, newspapers carried huge advertisements with Howard defending his country against the boat people and reminding voters that a 'vote for your Liberal team member protects our borders and supports the Prime Minister's team'.

So we can add to Neal's recombination of sovereign, disciplinary and national discourses and practices the possibility of an investigation into how the framing of issues as exceptional and acting decisively upon them is performed within the mediated politics of elections in liberal democracies. We shall return to this.

In any case, it is symptomatic that the word *decide* would appear in this election speech and that can act as a trigger for our second line of inquiry. The second line is this: that Guantánamo Bay does not exist in a domain of the evacuation of law, nor is it the materialization of a state of exception, but one that is densely overlaid with law, administrative procedure and review mechanisms which have the effect, as Fleur Johns has argued, of the 'annihilation of the exception' (2005). Thus not only is Agamben incorrect but so too are many international lawyers. We need, according to this argument, to question the 'black hole' assumption, that is, the assumption that 'there are no rights in Guantánamo' is the starting point for its analysis. Let us consider this view in a little more detail.

Johns argues (2005: 618) that far from a state of exception subject to a pure decision, Guantánamo Bay is a place 'filled to the brim with expertise, procedure, scrutiny and analysis'. The violence that occurs there is some distance from being a result of the existence of a juridical 'black hole'. Rather, '. . . the interactions of detainee and detainer in that jurisdiction are experienced as almost entirely pre-codified by the dictates of legal statutes. It is by this means ... that governmental violence is being effected' (Johns 2005: 627).

Among other pieces of evidence, Johns (2005: 630–1) quotes the description of these decisions by the Secretary for the Navy, Gordon England, speaking about the annual review process at a press briefing:

> There's no question there's judgment involved. I doubt if many of these are black and white cases. I would expect most are going to be grey ... I operate and oversee, organize the process, and I also make the ultimate decision ... we do have some guidelines ... the boards do have some guidelines. It will be a judgement based on facts, data available ... the best decision a reasonable person can make in this situation ... it's what is the situation today and going forward of a threat to America. And that is what we will decide, and that is what the decision is based on ... I believe the process is doing what we asked the process to do, which is to look at the data as unbiased as you can, from a reasonable point of view ... and I believe the process is working ...'

What emerges here is not a pure decision on the state of exception but the discussion of how a decision is 'cabined by broad policy directives, notions of reasonableness, and the institutional demand for standardization' (Johns 2005: 630). For Johns, the problem is in a sense the opposite of the one adapted from Schmitt by Agamben. It is not a case of the creation of a state of exception beyond the law but of the 'annihilation of the exception', a kind of evacuation of the responsibility entailed in the decision. The Navy Secretary, if we are to take his testimony at face value, is seeking to downplay the moment of decision. Johns (2005: 631) concludes her analysis of the Navy Secretary's briefing in which he explains a determination that a detainee was not an 'enemy combatant':

> This is not the language of Schmittian exceptionalism. Rather, it is suggestive of efforts to construct a series of normatively airtight spaces in which the prospect of agonizing over an impossible decision may be delimited and, wherever possible, avoided. As such, the jurisdiction at Guantánamo Bay is constituted, in Schmittian terms, in the liberal register of the norm ...

Johns's argument is extremely interesting because it demonstrates how law and techniques and rationalities of government are bound together in the decision on the detainees in Guantánamo. Thus there is an elaborate, multi-stage screening and evaluation process for each detainee involving, in the words of the public official responsible, 'an integrated team of interrogators, analysts, behavioural scientists and regional experts' working alongside lawyers and law enforcement officers (Johns 2005: 617). Indeed, the International Committee of the Red Cross has made claims implicating doctors and psychologists (the so-called Behavioral Science

Consultation Team informally known as Biscuit) in interrogation practices by advising interrogators on the state of detainees' health (Lewis 2004). The annihilation-of-the-exception argument would then meet the multiple-assemblage argument in that it allows us to view the practices of interrogation as a recombination of different kinds of powers, including those associated with the human sciences. Such a view would also be consistent with Darius Rejali's (1994) argument that modern forms of torture need to be viewed in relation to the techniques and expertise of the medical and behavioural sciences – of biopolitics.

The detainees at Guantánamo Bay have also, we should note, been given certain legal rights by the US Supreme Court in two rulings in June 2004 (Hamdi *et al.* v. Rumsfeld, Secretary of Defense, *et al.*; Rasul *et al.* v. Bush, President of the United States, *et al.*): first, to contest the factual basis of their detention before a neutral decision–maker; and second, to invoke the jurisdiction of US federal courts. In June 2006 (Hamdan v. Rumsfeld) it ruled that proposed Military Commissions were unauthorized by federal statute and violated international law. As a result of these decisions, the institutional network not only includes the work of an Administrative Review Board described above, and specially convened Military Commissions, but also a Combatant Status Review Tribunal established by the Deputy Secretary of Defense to determine whether they have been properly classified as 'enemy combatants', and the Military Commissions Act of 2006. 'Enemy combatant' has become a legal status which can be tested and has definite consequences. There is also an Office of Detainee Affairs to coordinate inquiries about the handling of detainees by US military police. From all this Guantánamo Bay is less a state of normless exception and more an example of an assemblage of expert know-how, techniques of administration, various courts and tribunals, and review processes.

For Johns, this is sufficient evidence to demonstrate that there is nothing like a decision in the pristine state – its 'absolute purity' – described by Schmitt ([1922] 1985b: 15). Nor is Guantánamo 'a space devoid of law, a zone of anomie in which all legal determinations ... are deactivated' (Agamben 2005: 50). Our two lines of inquiry join: the investigation of the juridical status of Guantánamo and the analysis into its material functioning demonstrate that it is a locale of intense legal and political contestation, procedure and review, of administrative process and human scientific expertise. What happens there can only be explained as a specific assemblage of sovereign, disciplinary, biopolitical, national, electoral and, yes, juridical, discourses and practices.

Does this mean that there are no decisions on the state of exception? Does it mean that such decisions have been so corralled by law, bureaucracy and expertise as to be unworthy of analysis? You will recall the tensions found in Schmitt's work between decisionist and institutionalist legal theory and personal and sociological accounts of decisive authority. From a legal point of view, there may be decisions that have a pristine character beyond legal precedent and where there is no pre-existent norm to follow. The extreme 'constitutional crisis' is perhaps the closest, such as the dismissal of a popular elected government by an appointed repre- sentative of the sovereign in Australia in 1975, or the US Supreme Court decision on the halting of the Florida recount in 2000. Even such cases invoke canons of legal interpretation and reasoning. However, from a sociological point of view sovereign decisions are made within definite institutional frameworks, mobilizing particular discursive and cultural elements, invoking fundamental constructions of friend/enemy opposi- tions, and operating within particular regimes of judging. Thus Australian Prime Minister Howard's declaration that 'we will decide who comes into the country' stresses a 'we' that condenses both his government and the Australian nation, and a 'them', first of all those seeking to enter Australia to gain asylum. The 'them' in this sentence will come to have multiple condensates: after 9/11, there will be a link between asylum seekers and terrorists. Paradoxically, the playing of the friend/enemy game will mean that the enemy in this sovereign political rhetoric will come to include both the Taliban regime and those who are fleeing from it, demonstrating that my enemy's enemy is not necessarily my friend. Fundamental to the maintenance of this opposition is the invocation of the language of emergency to an electorate both keen to appear humane and compassio- nate and intent upon preserving what it thought, and was constantly told, was a privileged (in this case, Australian) way of life. None of this – the electoral politics, the cultural and national values, not even the semiotic analysis of this utterance – can, however, deny that Howard had made a decision on the exception.

It would be a mistake, however, to think that Howard's decision utterly disregarded national law and international legal obligation. It was informed by his advisers based on legal advice. It works on the capacity of law to insufficiently prevent such decisions and their consequent actions. That such a decision and the statutes enacted to implement it could indeed be encompassed by law was confirmed by the Australian High Court's judgment in 2003 to refuse to strike down the so-called Tampa laws.[2]

As this example demonstrates, politics in contemporary liberal democ- racies is played out before an electorate with specific attributes including distaste for public and spectacular violence. Much of this electorate finds the use of violence consequent upon the state of exception repugnant and at the same time benefits from the definition of a form of life that the sovereign decision claims to defend. I use the word 'claim' here because the test of the efficacy of the sovereign decision on a state of exception in liberal democracies is not an objective standard of emergency or necessity but whether politicians can convince enough of their electorates that what they are doing is right. The capacity to convince of course would in turn depend on the values and norms of that electorate – and the entire insti- tutional and mediatized framework of political communication. The consummate politician of the emergency would be one who arrogated unto him- or herself the position of sovereign in Schmitt's sense, a position of decisive leadership while successfully appearing to give voice to the concerns of the people and nation through the various media. In the case of Prime Minister Howard, it was enough simply to enunciate the language of the exception without formally declaring a state of emergency.

My view is that the question of the state of exception needs to be understood against a contemporary authoritarian liberal-democratic electoral politics, played out as it is through the mass media and in terms of a largely two-party system. An executive declaration of an emergency, or even, as we have seen, a simple invocation of the language of emergency, is a claim for a radical 'securitization' of a particular issue which relies on a kind of 'aesthetics of horror' for its appeal to electorates (Buzan *et al.* 1998; Huysmans 1998). This certainly does not place actions outside law but it does relativize law and legal process in relation to fundamental security concerns. In the case of Guantánamo it has led to a recombination of different modalities of power including ones that seek revenge on an enemy for its defilement of the pristine body of the sovereign nation.

Still this process of securitization has its limits. If we invoke Norbert Elias's analysis of violence, we can see that the electorates to which the authoritarian liberal emergency must appeal are caught between a sociological and a political imperative. Sociologically, the sovereign decision, which can entail matters of life and death, is an abomination for much of the population and there is thus every attempt to suppress the 'necropolitical' character of such decision (Mbembe 2003). There is certainly a kind of denial of the full ramifications of the decision on the exception. On the other hand, politically, such electorates respond to the securitization of threat to the nation as a threat to their way of life (their *bios* in Agamben's terms) and thus may endorse strong action, including military interventions, when convinced of this threat or, via the media, subject to an aesthetics of horror (consider 9/11, the Bali, Madrid and London bombings). In order words, authoritarian liberalism is thereby constituted by a kind of tension between the popular distaste and liberal controls over the operation of legitimate violence and the recognition of the need for decisive action. While it might try to annihilate the sovereign decision and its attendant violence, authoritarian liberal rule is characterized by a sublimation of the decision onto various biopolitical, disciplinary, governmental and national discourses and practices, and as a necessary response to the threats to the security of national ways of life.

Against Agamben what we witness is not a permanent state of exception – such a notion would be meaningless anyway – but the interlacing of the techniques and discourses of the exception within specific assemblages of practices and power formations. The state of exception, whether formally declared or simply announced by employing a specific language, however much it punctuates the unity of the legal order, generates rather than evades legal contestation and review. Significantly, Agamben gives very little focus to the decision itself and its locale, which could prove very insightful.

In Schmitt's case, it might be argued that he is too fixated on the problem of the state and of state sovereignty and that, if we rid ourselves of that assumption, '... it is almost impossible not to conceive – as both political and exceptional – a much broader range of decisions, approached by or among a much broader range of events, aggregations or arrogations, than those which Schmitt entertained as such' (Johns 2005: 643). I would take this insight one step further: it is possible to conceive this much broader range of decisions concerned with human life and death as not only political and exceptional but as operations of sovereignty. What we see, according to this argument, is that every attempt is made to annihilate the exceptional and sovereign status of the decisions made at Guantánamo and to return them to the 'comfortable superficiality' of the liberal norm. The problem then is not that Guantánamo exists in a juridical black hole beyond the law but that there is an attempt to deny the operation of sovereignty as a decision on the exception which is its key *raison d'être*.

The point to make here is not that the legal norm has deprived the decision of its exceptional status *or* that sovereign decisions exist in a kind of pure, unmediated state entirely void of all normative considerations. Rather, we must accept the dual character of the sovereign decision. First, all forms of authoritative action and decision take place under definite historical, social and cultural conditions, are subject to particular administrative and procedural protocols, rely on certain forms of knowledge and expertise, and operate according to legal and quasi-legal norms of fairness and reasonableness. In other words there is no fundamental opposition between a decisionist notion of sovereignty and an institutionalist one, and the decision on the exception can be both personal and sociological. However, secondly, sovereign decisions on the exception, and on matters of life and death, cannot be reduced to expert knowledge, legal norm, or administrative procedure; they are circumscribed by such things but they are never wholly prescribed by them. To understand the operations of governmental practices is not simply to understand the expert knowledge that is deployed, the administrative procedure followed or the legal norm applied. It is to understand the place of the sovereign decision within such practices, and the derogation or arrogation, delegation or usurpation, of the right to exercise that decision.

The annihilation of sovereignty and liberalism

I think this last point can be made more broadly. The attempted annihilation of sovereignty, of the sovereign decision, and of the exception, in both mainstream contemporary social and political science and in governmental practice, replicates what we might view as a feature of liberal thinking and liberal ways of governing more generally. Consider another example: the case of therapeutic abortion subsequent to forms of prenatal or genetic screening mentioned in Chapter 4. While much of social and political science focuses on the annihilation of the territorial dimension of sovereignty in narratives of globalization and governance (see Table 3.1), here we shift our focus from the geopolitical back to the biopolitical. This case tries to annihilate the decision on an exception that actualizes a right of death.

Therapeutic abortion appears in relation to a process of risk assessment based on 'individual susceptibility'. Nikolas Rose (2001: 11) notes the following examples of the technology of such assessment: amniocentesis and the detection of abnormalities such as Down's Syndrome or in the number of X and Y chromosomes; chorionic villus sampling (CVS) and the detection of abnormalities in the DNA and the probabilities or certainty of a particular disorder such as Huntington's disease; genetic tests for a range of 'single-gene' diseases; tests for 'specific base sequences' which increase the likelihood of Alzheimer's, types of breast cancer and heart disease. Such technologies of assessment provide increased information to medical professionals, mothers and fathers prior to birth on the probability and risk susceptibility of a wide range of conditions. As Rose (2001: 12) then notes: 'While the calculation of risk often seems to promise a technical way of resolving ethical questions, these new kinds of susceptibility offer no clear-cut algorithm for the decisions of doctors or their actual or potential patients.'

What Rose has pinpointed in this statement is the relation beween life-politics (or what he calls 'etho-politics') and *decisions*. Indeed, given that these are decisions on a life deemed not to be worth living, or at least not worth living *with*, they are sovereign decisions. Given that such technologies and calculations lead to decisions on what level of risk is acceptable, or what kind of life falls within the normal frame of human existence, they are decisions on the exception. And, in deciding the exception, for example a life with Down's Syndrome, such decisions contribute very strongly to what constitutes a normal frame of life and, indeed, to what a population experiences as normal. They have a kind of self-confirming effect. The outcome of aggregated individual decisions might mean a population in which such children and adults are increasingly rare. In so far as certain of these technologies give rise to risk calculations as to susceptibility of certain diseases, then a normal frame of life comes to be defined in terms of acceptable levels of risk.

Decisions on the termination of pregnancy are no doubt very difficult and often troubling personal decisions and I do not wish to enter into the ethical debate here. However, at their heart is the kind of duality found in other cases of the sovereign decision on the exception. Here we find first a kind of horizon of promise for evasion, avoidance or subsumption of the decision on the termination of pregnancy by means of biomedical expertise, liberal norms, ethical procedures, forms of calculation and medical technologies. Thus the options presented are informed by different technical procedures, risk assessment and calculation, non-directive advice and dialogical relationships between a patient and her doctor and genetic counsellor, and so on. They may even take into account forms of collective action and identity, such as the movements of disability rights activists and groups. Such decisions are furthermore implicated in the advanced liberal norms of 'enterprising, self-actualising, responsible personhood' and become 'complex choices prudent individuals are obliged to make in their life strategies' (Rose 2001: 18–19).

On the other hand, however, if sovereignty is something that does not necessarily refer to the state but is an arrogation or delegation of the 'final decision' on an exception, then what faces the mother, parents or even professionals under such circumstances is a sovereign decision, a decision on 'the value or non-value of life', as Agamben might put it, or the exercise of a 'right of death', as Foucault would have said. In so far as this is a decision on killing – in this case a foetus – then it has something in common with the decisions made by police officers in everyday policing situations of when to use lethal force, and by governments engaged in military interventions for whatever purposes. In all such cases the decision on killing is 'cabined' by ethical regulations and even ethical values of the highest order, forms of expertise, particular kinds of technologies, modes of calculation, and so on. Indeed, all these decisions on killing can be associated with the highest values including the health, welfare, protection and security of the individual and the population, and the defence of human rights and prevention of genocide. In so far as the decision on termination of pregnancy is a decision on the exception, and on what therefore requires exceptional treatment, it exhibits the same features as the decisions on the detention of enemy combatants at Guantánamo. My argument is that these 'extreme' cases deserve the word 'decision' and deserve to be considered as a distinct kind of power which is irreducible to an advanced liberal rule through the shaping of choice, or a biopolitical concern to foster life. They are decisions on what it is necessary to do when confronted with what might be an exception to what is considered to be the normal form of life and of how to secure, protect and even enhance that life in the face of the exception. It is thus mistaken to follow Schmitt in the identification of the locus of the sovereign decision with the state. It is, however, important to recognize that the term *exception* can cover not only declared or undeclared emergencies but also the entire mass of exceptions to what are construed as the normal forms of life in contemporary liberal democracy, as we suggested in Chapter 5. It is the question of the decision on these exceptions that is raised by the multiple delegation, derogation and arrogation of sovereignty today.

Now, following Foucault, we would not want to limit the notion of sovereignty to a legal concept and to a discussion of the state and nor should we regard the exception as a purely legal concept. The virtue of Agamben's approach is that these concepts are broadened to encompass questions of the powers over life. However, just as sovereignty is neither limited to law nor to the state, as we have argued above, the exception cannot be restricted to a formally declared 'state of emergency' in which law is suspended and martial rule or emergency powers are brought into force. Agamben himself generalizes the notion of exception only by making the juridical state of exception a global and perpetual phenomenon, for example in his invocation of a global civil war. This kind of generalization simply deprives the concept of its dynamism in relation to the norm. If we follow Agamben, all we could say is that what first emerged as an exception has now become a new norm – hardly an earth-shattering insight. By contrast, I would suggest that the decision on the exception is present in every normalizing power and expert knowledge by which liberal forms of governing carve out the life of the self-determining individual (see Chapter 5).

What would distinguish styles or genres of liberal governing might be called the 'economy of the decision'. Perhaps we could say 'advanced liberal' ways of rule would operate through the shaping of the sovereign decision individuals make for themselves and their families such as in the right of individuals to make procreative and end-of-life decisions. It tends to derogate its sovereign power in such cases and to elide the decision with choice. Authoritarian liberal approaches, by contrast, might be ones that seek to reinscribe such decisions within the legal and authoritative framework of the state by denying access of certain categories of women (by age and sexual orientation, for example) to state medical insurance for IVF (in vitro fertilization) treatments and banning certain categories of abortion. They might attempt to limit the derogation of the sovereign decision (and its consequent violence) in such cases in the name of the sanctity of life while allowing certain delegations. For example, we have witnessed in the contemporary United States a politics that seeks to restrict the right to choose abortion or to disengage life-support systems (the Schiavo case) while creating new kinds of sovereign delegations such as that granted to police officers and to officials engaged in the War on Terror, such as air marshals. This latter style of liberalism might be called authoritarian liberalism. There is also a field of contestation within contemporary liberal democracies marked out by these two styles.

There are no privileged sites of the sovereign decision and, as I have argued throughout this book, liberal ways of governing are riddled with the sovereign decision and hence exceptionalism. We should not imagine that the call to decide has a privileged locus or loci, in the same way that Schmitt identifies it with the state. Rather than exhaustive, the following list is simply an inventory of some exemplary instances of the range of situations in which liberal norms of governing society can be viewed as entwined with sovereign decisions on the exception. These include:

1   The various states of exception allowed for and envisaged by constitutional law which include states of emergency, states of siege,

martial law, emergency powers, and so on. This is the classical state of exception of Schmitt and of Rossiter's constitutional dictatorship.

2 The possibility that states can claim exceptionality for themselves in an international context. A clear example of this has been the United States and its claim for exceptional status with regard to the International Criminal Court at the Hague, the Kyoto Protocol on greenhouse emission limitations, and the assertion of its right to conduct military intervention without approval by the United Nations' Security Council, and so on. In respect of the latter, other states in alliance with the United States, such as Britain, Australia and Denmark have also claimed this exceptionality.

3 The decision on the exception supported by expert knowledge of the human sciences within contemporary liberal-democratic practices of government. Such practices attempt to shape individual conduct by working on such aspects of the self as habits, disposition and character. In so doing they delineate, and continually redefine, the attributes of the autonomous citizenship and the normal form of life of the liberal-democratic social and political order (as we saw in Chapter 5). Such an order thus interweaves the governmental powers and practices that seek to shape the conduct of such autonomous or free individuals located within civil society with a mass of sovereign exceptions which define the space of various kinds of treatment, from training, therapy and discipline to punishment and imprisonment. In these cases, the exception is not a result of a generalized political crisis but something defined through the singular bodies of knowledge, observations and practices. These identify and act upon such things as problematic personal conduct from being workshy to bullying, pathological conditions from drug addiction to dementia, unsatisfactory performance in the workplace, and irresponsible, illegal and criminal identities from the deadbeat dad to drug trafficker. The normal frame of life would often seem to be nothing more than a kind of residue of the mass of exceptions.

4 The decision on the exception supported by expert knowledge of the life and biomedical sciences. Such exceptions include the brain-dead person or the foetus with abnormalities or a diagnosed susceptibility to certain diseases. Here we are again within a sovereign right to kill. While this decision remains overlaid with the aspirations and concerns of individuals, parents and family, with the counsel of experts, with the metrics of risk assessment, with the biotechnologies of testing and screening, and with legal restriction and ethical contestation and regulation, it nonetheless remains a decision on a life that it is judged not to be worth living.

5 A decision on the exception which warrants a radical revision rather than suspension of normal processes of law and the exercise of a right to kill in criminal matters or in response to security threats. The counter-terrorism legislation passed in many countries often presents

itself as a response to an urgent necessity without taking the form of a generalized state of exception.

Sovereignty, security and governing societies

To admit the possibility of an authoritarian liberalism as a feature of present practices and rationalities of governing society is to accept the continued salience of sovereignty and the decision on the exception in the contemporary task of governing society and to note transformations in the problematic of security. I have hence sought to sketch the place of sovereignty, security and the exception within various styles of government and note their implications for the task of governing societies in Table 8.1. If sovereignty is variously a right of death, a monopoly of the final decision and a rationality for the establishment of order, security might be broadly conceived as a concern with existential threats to life and a rationality for managing disorder. Security is a component of a rationality of government which is viewed as an ontological feature of contemporary human existence and which is germane to all domains that are conditions of human existence (Neocleous 2000). The 'delegation, derogation and arrogation of sovereignty' and the 'securitization' of all sorts of issues define the contours of key current problematics of governing societies.

The establishment of the territorial state bequeathed us sovereignty as the supreme power within a particular domain. State sovereignty is thus a condition and a limit of classical liberalism in that this territory bounds the process of civil society through which liberalism proposes to govern. Classical liberalism will approach the sovereign decision on the state of exception as a temporary suspension of law and its normal functioning and a response to a crisis threatening to its order (the state of emergency). As Rossiter showed ([1948] 2005), the sovereign may suspend the normal legal procedures and individual rights when faced with an emergency that threatens political order and democracy and invoke special security measures to manage that uncertainty until the cessation of threat, the restoration of order and, only then, the return to democracy. In this respect, special security measures are undertaken by agencies such as the police, the civil guard, special operations forces and the military. The key connective term, then, is the state of emergency.

Classical liberal styles of governing characterize as tyranny those who would seek to rule by emergency methods alone. The 'normal' business of governing is to put in place mechanisms that ensure the security of the necessary and nature-like processes that constitute civil society, including and especially the economy. These mechanisms would lead to such formations as the welfare state from the web of interventions and practices to support the processes and agencies of society. Citizenship would be conceived as a series of rights and obligations between the individual and state, between citizen and nation. Classical liberalism also depends upon the

Table 8.1 Sovereignty, security and governing societies

Styles or project of government	Sovereignty	Security	Key exceptions	Relation to project of governing societies
	Right of death. Monopoly of final decision. Establishing order.	Threat to life. Managing potential disorders, threats, uncertainty.		
Early modern establishment of the territorial state	Sovereignty as supreme power and as an end of government.	Techniques of the 'holding out' of the state against external and internal enemies, e.g. reason of state. Techniques of production of good order, e.g. police.	Civil war to be overcome.	Precondition for governing societies.
Classical liberalism	Condition of liberalism but to be limited. Establishes territorial enclosure of civil society.	Mechanisms of security within civil society. Relation to liberty. International vs domestic security issues.	Temporary state of emergency to be overcome to return to constitutional order.	Governing society as a container. Domestic and international security.
Advanced liberalism	Belief in supercession of national sovereignty. Annihilation of sovereign decision in choice.	Multilateral cooperation in face of global risks. Management of individual risk in life-planning.	Violations of human rights. Genocide.	World risk society. Cosmopolitan democracy. Governance.
Authoritarian liberalism	Strengthening states and international bodies to implement globalization policies. Exercising and delegating sovereignty.	Hyper-securitization. Pre-emptive intervention.	Mass of exceptions and practices defining normal frame of life. Creeping emergency.	Hierarchies and hegemons. Language of exception, necessity and emergency.

division between inside and outside, between the container-like pacific unit of domestic governing, where the multiple rationalities of social governing would flourish, and the world beyond it where each state or nation would pursue its own interests either by alliance, diplomacy or war.

The philosophy of neoliberalism and advanced liberal regimes of government claimed a supercession of sovereignty which was manifest in the processes of globalization that made the national state and national economy obsolete. The diminution of political authority would give rise to a new kind of rule, 'governance'. The new problematic of security would attempt to secure governmental mechanisms themselves – from the rule of law and controls on public expenditure to anti-corruption measures – to make specific regions of a global economy attractive to the flows of capital and investment. This new problematic is summed up by the phrase 'good governance'. For such programmes and styles of rule, citizenship would become a world citizenship without a world government, one in which individuals would have multiple identifications and allegiances, as much cosmopolitan and local as national. International security would mean defending the global economic order and intervening where universal human rights were threatened. The supercession of sovereignty on the international stage is accompanied by the sublimation of the decision by the construction of choices with the help and tutelage of experts and professionals found at the level of the individual, particularly in the domain of life politics. Life becomes a 'planning project' in the sense that the individual must plan and become the 'head office' of her or his own life and that it is up to the individual to make informed choices about life itself (Beck-Gernsheim 1996). At an international level, advanced liberalism promises a world without outsides, a world without exclusions and exceptions in a cosmopolitan order. The aporetic character of advanced liberalism, however, is demonstrated by the fact that it requires military intervention to defend a cosmopolitan order when faced with gross human rights abuses and genocide, and that, however sublimated, certain individual life-choices will remain decisions of the value of certain kinds of biological life. It produces the exception, the decision on the exception and the sovereign right of death in the very attempt to suppress or annihilate them.

Authoritarian liberal styles thus arise from the claims of advanced liberalism to have done away with sovereignty, including the territorial state, the decision and the exception. From its perspective, the 'new normal' of economic globalization and political cosmopolitanism did produce an outside: the losers in the processes of global economic competition, the criminals who would exploit globalization, and those who would attack it as morally bankrupt and politically corrupt. Authoritarian liberalism finds plenty of targets outside the cosmopolitan order: the fundamentalist, the terrorist, the drug trafficker, the people smuggler, the rogue state, the failed state, and so on. It finds plenty of exceptions, as we have seen. Authoritarian liberalism, as a programme and practice of rule, continues the suppression of the decision at the very same time that it sublimates it onto the mundane practices of policing, welfare and healthcare and proposes harsh solutions to the mass of exceptions generated by advanced liberal practices of rule. Moreover, it is not afraid to engage in radical securitization as a response to a mediated aesthetics of horror and atrocity which include pre-emptive military intervention, the restriction of due legal process, and the routine implantation of emergency measures. If Schmitt imagined a state of exception outside the law in order to return to law (as in classical liberalism), Rossiter a strictly delimited 'constitutional dictatorship' to preserve and return to democracy (in a robust liberal democracy), and Agamben the state of exception becoming the norm (in a global civil war), we must say that none has grasped the specificity of the contemporary authoritarian liberal style. The latter responds to its own processes of securitization with a creeping extension of emergency powers enunciated in the vocabulary of emergency, necessity, crisis, and so on. However, at its very core are the multiple delegations and arrogations of the decision on the exception and the implantation of the decision within the very fabric of normal life.

For an authoritarian liberal government, order is always 'at risk' and thus requires maintenance of close circumspection of individual and collective conduct. This entails the strict delegation of sovereignty onto multiple agents in everyday practices. Rather than, or in addition to, a formally announced 'state of emergency', states of exceptions are regularly invoked to enforce rapid legislative amendments, justify non-juridical detention, deportations of undesirables, summary use of lethal violence, and increased security forces. Given that existential threats and risks are held to be constitutive of living in the present, the task is to securitize as many domains as possible, by demonstrating that we must take extraordinary or exceptional measures.

We should make clear, however, that despite its reliance on sovereign powers and its tendency to hyper-securitization, authoritarian liberalism is not fascism. It relies on what might be called an 'aesthetics of horror', and fear of violent death, to compromise civil liberties and rights and to declare exceptional, extreme and urgent circumstances (Huysmans 1998). However, it neither celebrates a cult of death nor centralizes the right of death in the will of the leader, in the manner of fascism. Yet it is concerned to reinscribe freedoms and citizenship within obligation, authority and hierarchy, to employ coercive and punitive techniques on subpopulations of citizens and illegal aliens, and to defend society and homeland against personified threats in the forms of enemies. Authoritarian liberalism is a more or less coherent resultant of diverse practices and rationalities which are intrinsic to contemporary liberal forms of rule. This means that present approaches to governing societies cannot simply be viewed as an advanced liberal government concerned to shape and mobilize the aspirations, desires, choices and conduct of individuals and communities. Unfortunately, it has to be said, it has proved itself, even in its most benign and moralized forms, to be something more than that.

Conclusion

This chapter continues the discussion of the state of exception after Agamben exemplified by Guantánamo Bay. It uses two distinctive and pioneering studies to challenge the way in which exceptional practices and institutions such as the camp at Guantánamo Bay are in a state of norm-lessness outside law, administrative regulation, expertise and everyday life. I seek to show, following Andrew Neal, that there is plenty in the practices in this locale that activates and reanimates different techniques and rationalities of power – some sovereign, some disciplinary, and some national – and combines and recombines them in novel ways. Indeed, rather than being a radically undetermined decision on the exception, Guantánamo combines dense legal procedure and contestation, adminis-trative processes, policy directives, social and behavioural science expertise and indeed 'small-town' American normality, to seek an 'annihilation of the exception', as Fleur Johns puts it. I further these arguments by con-sidering the way in which exceptions are announced in the context of a liberal-democratic electoral system, given the 'civilizing process' which brings a popular distaste for the full ramifications of the exception and a widespread politics of security. I argue that authoritarian liberal rule is hence characterized by an annihilation of sovereignty broadly, and its decisionist elements in particular, a sublimation of the decision onto var-ious biopolitical, disciplinary, governmental and national discourses and practices, and a call to respond to the threats of security of a way of life.

I argue that these insights can be applied to contemporary liberal ways of governing more broadly. The latter is caught between the promise of the avoidance of the sovereign decision by sublimating it within expert advice, on the one hand, and the necessary delegation and arrogation of sovereign decisions, on the other. Such delegation and arrogation empowers specific moral persons from prospective parents to close family and from air marshals to police officers. I finally show how the division and exercise of sovereignty, its derogation, delegation and arrogation, the politics of security, and the vocabulary of exception, define key means of governing societies in contemporary authoritarian liberal rule.

Conclusion

I began this book by discussing the 'long twenty-first century' because I wanted to suggest that the first decade of the century appeared as a dense cascade of political events for those living both in what we considered 'liberal democracies' and those living outside their zones of safety and affluence. Controversial elections, terrorist actions, 'anti-globalization' protests and organizations, a focus on borders and their security, revelations about torture, the re-emergence of various kinds of camps, invasion and subsequent mayhem, forced into focus how we thought about politics and governing and the language with which we did so. While international events often dominated headlines, the treatment of subpopulations of refugees, the unemployed and welfare recipients, and public debates about aspects of minority culture, such as the clothing of Islamic women and gay marriage, scratched new lines of hierarchy, authority, obligation and exception across the putatively inclusive domestic surface of liberal societies.

I contend that much of mainstream social and political science and theory was unprepared for this long history and this has particular implications for how we might begin to rethink the topic of this book, 'governing societies'. I thus first sought to trace the historical conditions of the emergence of such a notion and to examine how that notion had fallen into disrepute.

The notion of governing societies, I have argued, had two major historical conditions which meant it was necessary to discuss both domestic and international sides of the question it posed. The first was the internal pacification of state territories in Europe and the emergence within their spaces of the relatively homogeneous population which would form the nation, and later the key aspirations and institutions of representative democracy and the welfare state. The second was the development of an international system of such territorial states which sublimated war onto the plane of relations between them within the framework of a Europe-centred world legal order. This order encompassed land and sea, state and colony, New and Old Worlds. These two conditions made it possible to think about governing in terms of a unified political apparatus, the government, which would have gained a sufficient monopoly of force to claim supremacy within a territory, and the relatively homogeneous and bounded population of a national society. This entity, the state, would act according to the defence and advancement of its national interests in the international arena.

By the 1990s, however, these conditions were held to have radically changed and to have made obsolete both the notion of governing societies on a domestic front and the idea of state sovereignty in the international arena. Changes in information and communication technology, the acceleration of international financial and currency transactions, new forms of mass media and travel, and much else beside, were summed up in 'globalization'. Globalization was the ineluctable force which was to break open the container of the nation-state and spill its social contents in all directions. It also made, it would be claimed, the aspiration of the national government of society impossible, particularly with the collapse of post-World War II Keynesian macro-economic policy and the Bretton Woods arrangements of financial and currency controls. On the parallel track of political and social thought, government was displaced by 'governance', a multi-layered affair within and outside the old nation-state boundaries, encompassing but subverting the claims of national government. Even sociologists would now speak of 'the death of the social' or of a 'sociology without society'. Economists would compare the value of transnational corporations with the gross domestic product of nation-states. Political scientists would speak of global governance conducted in a global civil society inhabited by international government and non-government organizations.

If anything bound the thesis of globalization together with the framework of governance more than a common distaste for the role of national government it was something that apparently brought these political metaphysics down to earth – the individual. The idea of the individual – suitably turned out as a sociological process word, 'individualization' – was held to be the necessary resultant of globalization and the presupposition of governance. The second modernity would be one in which the individual is placed in a situation in which all traditional and first-modern ascribed attributes would be open to problematization and the individual would thus be compelled to adopt a radical freedom to make itself, to narrate its past, plan its future and discover its own identity without reference to such certainties as lifelong jobs, predictable intimate lives or nationality. Governance would then be concerned with governing through this radically self-determining being and would no longer be able to rely on assumed authority and established hierarchy. Governing would thus be flattened, and take a network form. It would be inclusive and participatory. I called this form of governing through the ethical attributes and ethical culture of the individual 'culture-governance'.

This triple figure of globalization, individualization and governance marked out the intellectual coordinates with which we were urged to displace the idea of governing societies at the beginning of the new millennium. Each pointed to an important problem. One to the need for an analysis of the world order that had replaced the Cold War stand-off after 1989. The second to the ethical interrogation of individual and collective conduct and of individual freedom itself and the contestation over the legacies of the cultural transformations from the 1960s and the wind-up of the ideal of a welfare state. The third arose from the need to decentre political analysis from the nation-state after the 'micro-politics' of everyday life and expertise, the 'sub-politics' of social movements, and the meta-politics of international organizations. But the solutions proposed were rather too easy even by the standards of the 1990s. Globalization was not the One Big Thing of the new world order as the protestors had announced already at the World Trade Organization meeting in Seattle in 1999. The autonomous individual was an aspiration in programmes and policies given the dubious title of 'welfare reform' which used disciplinary means and compulsion to enforce work, family and community obligation as much as it was in dreams of a cosmopolitan democracy. A flattened governance was all very well for those who did not have to endure existence without any effective state structures and the chaos and genocide that ensued. After the irruptions of 9/11, the misadventures of military intervention in the Middle East, and the terror, the tortures and the camps, even those who believed that globalization would bring about the pacific march of liberal-democratic capitalism had changed their minds. Liberal globalizers rediscovered state sovereignty as the first principle of a civilized world order. American conservatives shifted from the end of history to the dynamics of state building.

The simple conclusion, reinforced by their prevarications and ambiguities, is that many current ways of thinking in the social and political sciences are showing only a creaking ability to come to terms with the emergent problems of the twenty-first century. It has become necessary to think against the grain of those sciences and theories. Only by doing so is it possible to think about our current political history.

I suspect that this thinking against the grain of the mainstream was one of the reasons that Michel Foucault's work on governmentality became prominent during the 1990s. As we have noted here, Foucault's lectures on government offer what in retrospect were prescient reflections on liberal and, more significantly, neoliberal forms of governing and a means for the analysis of practices of government in contemporary liberal democracies. We should also not underrate the empirical capacity of these analyses to render intelligible all manner of governing in liberal democracies, their objects, their techniques, their questioning and reasoning, their ethos and their ends.

There are two significant differences between Foucault's intellectual context and our own which, if not recognized, lead to a problematic take-up of his work. The first is that when Foucault was beginning his researches in France, Sartre would describe Marxism as the 'unsurpassable horizon of the age'. Today, we might say that conservative and social-democratic versions of liberalism and liberal democracy have grown so hegemonic as to make it almost impossible for us to think not only beyond them but about them in a manner that detaches ourselves from their self-descriptions and normative assertions. The second concerns the authority of science, particularly those of the social and human sciences. When he conceived of genealogies as 'anti-sciences' which contested 'the aspiration to power which is inherent in the claim to being a science' (2003: 9–10), Foucault was thinking of the then current pretensions of Marxism and psychoanalysis. Today the social sciences bother themselves less with the claim to science and more with the production of narratives whose apparent verisimilitude comes from their intimate relation to liberalism. If Foucault's move was to take liberalism seriously to make it the object of analysis, ours must be to ensure that we do not reproduce its premises. The context in Anglophone countries, in particular, during the 1980s and 1990s certainly affected the reception and development of governmentality analyses. I argue that due to the cultural dominance of a renewed and recharged form of liberalism, there was always the possibility of acceding to the soft normativity of liberalism itself. Thus I identify a tendency for this literature to reproduce the normative framework of liberal democracy and, in the absence of its own explicit value orientation, to have its description of the rationalities of neoliberalism stand as a proxy normative position. It is absolutely crucial, I contend, for this literature to place the following key claims of liberalism in abeyance: that liberalism is a form of government that respects individual liberty and seeks to work principally through forms of freedom; that liberalism is a form of limited government; and that liberalism is opposed to and may be a safeguard against authoritarian forms of rule. This is not because I contest the truth value of these claims. However, when confronted with the operations of liberal rule, these claims make possible the enormous extension of the formal apparatuses of sovereign government and allow all kinds of relationships to the project of governing through freedom. The latter include domestic forms of rule which enforce order, hierarchy and obligation in the service of freedom itself and international military interventions which can manage to justify all kinds of mayhem and war as a component of the liberation of popu-lations and the exportation of liberal democracy and the freedom it secures. This is not simply liberal hypocrisy as it is commonly thought but a result of a set of tensions entailed in the translation of liberal norms into policies and practices.

I have also argued against the tendency which the literature of gov-ernmentality shares with those of governance to imagine that the field of rule is exhausted by the multiple and heterogeneous forms of governing itself. I have called for a reinstatement of a much more multidimensional understanding of the field of power relations with a particular emphasis on biopolitics and sovereignty. While these postulates themselves sound rather abstract they have the effect of a rather different description of the politics of contemporary liberal-democratic societies. Contemporary liberal rule emerges as a political project linked to the use of force and violence, and the establishment of states of domination, as much as the shaping of liberty and the conduct of conduct. One key implication of this is that author-itarian liberal government is as much a possibility within our present and often appears as the reverse side of advanced liberal rule and intrinsically connected to its claims, its rationale and its ends. This is even more so when governing claims to take a non-political form, that is, when it claims to be purely economic or even ethical.

The rethinking of the governmentality approach led to a radical re-description of contemporary liberal rule which raised the authoritarian potential of liberalism. Contemporary liberal rule manifests the recurrent emergence of illiberal practices and rationalities which occur in the name of liberalism and in defence of its values. I argue that it is necessary to put aside the liberal assumption of a fundamental opposition between liberalism and authoritarian forms of rule. Authoritarianism is not simply that to which liberalism is implacably opposed and against which it offers safe-guards. Nor is it the ever-present danger against which liberalism must be vigilant. Rather, I contend, it is a permanent pole of liberal rule made possible by the liberal view of government as limited by the sphere of civil society external to it and the liberties of autonomous individuals within that sphere. The condition of possibility of thinking about the attributes of such free subjects is the division of populations according to the capacity for autonomy. The legal and political subject of liberalism is as much formed through exceptions to the norm of the autonomous individual as through the norm itself. The government/civil society split makes possible the enfolding, as I call it, of the processes, values and forms of conduct of a properly functioning and hence normatively binding domain external to governing onto the mode of governing itself. The upshot of this analysis was to show that the authoritarian side of liberal governing is intrinsic to liberalism itself and, further, that at least one version of current forms of liberal rule might be better thought of as authoritarian liberalism rather than neo- or advanced liberal rule.

The third part of the book does represent a genuine departure and adopts a far more exploratory posture than the earlier parts. The diagnoses of Part Two reveal the governmentality problematic at its breaking point by indicating the passages through which sovereign powers enter into the regimes of practices, techniques and even the rationalities said to constitute advanced liberalism. Sovereignty escapes its representation in much of the governance literature and critical-theoretical approaches to power as something historically and conceptually displaced. I conclude that if the undoubted insights gained by governmentality literature should be retained, they would need to be placed within a broader analytical framework. This is the occasion for 'bringing sovereignty back in' and reflecting upon its relation to violence and to the claims of state sovereignty to be a supreme power. I argue that it is necessary to place sovereignty and its relations to violence at the heart of the analysis of contemporary power relations, and thus of governing societies. I indicate two dualities concerning sovereignty. The first is between the enabling features of the sovereign claim to a monopoly of violence which both makes governing societies (both domestically and internationally) possible but also renders sovereign power terrifyingly responsible for all kinds of uses of force. The other is the notion of sovereignty as a supreme power which can be divided and dispersed, derogated and arrogated. In my discussion of a sovereign right of death I seek to rescue the analysis of sovereignty from ahistorical narratives of its transcendental status as constitutive of the political itself such as that found in Agamben, the bipolar narrative into which Foucault occasionally lapsed in which obsolete sovereignty gives way to more modern powers, or the more formal identification of sovereignty and state and sovereignty at the limit of law found in Schmitt. I suggest, in contrast, the need to keep in play the shifting relations between sovereignty, law, nation and state. Drawing on the many insights of these and other thinkers, finally, I contend that what is important from an analytical point of view is to be able to analyse the way that sovereignty enters into relations with discipline, government, biopower and other formations as they form various figurations of power and regimes of practices, reshape and recompose one another and combine and recombine in different forms.

Against the idea of sovereignty as a kind of originary and transcendent structure of the political, I contend that sovereignty must be understood in its shifting and variable manifestations, its historical conditions of existence, and the ways in which it is problematized. Against the idea of sovereignty as a right of final decision at the heart of the state, I seek to understand the multiple localizations and dispersal of the decision, its delegations and arrogations. And against the idea that sovereignty has been displaced by governance, or surpassed by a global civil society, I would stress the need to grasp how the changing forms of sovereignty enter into combination with other forms of power and rationalities and technologies of rule.

Such a position would seem, then, to have affinities with those who stress the re-emergence of the 'state of exception' and in particular Agamben's contention that the latter has become a permanent technique of government which has its most defining manifestation in the detention camps of the War on Terror such as that at Guantánamo Bay. More wildly, Agamben contends that the camp is the biopolitical *nomos* of modernity. Whatever the attractiveness of such gestures, I argue that they are immensely disabling for the analysis of contemporary liberalism and its approaches to governing societies. First, such camps are only one of many locales in which the call to decision has been promulgated. To restrict and specify the localization of sovereignty is to reproduce Schmitt's identification of sovereignty with the state. Secondly, rather than being outside the law, places like Guantánamo Bay are intense foci of legal regulation and contestation. Thirdly, the practices at such places can only be analysed as an assemblage of different power and discursive formations, containing sovereign, national and disciplinary elements and linkages to the cycles of electoral politics within liberal democracies. Far from being a declared state of exception at which law and governance recedes and at which a pure decision reigns, liberal governmentality seeks an annihilation of the exception and a sublimation of the moment for decision onto all kinds of expertise, administrative process, legal regulation and, indeed, everyday patterns and ways of life.

The implications of this book for 'governing societies' start with the idea that there is still much activity that can be described in any of the senses of such a term we outlined in the Introduction: as vision, as programme, as the routine activities of national government, as the overall strategic situation in a territorial state, and as many projects undertaken by international agencies. Secondly, the rationalities, techniques, practices and aims of governing societies cannot be understood without rethinking the issues of sovereignty as the kind of power capable of creating the conditions for the pacification of space necessary for them. Third, in the analysis of the regimes of practices that are constitutive of governing societies, it is important to understand how sovereign powers and the call to decision operate within them.

The diagnosis of contemporary liberalism contained here reveals a number of key points. The first is that 'the death of the social' narrative woven around notions of globalization and individualization should be viewed less as an authoritative description of the present and more as a rationality for a specific kind of governing of societies. This kind of governing stresses the moral or ethical character of specific populations as a key arena of political intervention and prescribes specific kinds of policy frameworks and techniques for the reform of industrial relations systems, the provision of public infrastructure, social welfare, healthcare and education. Rather than a programme of the withdrawal of the state in the face of the forces of global economic change and civil society, contemporary liberalism offered a comprehensive government of society by the agencies of government in tandem with those of civil society (domestic or global), particularly corporations and philanthropic bodies. When one considers the more authoritarian manifestations of this liberal governing, however, we find a renewed sense of the control over borders and movements of populations, the sovereign authority over a territory, the enforcement of obligation and the establishment of hierarchy. It would appear that the notion of governing society has somehow returned as a defence of society as a way of life built around liberal commercial imperatives and competition, and conceptions of freedom and personal responsibility. Moreover, in that defence, all kinds of concerns, from those of the environment to the supply of water and foodstuffs, as well as immigration and terrorism, are described in terms of security and its vocabulary. It would not be too hard to imagine that the notion of governing societies as a distinctive totality characterized by social order and disorder, solidarity and conflict, equality and inequality, poverty and prosperity, will soon return to the centre of our political vocabulary.

Neoliberalism is a strategy of governing society which corresponds to a characterless world – a world without markings and orientation, a 'scratchless' world of surfaces, flows and movements, of the erosion of the obstacles formerly presented by time and space, and a displacement of authority and hierarchy with governance and networks. Its paradigm is that of the free seas, and it is apt that such a strategy will style itself a 'world risk society'. Much contemporary social and political thought has cast us adrift in the dangerous waters of this spaceless universalism. By pointing out the sites of emergence of possible hegemons and new hierarchies, of division and exclusion, of violent, coercive and sovereign orderings, and of territorialities and appropriations, I hope we can regain some of the powers of criticism lost by that thought. By indicating some of the markings on the contemporary global and local landscape, and the persistence of orientations in spaces defined by territories and nations, I hope to have shown that the tasks of governing societies remain to be accomplished.

Notes

Introduction

1. The very different approaches and applications of the concept and frameworks of governance include those of Rhodes (1997), Kooiman (2003), Pierre and Peters (2000), Mayntz (1993), and Jessop (1998). Bang (2003) is an interesting recent overview with a range of heterodox positions and new approaches.
2. The treatment of these two women by the Australian immigration system is detailed in official reports by Palmer (2005) and the Australian Commonwealth Ombudsman (Commonwealth of Australia 2005). Rau spent six months in a prison and four in an immigration detention centre in 2004–05 and Solon spent over four years in a Catholic hospice in the Philippines after being deported in July 2001 despite the relevant government department knowing of its mistake in 2003. The former report comments on the department's operation: 'Cornelia Rau might have been considered a non-citizen but she was not a non-person, and nothing in the manner of her treatment should have allowed this accusation to have any basis in fact' (Palmer 2005: 214).
3. Schmitt's politics had national conservative, authoritarian liberal and some-time fascist shades before, during or after his collaboration with National Socialism. Among a large literature, representative views on the relation between Schmitt's political position and his theoretical work are expressed by Habermans (1987), Hirst (1988), Schwab (1996), Balakrishnan (2000), Müller (2004) and Kennedy (2004). That aspects of Schmitt's behaviour, including some of his writings, were morally reprehensible and his political choice to collaborate with Nazism thoroughly repugnant, is utterly beyond question. Nonetheless his work maintains at least some scientific and intellectual value as either style or object of analysis. This is attested to not only by his influence and debate with such diverse and influential figures as political philosopher Leo Strauss (see Meier 1995), the Hegelian Alexandre Kojève (Howse 2006), Walter Benjamin (Agamben 2005), and Hans Morgenthau and realist

international relations (Koskenniemi 2002: 413–509), but also by recent discussions by such critical political theorists as Chantal Mouffe, Slavoj Zizek, Jacques Derrida, Michael Hardt and Antonio Negri and Giorgio Agamben among others.

Chapter 1: Zombie Categories?

1. Hobbes surprisingly did little to explicate the mythological basis of the notion of the Leviathan and the image modern times has taken of the state consists of the drawing of the great man made up of smaller men which was the frontispiece to his book ([1651] 1996: xciii). The symbol is mentioned only three times in the book: in the introduction as the state as 'Artificall Man', as 'Mortall God' at the beginning of Part Two, 'Of Common-wealth', and at the end of Chapter XXVIII as being taken from the Book of Job (Hobbes [1651] 1996: 9, 120, 221). Schmitt ([1938] 1996b) explored the symbol and his understanding of its failure in his 1938 book on the subject. The Book of Job speaks of a struggle between two monsters, a sea-monster, the Leviathan, and a land-monster, Behemoth, in which the former emerges victorious. For Hobbes, Behemoth was the title he gave to his book on the English Civil War ([1679] 1840). I have discussed Schmitt's book and the image in the context of the political mythology of world order and the land and sea opposition in Schmitt's thought in Dean (2006b). I would note that a book highly critical of Schmitt's relation to Nazism, Franz Neumann's *Behemoth: The Structure and Practice of National Socialism* (1942) again uses the Leviathan–Behemoth myth to describe this specific political formation.
2. The Australian government passed Acts on counter-terrorism and on individual workplace agreements with unusual haste as this was being written in late 2005.
3. This and several of the citations in this section are to be found in the Oxford English Dictionary (OED) Online entries for government, govern, governing and society: http://dictionary.oed.com. Bentham's sentence appears under the entry for government.
4. In the OED Online entry for govern as a verb.
5. In the OED Online entry for society as a noun.

Chapter 3: Individualization

1. See the website: http://www.whitehouse.gov/government/fbci/ (accessed 11 May 2006).
2. A point made by Sakari Hanninen in a workshop on 'Obligation' at the University of Helsinki, November 2002.
3. This passage is quoted by Giddens (1998: 36). Interestingly, in view of his use of it (see below) to discuss the creation of social solidarity, he stops before the conjunction 'and' in the second last sentence. This omits both the key insights of the collective character of individualism and the individualization of responsibility for failure.

Chapter 4: Life and Death

1. At the time of writing, these lectures, delivered in 1977–78 and 1978–79 at the Collège de France, have only recently been published in French (Foucault 2004a, 2004b). Summaries of these lecture courses have been available in English for some time (Foucault 1997a, 1997b). They have been extensively drawn upon by Gordon (1991). The lecture of 1 February 1978 has been available in English for over twenty-five years (1979a) and in more recent versions (1991a, 2001a). Foucault's Tanner lectures delivered at Stanford in 1979 (1981, 2001b) also contain material covered in the 1977–78 lectures.

2. A point made by Colin Gordon (1980: 246–51) which I have tried to develop (Dean 1998b: 193–4; 1999: 69–70).

3. This second interpretation informs aspects of a recent critique of Foucault's texts on governmentality by Dupont and Pearce (2001). They claim that Foucault's own pieces on governmentality presuppose a kind of Hegelian teleology towards liberal government through self-government. All of the elements of Foucault's account add up to liberalism as the end of a history, as the owl of Minerva spreading its wings at dusk. I do not think this view, however provocative, can be sustained by Foucault's texts, which of course have been very fragmentary in this area prior to the publication of his lectures in French (2004a, 2004b). It relies on a forcing together of Foucault's work in the history of sexuality with his analysis of the 'arts of government' to produce such a teleology and a view of liberalism as a kind of inner force of 'governing through self-government' struggling to overcome certain obstacles. However, it does indicate a certain weakness in the architecture of studies of governmentality if they fail to take seriously the question of the heterogeneity of forms of power, particularly the relation between liberal ways of governing and sovereignty, or start to elide the programmatic rationality of a liberal conception of government with the logic of liberal practices of rule. If we fail to consider both of these issues, I would suggest, Dupont and Pearce may be correct in arguing that governmentality studies run the risk of promoting a version of the triumphalist historical narrative considered in this book.

4. Two excellent sociological accounts of the decisions on 'bare life' made in the context of various prenatal techniques and related forms of expertise are those of Barbara Katz Rothman (1994) and Kolker and Burke (1994). See also Beck-Gernsheim (1996) on the new powers over the planning of life. A comprehensive account of the area is Sharon Gaby's PhD thesis (2003).

5. A copy of the 1948 document is to be found at: http://www.unesco.org/education/information/50y/nfsunesco/doc/hum-rights.htm (accessed 11 May 2006).

6. In Australia, as in other settler societies of the former British Empire such as Canada and New Zealand, we have the rather strange situation in which the physical body of the sovereign is usually located outside the juridical–political order of the nation and its territory. Thus a sovereign decision on the state of exception was made in 1975 when an official appointed by the Prime Minister, the Governor-General, acting as a representative of Queen Elizabeth II, dismissed a popularly elected government and appointed the Leader of the Opposition as Prime Minister. These powers are referred to as 'reserve powers' under the Australian Constitution, which can be found at http://www.aph.gov.au/senate/general/constitution (accessed 14 June 2006), and its associated conventions. What is peculiar about the Australian polity and some other members of the Commonwealth group of nations is the actual

location of the sovereign in another nation, not that the sovereign is both inside and outside the juridical–political order.

7. Note that any characterization of Schmitt as an anti-liberal must account for the recent characterization of his position as authoritarian liberalism (Cristi 1998), and his 1932 address to a business association ([1932] 1998). It must also contend with Leo Strauss's (1996) brilliant demonstration that Schmitt fails to break free from the circle of liberalism.
8. The total character of liberalism was brought to my attention by Ilpo Helen's excellent essay (2000: 160). See Chapter 5 for further explication of this point.
9. Freedom could be the artefact of a legal and bureaucratic framework such as for the postwar German *Ordoliberalen* (Foucault 1997a: 77–8; Gordon 1991; Tribe 1995), of the generalization of market conditions for the Chicago School, and of the development of civilizational constraints for Hayek (1979).
10. O'Malley (1999) and Stenson (2000) provide helpful overviews of the range of punitive and policing practices and strategies respectively.

Chapter 5: Authoritarian Liberalism

1. See, for example, Foucault (1977), Valverde (1996), Stenson (1998), O'Malley (1999), Rose (1999: 233–73), and Hindess (2001).
2. As we said there of liberalism: 'It is a way of thinking ... which focuses especially on the place of the state in the overall government of society, and on the relation of law and more general forms of state regulation to other means of governing the conduct of the population' (Dean and Hindess 1998b: 7).
3. The language of the fold is suggested by Gilles Deleuze's (1998) reading of Foucault. I have attempted to use this language on several occasions to discuss aspects of the operation of power relations in liberal societies (Dean 1994b, 1995, 1996, 1999). Words such as 'explication', 'implication' and 'replication' have their etymological root in the Latin, *plico,* meaning fold.
4. Compare: 'The exclusions of the Enlightenment are therefore not practice-based contingent exceptions to a higher universal rule, but rather the expressions of the rule tying citizenship to certain moral "habits"' (Valverde 1996: 363).
5. Rice said in Paris in February 2005: 'Our charge is clear: we on the right side of freedom's divide have an obligation to help those unlucky enough to have been born on the wrong side of that divide.' From website: http://www.cnn.com/2005/WORLD/europe/02/08/rice/ (accessed 11 May 2006).
6. In a public lecture and seminar in the Department of Sociology, Macquarie University, July 2000.
7. Barry Hindess drew my attention to Smith's lectures in this regard. See his discussion (Hindess 2001: 99–100).

Chapter 6: Sovereignty and Violence

1. A copy of the UN Charter is found at: http://www.un.org/aboutun/charter/index.html (accessed 14 July 2006). Among the relevant articles are Articles 1, 2, 33 and 39. Article 2, paragraph 4 reads: 'All Members shall refrain in their international relations from the threat or use of force against the territorial

integrity or political independence of any state, or in any other manner inconsistent with the Purposes of the United Nations'.

2. For a popular account of the war in Kosovo in 1999 in these terms, see Ignatieff (2001). A postmodern elaboration of these notions, drawing most strongly on Virillo, is Der Derian (2001). For an excellent critique of notions of virtual war and an account of the limits of the Revolution in Military Affairs (RMA) see Hirst (2005: 136–51).

Chapter 7: State of Exception

1. Schmitt's exploration of the antithesis of land and sea begins with the Leviathan/Behemoth mythological conflict in his book on Hobbes ([1938] 1996b) and the 'children's tale' he wrote for his daughter, *Land and Sea* ([1942] 1997). It receives full elaboration in *Nomos of the Earth* ([1950] 2003), particularly in its first chapter. For commentary and critique of the myth elements of Schmitt's thinking see Connery (2001) and Dean (2006b).

2. See, for instance, the play, first performed in Australia in 2003, *Myth, Propaganda and Disaster in Nazi Germany and Contemporary America*, by Stephen Sewell. An archive of Abu Ghraib images is found at: http://www.thememoryhole.org/war/iraqis_tortured/index.htm (accessed 12 June 2006).

3. The information was located at: http://usinfo.state.gov/eur/Archive/2005/Nov/07-478256.html (accessed 14 January 2006).

4. The Constitution of the United States of America gives the designation, Commander in Chief, to the President who, under Article II, s. 2, 'shall be Commander in Chief of the Army and Navy of the United States, and of the Militia of the several States, when called into the actual Service of the United States'. The Constitution is available at: http://www.archives.gov/national-archives-experience/charters/constitution_transcript.html (accessed 14 June 2006). In this respect, Agamben's point seems ignorant of essential background knowledge. The Constitution would simply appear to be placing civilian authority over the military. However, the Secretary of Defense, Donald Rumsfeld, announced on 24 October 2002 that regional commanders of the armed forces would no longer be referred to as 'commanders-in-chief' and that the term would be reserved for the President. This would seem to support Agamben's point of the renewed salience of the term after 9/11 and in the War on Terror and the use of it to extend what is essentially a military power to one of civil authority. Rossiter's book is actually an argument on behalf of strong powers for the United States in the post-World War II era in order to ensure the long-term survival of democracy, and concludes: 'No sacrifice is too great for democracy, least of all the temporary sacrifice of democracy itself' ([1948] 2005: 314).

5. Schmitt was arrested by the Russians at the end of the war and then released. He was then arrested by the Americans and held prisoner for over a year. He was then arrested six months later, interrogated by a deputy public prosecutor for the Nuremberg tribunal, and then released when the prosecutor decided that there was no reason to pursue charges. Schmitt told his interrogator 'I wanted to give National Socialism my own meaning' (1987: 106) and admitted shame at the 'unspeakable' things he had written in the early days of the regime. Nevertheless, he refused to sign a de-Nazification certificate and appeared to believe, at least in the delirium of his American imprisonment,

that the Holocaust and the destruction of Germany were part of a dialectical theology of revenge and restitution (Balakrishnan 2000: 252–9).

Chapter 8: Contemporary Liberal Exceptionalism

1. Even the Nazi camps had many forms, contained different populations and changed their function (Diken and Lausten 2005: 46–50). Rather than a single form with a necessary and essential logic, the movement from slave-labour camp to terror-labour and death camp devoted to systematic extermination of 'sub-races' in Germany was both somewhat contingent and unpredictable, dependent not only upon the decision on the 'final solution' in December 1941, but policies regarding settlement of 'superior races' in the East and the kinds of resources available for the design and building of the camps. For a chilling history of the pragmatics of the design, planning and implementation of what we now know as Auschwitz, *prior* to its use as the systematic extermination machine of modernity, see Pelt (1994).
2. I thank Fleur Johns for making this point.

References

Agamben, G. (1998) *Homo Sacer: Sovereign Power and Bare Life*, trans. D. Heller-Roazen. Stanford, CA: Stanford University Press.

Agamben, G. (2000) *Means without Ends: Notes on Politics*, trans. V. Binetti and C. Casarino. Minneapolis, MN: University of Minnesota Press.

Agamben, G. (2005) *State of Exception*, trans. K. Atell. Chicago, IL: University of Chicago Press.

Anderson, B. (1983) *Imagined Communities*. London: Verso.

Aristotle (1957) *Politics*, trans. H. Rackman. London: Heinemann.

Ashenden, S. (1996) Reflexive governance and child sexual abuse: liberal welfare rationality and the Cleveland Inquiry, *Economy and Society*, 25 (1): 64–88.

Australian Department of Family and Community Services (2000) *Participation Support for a More Equitable Society: Welfare Reform Final Report*. Canberra: Australian Government Printing Service.

Balakrishnan, G. (2000) *The Enemy: An Intellectual Portrait of Carl Schmitt*. London: Verso.

Bang, H. (ed.) (2003) *Governance as Social and Political Communication*. Manchester: University of Manchester Press.

Barry, A., Osborne, T. and Rose, N. (eds) (1996) *Foucault and Political Reason: Liberalism, Neo-liberalism and Rationalities of Government*. London: UCL Press.

Barry, J., Hirsh, M. and Isikoff, M. (2004) The roots of torture, *Newsweek*, 24 May. http://msnbc.msn.com/id/4989436/site/newsweek/ (accessed 27 May 2004).

Bataille, G. (1991) *The Accursed Share: An Essay in General Economy, Vol. 3: Sovereignty*, trans. R. Hurley. New York: Zone Books.

Baudrillard J. (1983) *In the Shadow of the Silent Majorities . . . or The End of the Social*. New York: Semiotext(e).

Bauman, Z. (2005) Holocaust, in T. Bennett, L. Grossberg and M. Morris (eds) *New Keywords: A Revised Vocabulary of Culture and Society*. Oxford: Blackwell.

Beasley-Murray, J. (2005) The common enemy: tyrants and pirates, *South Atlantic Quarterly*, 104 (2): 217–25.

Beck, U. (1989) On the way to the industrial risk society? Outline of an argument, *Thesis Eleven*, 23: 86–103.

Beck, U. (1992a) From industrial society to risk society, *Theory, Culture and Society*, 9: 97–123.

Beck, U. (1992b) *Risk Society: Towards a New Modernity*. London: Sage Publications.

Beck, U. (1998) The cosmopolitan manifesto, *New Statesman*, 20 March.

Beck, U. (1999) *World Risk Society*. Cambridge: Polity.

Beck, U. (2000a) The cosmopolitan perspective: sociology of the second age of modernity, *British Journal of Sociology*, 51 (1): 79–105.

Beck, U. (2000b) *What is Globalization?*, trans. P. Camiller. Cambridge: Polity.

Beck, U. (2002) The terrorist threat: world risk society revisited, *Theory, Culture and Society*, 19 (4): 39–55.

Beck, U. and Beck-Gernsheim, E. (2002) *Individualization: Individualized Individualism and its Social and Political Consequences*. London: Sage Publications.

Beck-Gernsheim, E. (1996) Life as a planning project, in S. Lash, B. Szerszynski and B. Wynne (eds) *Risk, Environment and Modernity: Towards a New Ecology*. London: Sage Publications.

Benjamin, W. ([1921] 1978) Critique of violence, in *Reflections: Essays, Aphorisms, Autobiographical Writings*, trans. E. Jephcott. New York: Schocken Books.

Bentham ([1789] 1996) *An Introduction to the Principles of Morals and Legislation*. Oxford: Clarendon Press.

Berlin, I. ([1958] 1997) Two concepts of liberty, in *The Proper Study of Mankind*. London: Chatto and Windus.

Bodin, J. ([1576] 1955) *Six Books of the Commonwealth*, abridged and trans. M.J. Tooley. Oxford: Basil Blackwell.

Bodin, J. ([1576] 1992) *On Sovereignty: Four Chapters from The Six Books of the Commonwealth*, trans. J.H. Franklin. Cambridge: Cambridge University Press.

Bourdieu, P. (1990) *The Logic of Practice*. Cambridge: Polity.

Bull, H. (1977) *The Anarchical Society: A Study of World Order in Politics*. London: Macmillan.

Bush, G.W. (2001) Statement by the President in his Address to the Nation, 11 September, 2001. http://www.whitehouse.gov/news/releases/2001/09/20010911-16.html (accessed 4 May 2006).

Bush, G.W. (2006) Speech on Immigration, *New York Times*, 15 March.

Buzan, B., Waever, O. and de Wilde, J. (1998) *Security: A New Framework for Analysis*. Boulder, CO: Lynne Rienner.

Callon, M. and Latour, B. (1981) Unscrewing the big Leviathan: how actors macrostructure reality and how sociologists help them to do so, in K. Knorr-Cetina and A. Cicourel (eds) *Advances in Social Theory*. London: Routledge and Kegan Paul.

Canguilhem, G. (1991) *The Normal and the Pathological*, trans. C.R. Fawcett with R.S. Cohen. New York: Zone Books.

Carlsson, I., Han, S-J. and Kupolati, R.M. (1999) Report of the Independent Inquiry into the actions of the United Nations during the genocide in Rwanda. United Nations Security Council, 15 December.

Castells, M. (2000a) *The Information Age, Vol. 1: The Rise of the Network Society*. Oxford: Basil Blackwell.

Castells, M. (2000b) The network society, in D. Held and A. McGrew (eds) *The Global Transformations Reader*. Cambridge: Polity.

Checkland, S.G. and Checkland, E.O. (eds) (1974) *The Poor Law Report of 1834*. Harmondsworth: Penguin.

Commonwealth of Australia (2005) *Inquiry into the Circumstances of the Vivian Alvarez Matter*. Canberra: Commonwealth Ombudsman.

Connery, C. (2001) Ideologies of land and sea: Alfred Thayer Mahan, Carl Schmitt and the shaping of global myth elements, *boundary 2*, 28 (2): 173–201.

Connolly, W. (1999) *Why I Am Not a Secularist*. Minneapolis, MN: University of Minnesota Press.

Cooper, R. (2003) *The Breaking of Nations: Order and Chaos in the Twenty-first Century*. New York: Grove Press.

Corrigan, P. and Sayer, D. (1985) *The Great Arch: English State Formation as Cultural Revolution*. Oxford: Basil Blackwell.

Cristi, R. (1998) *Carl Schmitt and Authoritarian Liberalism: Strong State, Free Economy*. Cardiff: University of Wales Press.

Crozier, M., Huntingon, S.P. and Watanuki, J. (1975) *The Crisis of Democracy: Report on the Governability of Democracies to the Trilateral Commission*. New York: New York University Press.

Cruikshank, B. (1998) Moral entitlement: personal autonomy and political reproduction, in S. Hänninen (ed.) *The Displacement of Social Policies*. Jväskylä: SoPhi.

Cruikshank, B. (1999) *The Will to Empower: Democratic Citizens and Other Subjects*. Ithaca, NY: Cornell University Press.

Danilenko, G.M. (1991) International *jus cogens*: issues of law-making, *European Journal of International Law*, 2 (1): 42–65.

Dean, M. (1991) *The Constitution of Poverty: Toward a Genealogy of Liberal Governance*. London: Routledge.

Dean, M. (1994a) *Critical and Effective Histories: Foucault's Methods and Historical Sociology*. London: Routledge.

Dean, M. (1994b) 'A social structure of many souls': moral regulation, government and self-formation, *Canadian Journal of Sociology*, 19 (2): 145–68.

Dean, M. (1995) Governing the unemployed self in an active society, *Economy and Society*, 24 (4): 559–83.

Dean, M. (1996) Foucault, government and the enfolding of authority, in A. Barry, T. Osborne and N. Rose (eds) *Foucault and Political Reason: Liberalism, Neo-Liberalism and Rationalities of Government*. London: UCL Press.

Dean, M. (1998a) Administering asceticism: re-working the ethical life of the unemployed citizen, in M. Dean and B. Hindess (eds) *Governing Australia: Studies in Contemporary Rationalities of Government*. Cambridge: Cambridge University Press.

Dean, M. (1998b) Questions of method, in R. Williams and I. Velody (eds) *The Politics of Constructionism*. London: Sage Publications.

Dean, M. (1999) *Governmentality: Power and Rule in Modern Society*. London: Sage Publications.

Dean, M. (2001) 'Demonic societies': liberalism, biopolitics and sovereignty, in T.B. Hansen and F. Stepputat (eds) *States of Imagination: Ethnographic Explorations of the Postcolonial State*. Durham, NC: Duke University Press.

Dean, M. (2002a) Liberal government and authoritarianism, *Economy and Society*, 31 (1): 37–61.

Dean, M. (2002b) Powers of life and death beyond governmentality, *Cultural Values: Journal of Cultural Research*, 6 (1/2): 119–38.

Dean, M. (2003a) Culture governance and individualisation, in H. Bang (ed.) *Governance as Social and Political Communication*. Manchester: Manchester University Press.

Dean, M. (2003b) Empire and governmentality, *Distinktion*, 6: 111–22.

Dean, M. (2004) Four theses on the powers of life and death, *Contretemps*, 5: 16–29. http://www.usyd.edu.au/contretemps/ (accessed 15 April 2006).

Dean, M. (2006a) Military intervention as police action?, in M. Dubber and M. Valverde (eds) *The New Police Science*. Stanford, CA: Stanford University Press.

Dean, M. (2006b) The political mythology of world order: Carl Schmitt's *nomos*, *Theory, Culture and Society*, 23 (5): 1–22.

Dean, M. and Hindess, B. (eds) (1998a) *Governing Australia: Studies in Contemporary Rationalities of Government*. Cambridge: Cambridge University Press.

Dean, M. and Hindess, B. (1998b) Introduction: society, government, liberalism, in

Governing Australia: Studies in Contemporary Rationalities of Government. Cambridge: Cambridge University Press.

Deleuze, G. (1979) Foreword: The rise of the social, in J. Donzelot, *The Policing of Families*. New York: Pantheon.

Deleuze, G. (1995) Postscript on control societies, in *Negotiations*. New York: Columbia University Press.

Deleuze, G. (1998) *Foucault*. Minneapolis, MN: University of Minnesota Press.

Der Derian, J. (2001) *Virtual War: Mapping the Military–Industrial–Media-Entertainment Network*. Boulder, CO: Westview Press.

Der Derian, J. (2002) Network war, *Theory and Event* 5 (4). http://muse.jhu.edu/journals/theory_and_event/v005/5.4derderian.html (accessed 11 May 2006).

Diken, B. and Lausten, C.B. (2005) *The Culture of Exception: Sociology Faces the Camp*. London: Routledge.

Donzelot, J. (1979a) *The Policing of Families*, trans. R. Hurley. New York: Pantheon.

Donzelot, J. (1979b) The poverty of political culture, *Ideology and Consciousness*, 5: 73–86.

Dubber, M. (2005) *The Police Power: Patriarchy and the Foundations of American Government*. New York: Columbia University Press.

Dupont, D. and Pearce, F. (2001) Foucault contra Foucault, *Theoretical Criminology*, 5 (2): 123–58.

Durkheim, E. ([1893] 1997) *The Division of Labour in Society*, trans W.D. Halls. New York: The Free Press.

Ehrenreich, B. (2001) Working classes: dialogues with James Fallows, *The Atlantic Online*, 2 May. www.theatlantic.com/jf2001–05-02 (accessed 21 August 2001).

Elias, N. (1978) *The Civilizing Process, Vol. 1: The History of Manners*, trans. E. Jephcott. New York: Urizen.

Elias, N. (1997) *The Germans*, trans. E. Dunning and S. Mennell. Cambridge: Polity.

Elias, N. and Dunning, E. (1986) *Quest for Excitement: Sport and Leisure in the Civilizing Process*. Oxford: Blackwell.

Etzioni, A. (1995) *The Spirit of Community: Rights, Responsibilities and the Communitarian Agenda*. London: Fontana.

Etzioni, A. (1996) *The New Golden Rule: Community and Morality in a Democratic Society*. New York: Basic Books.

Ewald, F. (1991) Insurance and risk, in G. Burchell, C. Gordon and P. Miller (eds) *The Foucault Effect: Studies in Governmentality*. London: Harvester Wheatsheaf.

Ferguson, N. (2004) *Colossus: The Price of America's Empire*. New York: Penguin Press.

Foucault, M. (1977) *Discipline and Punish: The Birth of the Prison*, trans. A. Sheridan. London: Allen Lane.

Foucault, M. (1979a) *History of Sexuality, Vol. 1: An Introduction*, trans. R. Hurley. London: Allen Lane.

Foucault, M. (1979b) On governmentality, *Ideology and Consciousness*, 6: 5–21.

Foucault, M. (1980) *Power/Knowledge*. Brighton: Harvester.

Foucault, M. (1981) *Omnes et singulatim*: towards a criticism of 'political reason', in S. McMurrin (ed.) *The Tanner Lectures on Human Values, Vol. 2*. Salt Lake City: University of Utah Press.

Foucault, M. (1982) The subject and power, in H. Dreyfus and P. Rabinow, *Michel Foucault: Beyond Structuralism and Hermeneutics*. Brighton: Harvester.

Foucault, M. (1985) *The History of Sexuality, Vol. 2: The Use of Pleasure*, trans. R. Hurley. New York: Pantheon.

Foucault, M. (1988a) The ethic of the care of the self as a practice of freedom, in J. Bernauer and D. Rasmussen (eds) *The Final Foucault*. Cambridge, MA: MIT Press.

Foucault, M. (1988b) Technologies of the self, in L.H. Martin, H. Gutman and P.H. Hutton (eds) *Technologies of the Self: A Seminar with Michel Foucault*. London: Tavistock.

Foucault, M. (1991a) Governmentality, in G. Burchell, C. Gordon and P. Miller (eds) *The Foucault Effect: Studies in Governmentality*. London: Harvester Wheatsheaf.

Foucault, M. (1991b) Questions of method, in G. Burchell, C. Gordon and P. Miller (eds), *The Foucault Effect: Studies in Governmentality*. London: Harvester Wheatsheaf.

Foucault, M. (1997a) The birth of biopolitics, in *The Essential Works 1954–1984, Vol. 1: Ethics, Subjectivity and Truth*. New York: The New Press.

Foucault, M. (1997b) Security, territory and population, in *The Essential Works 1954–1984, Vol. 1: Ethics, Subjectivity and Truth*. New York: The New Press.

Foucault, M. (2001a) Governmentality, in *The Essential Works 1954–1984. Vol. 3: Power*. London: Allen Lane.

Foucault, M. (2001b) *Omnes et singulatum*: toward a critique of 'political reason', in *The Essential Works 1954–1984, Vol. 3: Power*. London: Allen Lane.

Foucault, M. (2001c) The risks of security, in *The Essential Works 1954–1984, Vol. 3: Power*. London: Allen Lane.

Foucault, M. (2001d) The subject and power, in *The Essential Works 1954–1984, Vol. 3: Power*. London: Allen Lane.

Foucault, M. (2003) *Society Must be Defended*, trans. D. Macey. New York: Picador.

Foucault, M. (2004a) *Naissance de la Biopolitique*. Paris: Gallimard Seuil.

Foucault, M. (2004b) *Sécurité, Territoire, Population*. Paris: Gallimard Seuil.

Foucher, M. (2001) The geopolitics of frontlines and borderlines, in J. Lévy (ed.) *From Geopolitics to Global Politics: A French Connection*. London: Frank Cass.

Fraser, N. and Gordon, L. (1994) A genealogy of dependency: tracing a keyword of the US welfare state, *Signs*, 19 (2): 309–36.

Friedman, T. (2000) *The Lexus and the Olive Tree*. London: HarperCollins.

Friedman, T. (2005) *The World is Flat: A Brief History of the Globalized World in the 21st Century*. London: Allen Lane.

Friedman, T. (2006) Order versus disorder, *New York Times*, 21 July.

Fukuyama, F. (1992) *The End of History and the Last Man*. London: Hamish Hamilton.

Fukuyama, F. (2004) *State-Building: Governance and World Order in the 21st Century*. Ithaca, NY: Cornell University Press.

Gaby, S. (2003) The ethical pregnancy: reproductive choice in the context of prenatal testing. PhD thesis, Macquarie University.

Geertz, C. (1973) *The Interpretation of Cultures*. New York: Basic Books.

Giddens, A. (1985) *The Nation-State and Violence*. Cambridge: Polity.

Giddens, A. (1991) *Modernity and Self-identity*. Cambridge: Polity.

Giddens, A. (1994) *Beyond Left and Right: The Future of Radical Politics*. Cambridge: Polity.

Giddens, A. (1998) *The Third Way: The Renewal of Social Democracy*. Cambridge: Polity.

Gierke, O. ([1913] 1957) *Natural Law and the Theory of Society 1500–1800*, trans. E. Barker. Boston, MA: Beacon Press.

Giesen, K.-G. (2004) The postnational constellation: Habermas and the 'second modernity', *Res Publica*, 10 (1): 1–13.

Gordon, C. (1980) Afterword, in M. Foucault, *Power/Knowledge*. Brighton: Harvester.

Gordon, C. (1986) Question, ethos, event, *Economy and Society*, 15 (1): 73–87.

Gordon, C. (1991) Introduction, in G. Burchell, C. Gordon and P. Miller (eds) *The Foucault Effect: Studies in Governmentality*. London: Harvester Wheatsheaf.

Greenberg, K.J. and Dratel, J.L. (eds) (2005) *The Torture Papers: The Road to Abu Ghraib*. New York: Cambridge University Press.

Habermas, J. (1975) *Legitimation Crisis*, trans. T. McCarthy. Boston, MA: Beacon Press.

Habermas, J. (1985) Modernity: an incomplete project, in H. Foster (ed.) *Postmodern Culture*. London: Pluto.

Habermas, J. (1987) Sovereignty and *führerdemokratie*, *Times Literary Supplement*, 26 September.

Habermas, J. (2000) Bestiality and humanity: a war on the border between law and morality. http://www.theglobalsite.ac.uk/press/011habermas.htm (accessed 19 June 2006).

Habermas, J. (2001) *The Postnational Constellation: Political Essays*, trans. M. Pensky. Cambridge: Polity.

Hall, S. (1992) The question of cultural identity, in S. Hall, D. Held and T. McGrew (eds) *Modernity and its Futures*. Cambridge: Polity.

Hardt, M. and Negri, A. (2000) *Empire*. Cambridge, MA: Harvard University Press.

Hardt, M. and Negri, A. (2004) *Multitude*. London: Allen Lane.

Harris, L. (2004) *Civilization and its Enemies: The Next Stage of History*. New York: Free Press.

Hayek, F.A. (1979) *Law, Legislation and Liberty, Vol. 3: The Political Order of a Free People*. London: Routledge and Kegan Paul.

Held, D. (2000) International law, in D. Held and A. McGrew (eds) *The Global Transformations Reader: An Introduction to the Globalization Debate*. Cambridge: Polity Press.

Held, D. (2004a) *Global Covenant: The Social Democratic Alternative to the Washington Consensus*. Cambridge: Polity Press.

Held, D. (2004b) Inescapably side by side: an interview, *Polity*, February. http://www.globalpolicy.org/globaliz/define/2004/04heldinterview.htm (accessed 11 May 2006).

Held, D. and Hirst, P. (2002) Globalisation after 11 September: the argument of our time, *Open Democracy*, 24–31 January. http://www.opendemocracy.net/content/articles/PDF/637.pdf (accessed 11 May 2006).

Held, D. and McGrew, A. (eds.) (2000) *The Global Transformations Reader: An Introduction to the Globalization Debate*. Cambridge: Polity.

Held, D. and McGrew, A. (2002) *Globalization/Anti-Globalization*. Cambridge: Polity Press.

Held, D., McGrew, A., Goldblatt, D. and Perraton, J. (1999) *Global Transformations*. Cambridge: Polity.

Helen, I. (2000) Welfare and its vicissitudes, *Acta Sociologica*, 43: 157–64.

Hindess, B. (1996) *Discourses of Power: From Hobbes to Foucault*. Oxford: Blackwell.

Hindess, B. (1997) Politics and governmentality, *Economy and Society*, 26 (2): 257–72.

Hindess, B. (1998) Neo-liberalism and the national economy, in M. Dean and B. Hindess (eds) *Governing Australia: Studies in Contemporary Rationalities of Government*. Cambridge: Cambridge University Press.

Hindess, B. (2001) The liberal government of unfreedom, *Alternatives: Social Transformation and Humane Governance*, 26 (1): 93–111.

Hindess, B. (2005) Sovereignty, in T. Bennett, L. Grossberg and M. Morris (eds) *New Keywords: A Revised Vocabulary of Culture and Society*. Oxford: Blackwell.

Hirst, P. (1988) Carl Schmitt: decisionism and politics, *Economy and Society*, 17 (2), 272–81.

Hirst, P. (1993) *Associative Democracy: New Forms of Economic and Social Governance*. Cambridge: Polity Press.

Hirst, P. (2005) *Space and Power: Politics, War and Architecture*. Cambridge: Polity.

Hirst, P. and Thompson, G. (1999) *Globalization in Question: The International Economy and the Possibilities of Governance*, 2nd edn. Cambridge: Polity.

Hobbes, T. (1651) *Philosophicall Rudiments Concerning Government and Society*. London: R. Royston. http://socserv2.socsci.mcmaster.ca/~econ/ugcm/3ll3/hobbes/hobbes1 (accessed 13 July 2006).

Hobbes, T. ([1651] 1996) *Leviathan*. Cambridge: Cambridge University Press.

Hobbes, T. ([1679] 1840) *Behemoth: The History of the Causes of the Civil Wars of England*, in *Works, Vol. 6*. London: John Bohn.

Holmes, S. (1993) *The Anatomy of Antiliberalism*. Cambridge, MA: Harvard University Press.

Holmes, S. (1995) *Passions and Constraint: On the Theory of Liberal Democracy*. Chicago, IL: University of Chicago Press.

Howard, J.W. (2001) Election Speech, 6 December. http://afr.com/election2001/transcripts/2001/12/06/FFX4PNXV8TC.html (accessed 11 May 2006).

Howse, R. (2006) Europe and the new world order: lessons from Alexandre Kojève's engagement with Schmitt's 'Nomos of the Earth', *Leiden Journal of International Law*, 19 (1): 93–103.

Hunter, I. (1990) Personality as a vocation: the political rationality of the humanities, *Economy and Society*, 19 (4): 391–430.

Hunter, I. (1998) Uncivil society: liberal government and the deconfessionalisation of politics, in M. Dean and B. Hindess (eds) *Governing Australia: Studies in Contemporary Rationalities of Government*. Cambridge: Cambridge University Press.

Huntington, S.P. (1996) *The Clash of Civilizations and the Remaking of World Order*. New York: Simon and Schuster.

Huysmans, J. (1998) The question of the limit: desecuritisation and the aesthetics of horror in political realism, *Millennium: Journal of International Studies*, 27 (3): 569–89.

Ignatieff, M. (2001) *Virtual War*. London: Vintage.

Jessop, B. (1998) The rise of governance and the risks of failure: the case of economic development, *International Social Science Journal*, 50 (1): 29–45.

Johns, F. (2005) Guantánamo Bay and the annihilation of the exception, *European Journal of International Law*, 16 (4): 613–35.

Kagan, R. (2002) Power and weakness, *Policy Review*, June–July: 3–28.

Kant, I. (1980) Perpetual peace, in *Kant's Political Writings*, ed. H. Reiss, trans. H.B. Nisbet. Cambridge: Cambridge University Press.

Kantorowicz, E. (1957) *The King's Two Bodies: A Study in Mediaeval Political Theology*. Princeton, NJ: Princeton University Press.

Kaufmann, D. (2005) Debunking myths on worldwide governance and corruption. David B. Goodman lecture, University of Toronto, 10 February. http://www.worldbank.org/wbi/governance/events/Goodman_Toronto_0205_w.pdf (accessed 29 December 2005).

Kennedy, E. (2004) *Constitutional Failure: Carl Schmitt in Weimar*. Durham, NC: Duke University Press.

Kettle, M. (2001) Bush pours dollars into gospel mission, *The Guardian Weekly*, 8–14 February.

Khan, I. (2005) Foreword, in *Amnesty International 2005 Report: The State of the World's Human Rights*. http://web.amnesty.org/report2005/ (accessed 8 February 2007).

Knemeyer, F.-L. (1980) Polizei, *Economy and Society*, 9 (2): 172–96.

Kolker, A. and Burke, B.M. (1994) *Prenatal Testing: A Sociological Perspective*. Westport, CT: Bergen and Garvey.

Kooiman, J. (ed.) (1993) *Modern Governance: New Government–Society Interactions*. London: Sage Publications.

Kooiman, J. (2003) *Governing as Governance*. London: Sage Publications.

Koskenniemi, M. (2002) *The Gentle Civilizer of Nations: The Rise and Fall of International Law 1870–1960*. Cambridge: Cambridge University Press.

Koskenniemi, M. (2004) International law as political theology: how to read *Nomos der Erde?*, *Constellations*, 11 (4): 492–511.

Krasner, S. (2000) Compromising Westphalia, in D. Held and A. McGrew (eds) *The Global Transformations Reader: An Introduction to the Globalization Debate*. Cambridge: Polity.

Larner, W. (1998) Globalisation and spatial imaginaries in New Zealand, *Environment and Planning D: Society and Space*, 16 (5): 599–614.

Larner, W. and Walters, W. (2004) Globalization as governmentality, *Alternatives: Global, Local, Political*, 29 (5): 495–514.

Latham, M. (1998) *Civilising Global Capital: New Thinking for Australian Labor*, Sydney: Allen and Unwin.

Lewis, N.A. (2004) Red Cross finds detainee abuse in Guantanamo, *New York Times*, 30 November.

Lippert, R. (1998) Rationalities and refugee resettlement, *Economy and Society*, 27 (4): 380–406.

Lippert, R. (2004) Sanctuary practices, rationalities, and sovereignties, *Alternatives: Global, Local, Political*, 29 (5): 535–55.

Luhmann, N. (1997) Limits of steering, *Theory, Culture and Society*, 14 (1): 41–57.

Lund, B. (1999) 'Ask not what your community can do for you': obligations, New Labour and welfare reform, *Critical Social Policy*, 19 (4): 447–62.

MacDonagh, O. (1958) The nineteenth century revolution in government: a reappraisal, *The Historical Journal*, 1 (1): 52–67.

Mahan, A. T. (1894) Possibilities of an Anglo-American reunion, *The North American Review*, 159: 551–63.

Marinetto, M. (2003) Governing beyond the centre: a critique of the Anglo-Governance School, *Political Studies*, 51 (3): 592–608.

Marr, D. and Wilkinson, M. (2004) *Dark Victory*. Sydney: Allen and Unwin.

Marshall, T.H. ([1949] 1963) Citizenship and social class, in *Sociology at the Crossroads and Other Essays*. London: Heinemann.

Mauss, M. (1979) Techniques of the body, in *Sociology and Psychology*, trans. B. Brewster. London: Routledge and Kegan Paul.

Mayntz, R. (1993) Governing failures and the problem of governability: some comments on a theoretical paradigm, in J. Kooiman (ed.) *Modern Governance: New Government–Society Interactions*. London: Sage Publications.

Mbembe, A. (2003) Necropolitics, *Public Culture*, 15 (1): 11–40.

Mead, L. (1986) *Beyond Entitlement: The Social Obligations of Citizenship*. New York: Free Press.

Mead, L. (ed.) (1997) *The New Paternalism: Supervisory Approaches to Poverty*. Washington, DC: Brookings Institution.

Meier, H. (1995) *Carl Schmitt and Leo Strauss: The Hidden Dialogue*, trans. J. Harvey Lomax. Chicago, IL: University of Chicago Press.

Mill, J. S. ([1861] 1974) Representative government, in *Three Essays: On Liberty, Representative Government, The Subjection of Women*. London: Oxford University Press.

Miller, C.M. (2005) Police 'showdown' averted, *Miami Herald*, 26 March.

Miller, P. and Rose, N. (1990) Governing economic life, *Economy and Society*, 19 (1): 1–31.

Minogue, M., Polidano, C. and Hulme, D. (eds) (1998) *Beyond the New Public Management: Changing Ideas and Practices of Governance*. Cheltenham: Edward Elgar.

Minson, J. (1985) *Genealogies of Morals: Nietzsche, Foucault, Donzelot and the Eccentricity of Ethics*. London: Macmillan.

Müller, J.-W. (2004) *A Dangerous Mind: Carl Schmitt in Post-war European Thought*. New Haven, CT: Yale University Press.

Neal, A. (2005a) Foucault in Guantánamo: national, sovereign, disciplinary exceptionalism. http://libertysecurity.org/article199.html (accessed 8 November 2005).

Neal, A. (2005b) Review of the literature on the 'state of exception' and the application of this concept to contemporary politics. http://libertysecurity.org/article169.html (accessed 8 November 2005).

Neal, A. (2006a) Foucault in Guantánamo: towards an archaeology of the exception, *Security Dialogue*, 37 (1): 31–46.

Neal, A. (2006b) The politics of the exception: theorizing discourses of liberty and security. PhD thesis, Keele University.

Neocleous, M. (2000) Against security, *Radical Philosophy*, 100: 7–15.

Neocleous, M. (2003) *Imagining the State*. Maidenhead: Open University Press.

Neocleous, M. (2005) *The Monstrous and the Dead: Burke, Marx, Fascism*. Cardiff: University of Wales.

Neumann, F. (1942) *Behemoth: The Structure and Practice of National Socialism*. London: Victor Gollancz.

Nietzsche, F. (2004) Thus Spake Zarathustra: A Book for All and None, trans. T. Common, *eBooks@Adelaide*. http://etext.library.adelaide.edu.au/n/nietzsche/friedrich/n67a/index.html

Nye, J. (2004) *Soft Power: The Means to Success in World Politics*. New York: Public Affairs.

O'Connor, J. (1973) *The Fiscal Crisis of the State*. New York: St Martin's Press.

Oestreich, G. (1982) *Neostoicism and the Early Modern State*, trans. D. McLintock. Cambridge: Cambridge University Press.

Offe, C. (1984) *Contradictions of the Welfare State*. London: Hutchinson.

Olasky, M. (2000) *Compassionate Conservatism: What it is, What it Does, and How it Can Transform America*. New York: Free Press.

O'Malley, P. (1992) Risk, power and crime prevention, *Economy and Society*, 21 (2): 252–75.

O'Malley, P. (1999) Volatile and contradictory punishment, *Theoretical Criminology* 3 (2): 175–96.

Osborne, D. and Gaebler, T. (1993) *Reinventing Government: How the Entrepreneurial Spirit is Transforming the Public Sector*. New York: Plume Books.

Palmer, M. (2005) *Inquiry into the Circumstances of the Immigration Detention of Cornelia Rau*. Canberra: Attorney General's Department.

Parris, H. (1960) The nineteenth century revolution in government: a reappraisal reappraised, *The Historical Journal*, 3 (1): 17–36.

Peck, J. (1998) Workfare: a geopolitical etymology, *Environment and Planning D: Society and Space*, 16: 133–61.

Peck, J. (2001) Neoliberalizing states: thin policies/hard outcomes, *Progress in Human Geography*, 25 (3): 445–55.

Pelt, R.J. van (1994) Auschwitz: from architect's promise to inmate's perdition, *Modernism/Modernity*, 1 (1): 80–120.

Pierre, J. and Peters, B.G. (2000) *Governance, Politics and the State*. London: Macmillan.

Polanyi, K. (1957) *The Great Transformation*. Boston: Beacon Press.

Procacci, G. (1998) Poor citizens: social citizenship and the crisis of the welfare state, in S. Hänninen (ed.) *The Displacement of Social Policies*. Jväskylä: SoPhi.

Project for the New American Century (2000) *Rebuilding America's Defenses: Strategy, Forces and Resources for a New Century*. http://www.newamericancentury.org/RebuildingAmericasDefenses.pdf (accessed 11 May 2006).

Putnam, R.D. (1995) Bowling alone: America's declining social capital, *Journal of Democracy*, 6 (1): 65–78.

Rasul, S., Iqbal, A. and Ahmed, R. (2004) Composite statement: detention in Afghanistan and Guantanamo Bay. http://www.ccr-ny.org/v2/reports/docs/Gitmo-compositestatementFINAL23july04.pdf (accessed 19 June 2006).

Rejali, D. (1994) *Torture and Modernity: Self and State in Modern Iran*. Boulder, CO: Westview Press.

Rhodes, R.A.W. (1994) The hollowing out of the state: the changing nature of the public service in Britain, *Political Quarterly*, 65 (2): 138–51.

Rhodes, R.A.W. (1996) The new governance: governing without government, *Political Studies*, 44 (3): 652–67.

Rhodes, R.A.W. (1997) *Understanding Governance: Policy Networks, Reflexivity and Accountability*. Buckingham: Open University Press.

Rose, N. (1996) The death of the social? Re-figuring the territory of government, *Economy and Society*, 23 (5): 327–56.

Rose, N. (1999) *Powers of Freedom: Reframing Political Thought*. Cambridge: Cambridge University Press.

Rose, N. (2001) The politics of life itself, *Theory, Culture and Society*, 18 (6): 1–30.

Rose, N. and Miller, P. (1992) Political power beyond the State: problematics of government, *British Journal of Sociology*, 43 (2): 173–205.

Rosenau, J. (2000) Governance in a globalising world, in D. Held and A. McGrew (eds) *The Global Transformations Reader*. Cambridge: Polity.

Rosenau, J.N. and Czempiel, E.-O. (1992) *Governance without Government: Order and Change in World Politics*. Cambridge: Cambridge University Press.

Rossiter, C. ([1948] 2005) *Constitutional Dictatorship: Crisis Government in the Modern Democracies*. New Brunswick: Transaction.

Rothman, B.K. (1994) *The Tentative Pregnancy: Amniocentesis and the Sexual Politics of Motherhood*. London: HarperCollins.

Schmitt, C. ([1926] 1985a) *The Crisis of Parliamentary Democracy*, trans. E. Kennedy. Cambridge, MA: MIT Press.

Schmitt, C. ([1922] 1985b) *Political Theology: Four Chapters on the Concept of Sovereignty*, trans. G. Schwab. Cambridge, MA: MIT Press.

Schmitt, C. (1987) Interrogation of Carl Schmitt by Robert Kempner (I-III), *Telos*, 72: 97–107.

Schmitt, C. (1993) The age of neutralizations and depoliticizations, *Telos*, 96: 130–42.

Schmitt, C. ([1932] 1996a) *The Concept of the Political*, trans. G. Schwab. Chicago, IL: University of Chicago Press.

Schmitt, C. ([1938] 1996b) *The Leviathan in the State Theory of Thomas Hobbes: Meaning and Failure of a Political Symbol*, trans. G. Schwab and E. Hilfstein. Westport, CT: Greenwood Press.

Schmitt, C. ([1942] 1997) *Land and Sea*, trans. S. Draghici. Corvallis, OR: Plutarch Press.

Schmitt, C. ([1932] 1998) Strong state and sound economy, in R. Cristi, *Carl Schmitt and Authoritarian Liberalism: Stong State, Free Economy*. Cardiff: University of Wales Press.

Schmitt, C. ([1950] 2003) *The Nomos of the Earth in the International Law of Jus Publicum Europaeum*, trans. G. Ulmen. New York: Telos Press.

Schram, S.F. (1995) *Words of Welfare: The Poverty of Social Science and the Social Science of Poverty*. Minneapolis, MN: University of Minnesota Press.

Schram, S.F. (2000) *After Welfare: The Culture of Postindustrial Social Policy*. New York: New York University Press.

Schwab, G. (1996) Introduction, in C. Schmitt, *The Leviathan in the State Theory of Thomas Hobbes: Meaning and Failure of a Political Symbol,* trans. G. Schwab and E. Hilfstein. Westport, CT: Greenwood Press.

Senellart, M. (2004) Situation du cours, in M. Foucault, *Sécurité, Territoire, Population*. Paris: Gallimard Seuil.

Sieyès, E.-J. ([1789] 1963) *What is the Third Estate?*, trans. M. Blondel. London: Pall Mall.

Skelcher, C. (2000) Changing images of the state: overloaded, hollowed-out, congested, *Public Policy and Administration*, 15 (3): 3–19.

Skinner, Q. (1989) The state, in T. Ball, J. Farr and R.L. Hanson (eds) *Political Innovation and Conceptual Change*. Cambridge: Cambridge University Press.

Skinner, Q. (1998) *Liberty before Liberalism*. Cambridge: Cambridge University Press.

Smith, A. ([1776] 1976) *An Inquiry into the Nature and Causes of the Wealth of Nations, Vol. 1*. London: Oxford University Press.

Smith, A. ([1752–4] 1978) *Lectures on Jurisprudence*. Oxford: Clarendon Press.

Smith, A. ([1759] 2002) *The Theory of Moral Sentiments*. Cambridge: Cambridge University Press.

Spence, K. (2005) World risk society and war against terror, *Political Studies*, 53 (2): 284–302.

Stehr, N. and Ericson, R.V. (2000) The ungovernability of modern societies: states, democracies, markets, participation and citizens, in R.V. Ericson and N. Stehr (eds) *Governing Modern Societies*. Toronto: University of Toronto Press.

Stenson, K. (1998) Beyond histories of the present, *Economy and Society*, 27 (4): 333–52.

Stenson, K. (2000) Crime control, social policy and liberalism, in G. Lewis, S. Gewirtz and J. Clarke (eds) *Rethinking Social Policy*. London: Sage Publications.

Stenson, K. (2005) Sovereignty, biopolitics and the local government of crime, *Theoretical Criminology*, 9 (3): 267–87.

Stenson, K. and Edwards, A. (2001) Rethinking crime control in advanced liberal government, in K. Stenson and R. Sullivan (eds) *Crime, Risk and Justice*. Cullompton: Willan Press.

Steyn, J. (2004) Guantanamo Bay: the legal black hole, *International and Comparative Law Quarterly*, 53 (1): 1–15.

Strange, S. (2000) The declining authority of states, in D. Held and A. McGrew (eds) *The Global Transformations Reader: An Introduction to the Globalization Debate*. Cambridge: Polity.

Strauss, L. (1996) Notes, in C. Schmitt, *The Concept of the Political*, Chicago, IL: University of Chicago Press.

Sutherland, G. (ed.) (1972) *Studies in the Growth of Nineteenth-Century Government*. London: Routledge and Kegan Paul.

Thatcher, M. (1993) *The Downing Street Years*, London: HarperCollins.

Theodore, N. and Peck, J. (1999) Welfare-to-work: national problems, local solutions, *Critical Social Policy*, 19 (4): 485–510.

Thompson, G. F. (2004) Is all the world a complex network?, *Economy and Society*, 33 (3): 411–24.

Tingle, L. and Gotting, P. (1999) Christian jobs check defended, *Sydney Morning Herald*, 30 December.

Tribe, K. (1995) *Strategies of Economic Order: German Economic Discourse 1750–1950*. Cambridge: Cambridge University Press.

Tully, J. (ed.) (1988) *Meaning and Context: Quentin Skinner and his Critics*. Cambridge: Cambridge University Press.

Tully, J. (1995) *Strange Multiplicity: Constitutionalism in an Age of Diversity*. Cambridge: Cambridge University Press.

Ulmen, G. (1996) Just wars of just enemies?, *Telos*, 109: 99–112.

Urry, J. (2000) *Sociology without Society*. London: Routledge.

Valverde, M. (1996), 'Despotism' and ethical governance, *Economy and Society*, 25 (3): 357–72.

Walters, W. (2004) The frontiers of the European Union: a geostrategic perspective, *Geopolitics*, 9 (3): 674–98.

Weber, M. ([1918] 1972) Politics as a vocation, in H.H. Gerth and C. Wright Mills (eds) *From Max Weber*. London: Routledge and Kegan Paul.

Weber, M. (1978) *Economy and Society: An Outline of Interpretive Sociology*, Vol. 1. Berkeley, CA: University of California Press.

Young of Graffam, Lord (1992) Enterprise regained, in P. Heelas and P. Morris (eds) *The Values of Enterprise Culture: The Moral Debate*. London: Routledge.

Zacher, M. (1993) The decaying pillars of the Westphalian Temple, in J.N. Rosenau and E.-O. Czempiel (eds) *Governance without Government: Order and Change in World Politics*. Cambridge: Cambridge University Press.

Index